The Broken Rainbow:
Mysterious Dark Karma

Dr. Julio Antonio del Marmol
"The Cuban Lightning"

Based on a True Spy Story

© Copyright 2022 Dr. Julio Antonio del Marmol.

All rights reserved. No part of this publication may be reproduced, stored in a retrieval system, or transmitted, in any form or by any means, electronic, mechanical,
photocopying, recording, or otherwise, without the written prior permission of the author.

ISBN: 978-1-68588-037-8 (sc)
ISBN: 978-1-68588-038-5 (hc)
ISBN: 978-1-68588-039-2 (e)

Because of the dynamic nature of the Internet, any web addresses or links contained in this book may have changed since publication and may no longer be valid.

Any people depicted in stock imagery provided by Thinkstock are models, and such images are being used for illustrative purposes only.
Certain stock imagery © Thinkstock.

Cuban Lightning Publications, Int rev. 12/07/2016
www.cuban-lightning.com

The Broken Rainbow: Mysterious Dark Karma

Based on a True Spy Story by Dr. Julio Antonio del Marmol

<u>Nazi Germany 1930's: the Dark Angels follow from one continent's socialist revolution to that of another's</u>

A Jewish shoemaker and his family live a quiet life in the German village of Blankenfeld-Mahlow while anti-Jewish sentiment grows in pre-World War II Europe. Hitler is rising to power, and the signs are everywhere as the Jews' rights are slowly taken away. A mysterious woman reveals the sign of the Broken Rainbow will show that a Dark Angel has appeared on earth. When a Nazi officer tries to rape young daughter Sarah, her father and brother end up in a prison camp while she barely escapes. The family is divided and even with the help of a Nazi Captain friend of the family, Sarah's brother and father are killed in an escape attempt. Her grandfather dies since Jews have little access to medical attention. Captain Volker, helped by the local village physician, a secret agent for Allied intelligence, made unbelievable progress in saving hundreds if not thousands of Jews beneath the very noses of the SS and Gestapo. The global intelligence community for the Allies had assessed that the rise of Hitler would do nothing good for the world and planted Dr. Emilio del Marmol in the local hospital as an obstetrician, gynecologist, and pediatrician, pretending to work with the Nazis. In reality, he would secretly convey medicines, food, and weapons to the pockets of resistance operating in the forests of the German mountains and was close enough to Berlin to keep an eye on Nazi plans. He became a beacon of hope to many Jews for surviving the Nazi genocide. Both men, working in absolute secrecy, risked their very lives for several years until they were discovered and Captain Volker was executed, while Dr. del Marmol managed to escape to Spain and from there to his native country of Cuba. Captain Volker takes Sarah and her family to the train station where he helps them escape to Spain with counterfeit documents, sacrificing his own future and career to do so.

In Spain the persecution continues with a corrupt police force, and after further incidents the family flees to Cuba. During the journey, Grandmother Livka dies, but the rest of the family and children make it to Cuba, where all seems well for a while. Sarah meets a young pilot, Ramon, who goes off to fight the Axis in World War II. Ramon is killed in action, leaving a son named Miguel Angel.

Years later, in the little town of Pinar del Rio, Cuba, in the sky we can see a huge broken rainbow in the morning of January 1, 1959, the date the Cuban revolution took power. A young boy, Julio Antonio del Marmol, also known as el Commandantico, lives in the same neighborhood of Pinar del Rio and becomes the best friend of Sarah's son; Miguel Angel grows up in the time of the Cuban revolution and becomes a passionate, innocent follower of Fidel Castro and Che Guevara. He becomes a teacher for the revolution, sent to the poor to educate them about the merits of communism and to indoctrinate all to the new doctrine of the regime.

However, Che Guevara and the communists have no room for his God or his Jewish faith in their revolution, and when Miguel Angel refuses to renounce God, he is sent to mandatory military service as a punishment.

There he reunites with Julio Antonio. He also has been resistant to the fanatic indoctrination and is being punished for the same crime. The pair become good friends with Hernesto and escape the service with his help. While in service Miguel Angel discovers his teenage love, Flora, is pregnant, and they decide to marry. Before his service is over, however, the communists find his hidden Jewish prayer book and send him to prison, but in a daring escape his uncles free him as he dives into a river to avoid gunfire. Now partially paralyzed, he hides out until he can flee with his family to the United States.

In the U.S., medical doctors reverse his paralysis and three years later he joins the military and finds himself in Bolivia fighting Che Guevara. He fights for freedom and his family, and soon finds himself face to face with Che himself! Find out the true story of how Che Guevara spent his last moments from a man who witnessed this historical event. From one continent to another, history mysteriously repeats itself. Watch for **The Broken Rainbow** in the sky, for a sign showing that another Dark Angel has come to earth to persecute God's people.

The Communist Dream

The communist is a lonely, irrational beast that hides from view in the guise of a normal man. This man is supposedly bringing peace, love, happiness, and order to our world. To the rest of rational beings these promises are something we all love but if we allow him to take power we will never get to see. This man will proclaim to be himself the king.

He is the only one allowed the privilege and power to make the same mistakes again and again, against the laws of God and Nature, dragging with him a minority of fools in pursuit of a Utopian dream. This lonely and irrational beast, unless stopped in time, will not just destroy itself but also all of humanity, drowning everyone in the sea. If not stopped, the lonely, irrational beast will finally accomplish the communist Utopian dream.

The world will then be one in which none of us exist. The mask of the being is off now, and the world is now in the hands of Satan and evil, irrational beings. Is that what you want to see? For the sake of you, your family and country, and the rest of humanity, let's stop this in time and send Satan with his communist disciples to Hell where they belong. Let them enjoy there their Utopian dream.

Dr. Julio Antonio del Marmol

Integrity and Reciprocity

With no integrity and reciprocity, love dies, and the exchange can avert discord and misery that eventually feeds and makes larger the distrust that will grow deep roots into your heart destroy all the beauty, noble, and good intentions without distinction of sex for all of humanity.

Dr. Julio Antonio del Marmol

Dedication

    To those who have had to leave family, country, and even everything they owned behind because of persecution by unscrupulous dictators with extreme political and religious ideologies in order to pursue freedom, happiness, and a dignified life. These people have only sought the most precious gift any human being has: the ability to practice the religion or beliefs they choose for themselves.
    Dr. Julio Antonio del Marmol

Prologue

**Blankenfeld-Mahlow Village, Germany
1933**

My uncle was involved in helping the family of my dear friend Miguel Angel. Like everything else he did in his life, he left me extensive notes which I include here to tell the story of the Baumann family.

Blankenfeld-Mahlow was a small village just outside of Berlin in those early 1930's, with horse-drawn vehicles still more common that automotive ones. The overcast sky was darkening with the onset of evening, and a light dusting of snow could be seen on the roofs of the buildings in the village. Two working men leaned against the support poles of a storefront.

One said to the other, "Another week finished, my friend."

The other replied, "About time to have some beer!"

The two men laughed as they walked off towards the beer house. The rhythmic sound of hammering came from one of the nearby shops; but not the hard crack of nails driven into wood but instead the softer thump of nails pounded into leather.

The only reason the sound was so loud was that the door to the cobbler's shop was slightly ajar. It was a worn wooden structure, wooden crates and barrels were piled up on either side of the door. Snow accented the tops of the surfaces quaintly.

It was typical of shops in those days for the family's living quarters to be attached to the same structure as the business. As a young man hammered nails into a boot methodically, rhythmically with practiced skill, inside the house a mother and daughter prepared the table for dinner.

A silver spice tower stood in the middle of the table as other silver Judaica decorated the room. The mother, Rose, wore a simple dress and apron. Her features were distinctly Jewish with her dark hair and eyes, and she continued about her preparations peacefully and methodically.

Her daughter, Sarah, was twelve, blonde hair and blue eyed, tall for her age and had a figure already blooming into womanhood. She laid out the plates happily with a smile in her eyes.

A small boy of about six ran through the dining room until his mother stopped him. "Englebert, go tell David and your father that it is time."

"Yes, mother," Englebert replied. Sarah smiled at him as he ran with childlike energy into the shop.

The father, Jacob Baumann, was a middle-aged man. Englebert found him leaning over a table cutting leather for shoes. The sound of hammering was heard again as Jacob straightened up to examine his work. His face was lined by pleasant—a worker's face. His hair was a dusty grey, his brown eyes showed both deep emotion and strength.

Englebert said, "Father, it's time for Sabbath dinner."

The Broken Rainbow: Mysterious Dark Karma

The young man, Jacob's oldest son David, stopped his hammering. He was about nineteen, very thin, and was dressed in working clothes. He smiled at his younger brother. Jacob looked at Englebert warmly, put his tools down, and clapped his hands. "So, Englebert, did you wash your hands?"

"No, father, but I will right now!" Englebert ran out of the shop as David and Jacob cleaned up the shop.

Back in the house, two other boys sat at the table; they were Solomon Junior, aged ten, and Jacob Junior, aged eight. They impatiently waited for everyone to be ready, fidgeting as they watched Rose and Sarah.

Rose placed candles in silver candlesticks as Sarah laid out the tableware. Sarah was now wearing her lace Sabbath shawl as she laid out the Challah[1] in a basket covered by a cloth with the Star of David embroidered on it. The silver Kiddush cup[2] sat on the table near the side where Jacob walked in with David, who was wiping his hands on a towel.

Rose looked up at him and simply said, "Jacob." She planted a kiss on her husband's cheek.

"Is everyone ready?" Jacob asked. "Where is Englebert?"

Englebert popped his head up from under the table. "Here, Father! Did I surprise you?"

---

[1] Ritual bread of Ashkenazi Jewish origin made of dough from which a small portion is set aside as an offering.

[2] A silver wine cup marked with scenes of Jerusalem and engraved with the Kiddush in Hebrew. Kiddush refers to sanctification or being set apart.

Jacob looked at him disapprovingly but then he smiled. "Yes, son, but now it is time to be serious. Take your seat."

Rose lit the candles, pulled her shawl over her eyes, and began the prayer. "Blessed are you, Lord our God, sovereign of the universe, Who has sanctified us with His commandments and commanded us to light the lights of Sabbath."

Everyone sat down. Jacob poured the wine into the Kiddush cup and then prayed the Kiddush. "And there was evening and there was morning, a sixth day. The heavens and the earth were finished, the whole host of them. And on the seventh day God completed his work that He had done, and He rested on the seventh day from all His work. And God blessed the seventh day, and sanctified it because in it He had rested from all His work that God had created to do. Blessed are you, Lord our God, sovereign of the universe Who creates the fruit of the vine."

The family said in unison, "Amen."

Jacob continued, "Blessed are You, Lord our God, King of the universe, who has sanctified us with His commandments, has desired us, and has given us, in love and good will, His holy Shabbat as a heritage, in remembrance of the work of Creation; the first of the holy festivals, commemorating the Exodus from Egypt. For You have chosen us and sanctified us from among all the nations, and with love and good will given us Your holy Shabbat as a heritage. Blessed are You, Lord, who sanctifies the Shabbat."

Again, the family said in unison, "Amen."

Jacob drank from the cup and then reverently passed it around for the family to drink from it. Outside, as darkness enveloped the small village, it began to snow, the flakes drifting down to rest on the roofs and streets of the town.

Two days later, Jacob entered the shop from the back to prepare it for opening. He carefully checked the shoes on display before the window in front of the shop as David swept up in the workshop area. Jacob unlocked the front door and began to check his merchandise once more, straightening any crooked pairs of shoes that he might have missed before.

A small bell tinkled as a man entered the shop. He was a dark-haired German man in his twenties with an intense but friendly look as he strode up to Jacob. "*Guten Morgen*[3]," he said by way of greeting.

Jacob replied, "Ah, *guten Morgen, Herr Kiel*[4]. I have your order ready. I'll just go get it from the back."

Jacob went into the back, and after a moment David came out to greet their customer. "Volker! *Guten Morgen!*"

"Ah, David! It is nice to see you, it's been a little while. I swear you have grown a foot in the last month."

David looked embarrassed, and it was clear they were good friends. "Well...."

Jacob emerged with a box and said with a smile, "I think you will find these to your liking." He opened the box and presented the shoes to Volker.

"Wunderbar! As usual, you do excellent work, my friends."

"Will we see you at the cottage this week? You are always invited when we go."

---

[3] Good morning
[4] Good morning, Mr. Kiel

"Yes, yes—I would like that very much. A little drink, a little smoke, a little conversation."

Jacob laughed. "Well, if you want that, come to the beer house tonight!"

Volker reached into his pocket and pulled out some money to hand to Jacob. "Here you are. I must go for now. I will see you at the cottage." He smiled and waved as he left with the box.

Later that night, Jacob was drinking with some friends at the beer house, laughing and talking, generally having a good time. He finished his beer, said goodbye to his friends, and walked out the door to head home. Jacob walked away from the tavern, the sounds of merriment fading as the distance increased.

A few scattered lamps dimly lit the street. He put his scarf up around his face to avert the cold. He strode home leisurely, but suddenly a Gypsy woman darted out from an alley to stand in front of him.

"You are to come with me," she said. Her finger pointed at Jacob as he found himself held by her intense green eyes. The Gypsy was a middle-aged woman with a brown shawl, heavy eye makeup, and rings on every finger. She was older yet still profoundly beautiful. Jacob did not respond. She said, "Come. I have words for you. I have seen your coming tonight."

Jacob said, "I don't believe in your magic, woman."

He tried to walk past her, but she interposed herself in his path once again. "It is about your sons...." He shouldered past her and kept walking. "And your beautiful daughter."

He stopped. After a moment, Jacob turned around to face her, feeling much more sober. "What about my daughter?"

The Broken Rainbow: Mysterious Dark Karma

The Gypsy took him to a dimly lit and cramped parlor that held just enough room for her and Jacob to sit around a small table. Arcane implements adorned the walls along with religious symbols, including a cross, a Star of David, and a Buddha. She cleared a crystal ball from the table and put it away.

She said, "Do you know of the Dark One? The one who opposes all that is good?"

Jacob replied simply with, "Satan."

"He goes by many names." She gestured to the various religious symbols on the wall. "He sends ahead of him his messengers, his servants to prepare his way to come into this world. He is coming and they are here to make things ready. One is already here."

She gestured towards a newspaper sitting on a nearby table. The headline read, "Nazi Party Makes Gains."

Jacob asked, "What does this have to do with me and my family?"

"Your family is special. The Dark Angels and your family are connected. Their shadow is over you." Jacob looked concerned. She continued, "There are three of them. Your own children, a seed will come from them. One such seed will see a Dark Angel fall. The sign of these dark servants is this: a broken rainbow."

Jacob finally laughed and broke the spell in the room. "A broken rainbow? Go back to your crystal ball, woman."

He got up to leave. She said, "But first, your seed will suffer."

"What? What do you mean?"

"There will be pain. Your son, your daughter."

For a moment, Jacob looked serious and concerned, but then he shook it off. "I told you I don't believe in your magic."

She closed her eyes to see the vision in her head. "A rainbow, broken in pieces."

The room shook with a sudden earthquake. A few of her objects fell to the floor. She remained with her eyes closed while Jacob looked panicked. The earthquake stopped and he stared at the woman, who opened her eyes, breaking out of her trance. He hurriedly placed some money on the table and rushed out.

After a moment, the woman rose to pick up her mess. She walked over to where the Star of David lay on the floor, picked it up, and hung it back on the wall.

1 The First Revelation

The Broken Rainbow: Mysterious Dark Karma

Chapter 1: Dark Karma's First Appearance

2 Hitler Youth Corps

The next day, Sarah and Rose were packing food for their trip to the cottage. Rose called out, "David! David!"

David walked in with the awkwardness of a tall, gangly youth. "Yes, Mother?"

"Take your brothers and make sure they get everything ready to visit the cottage."

"Yes, Mother."

As he walked out, Sarah said, "I love going to our cottage. It's so peaceful there."

Rose replied, "Well remember to thank your father for all his hard work; without that we wouldn't have the cottage."

"I will, Mother."

They joined the rest of the family as they walked outside where the Baumanns had loaded up their carriage pulled by a four-horse team for the trip to the cottage. David and Jacob were finishing loading the carriage while the women and two young boys got seated inside it. An automobile drove by.

Sarah said, "I wonder what it is like to ride in one of those autos."

Rose frowned and replied, "Too loud, if you ask me."

Solomon Jr. said, "I'm going to have my own auto when I grow up."

"Me, too," Jacob Jr. chimed in.

Englebert said, "I'm going to have two of them!"

Rose asked, "Two? Englebert, what would you do with two autos? You could only drive one at a time."

"Well," he replied thoughtfully, "I would let Sarah drive one. Then we could drive together."

"Thank you, Englebert," Sarah said.

Rose said, "Why would you do that? If you were going to the same place, you should take the same auto. It would be silly to take two autos."

Sarah giggled as Solomon and Jacob Jr. looked out the carriage window.

Jacob and David finished loading the carriage and climbed up into the driver's box where Jacob took the reins. He cracked the whip over the horses, and they drove away. The carriage rolled across beautiful snow-covered hills and trees down a country road. Occasionally another carriage or automobile passed them.

Inside the carriage Solomon and Jacob Jr. continued to happily look out the window. Rose and Sarah talked while Englebert watched. Rose asked, "How are your ballet classes?"

"They are going well. Frau Meier says I could win the regional contest."

"You will, Sarah!" Englebert exclaimed. "You will win all the competitions!"

"Well," Sarah said modestly, "I've only won one of them."

Rose said, "I'm more concerned with those outfits the girls wear. Did you see Heidi? Her mother shouldn't let her wear makeup at such a young age."

"How old do you think a girl should be to wear makeup, Mother?" Sarah asked.

"More than twelve, like you and Heidi!" Sarah giggled. Rose continued, "You know I love you, Sarah. I just want you to watch out for those boys."

"I know, Mother," Sarah replied.

Englebert said, "Don't worry, Sarah. I'll watch out for you!"

"Oh?" Sarah asked in amusement. "What will you do?"

"If anybody bothers you," Englebert said confidently, "I'll punch 'em in the nose!"

"You most certainly will not!" Rose admonished him. Sarah laughed.

The horses and carriage drew up to the cottage. It was a lovely wooden structure with a covered porch, the roof still adorned with snow. There are some pens with chickens and a couple of happy dogs run around. Another horse-drawn carriage, the horses still in the harness, were already on the side.

David held the reins and halted the carriage. As he and Jacob climbed down, he said, "Mother! Sarah! Boys! We're here!"

The door to the carriage burst open and the boys ran out to start running around, playing with the dogs, and looking at the chickens. Sarah helped her mother down while David and Jacob grabbed some bags from the back of the carriage.

The boys burst through the cottage's front door to find their grandfather, Solomon, and grandmother, Rivka, there to welcome them. The boys ran excitedly to get their hugs, exclaiming, "Grandfather! Grandmother!"

Rose and Sarah followed the boys through the front door, Jacob and David bringing up the rear with some of the family's luggage. Jacob said, "Mother, Father, it is good to see you."

Solomon and Rivka greeted everyone with friendly hugs and kisses. Jacob asked, "David, can you get the rest?" David nodded and went back out the door as the boys started once more to run around excitedly. Jacob turned to his father and asked, "How are you doing, Father?"

"Well, I'm not getting any younger."

Rivka glanced at her husband and said to Jacob, "Oh, don't mind him—he's just fine."

David came back in and set down the last bag. Englebert tripped over it as he ran around. Jacob said, "Englebert! Boys! Go play outside!" The boys acknowledged his admonition and ran outside.

Rose, Jacob, Solomon, and Rivka sat down on the comfortable furniture around a table as they started to chat and catch each other up. After a few moments, Rose stood up and said, "I'll make some tea."

The Broken Rainbow: Mysterious Dark Karma

As she walked into the kitchen, Solomon said, "So, anything interesting happening in Starnberg these days?"

Jacob shook his head. "Not much, just working hard in the store. David has gotten so good that he could run the shop without me."

Livka asked, "How are the young ones?"

Jacob smiled. "Well, Solomon Jr. is growing so fast that I had to make him new shoes. Soon he will be good enough to make his own. Jacob Jr. is learning well also. Of course, Englebert is as lively as ever."

Solomon grunted. "You'd think something interesting would happen in town. It's so quiet up here."

Jacob said a little tentatively, "Well, Father, one night something *did* happen. I know you don't believe in the Lord…." Livka shifted nervously as the uncomfortable topic entered the conversation and Solomon frowned. Undeterred, Jacob plunged on. "Something happened. I haven't even told Rose yet. Late at night a few days ago, a Gypsy woman stopped me in town. She said she saw me coming."

"Foolishness," Solomon snorted.

"That is what I thought, Father," Jacob agreed. "Especially when she started talking about a broken rainbow."

Rose entered with a tray of tea and heard the last remark. "A rainbow?" she asked. That reminds me, Jacob—the other day I saw a rainbow in the sky. I haven't seen one for years." She passed out the tea. "But it was the strangest thing. Just after it appeared, it broke into pieces."

"When was this, Rose?" Livka asked.

"I remember it was the same day that man, Adolf Hitler, was appointed to the government. I had just heard about it on the radio."

"I still say it's foolishness," Solomon grumbled.

"What is, Solomon?" Rose asked.

"Ask Jacob. It's his foolishness, not mine," the old man answered.

"I haven't told you about it yet, Rose," Jacob said. "A fortune teller stopped me on the way back from the beer house Monday night."

"She did?" Rose asked.

"Yes, and she insisted that I hear what she had to say. I, of course, wanted to get home, but she was very persistent. Then she mentioned Sarah."

"Sarah!?" Rose exclaimed.

"So, I went in. She told me something about Satan, the Dark One coming into the world. That he is first sending his disciples to prepare the way."

"Oh, my," Livka murmured.

"Then she said that my seed would see one of these Dark Angels fall and be defeated. And that my family would suffer."

"Why would you believe such crazy talk?" Solomon demanded.

"I told you, Father, I didn't," Jacob replied. "But then, as she was finishing, she spoke about a rainbow. A broken rainbow. And then there was an earthquake. Everything shook!"

Solomon looked skeptical. "It was probably all that beer you had that night."

"Solomon!" Livka gasped.

"And *I* saw the broken rainbow," Rose mused. "What do you think it means?"

Jacob shrugged. "Maybe Father is right. Foolishness." It was clear from his expression that he was himself unconvinced. A moment later they heard the sounds of horses outside.

Rose said, "Well, it seems our friends are here. I'll go start dinner."

Later, the family dinner included Volker Kiel and another friend of the family, Hans Klaus, a blonde man in his thirties, who looked at Rose and said, "Wonderful dinner as always, Frau Baumann."

Rose smiled. "And you are a wonderful eater as always, Hans."

"No, no," Hans disagreed with a smile, "what I'm really good at is the drinking!"

Everyone laughed and Volker said with a chuckle, "I'll agree with that, Hans."

Jacob said, "Well, then, we should begin with the drinking, yes?"

Volker smiled. "I'm in favor of that, and I'm sure Hans is as well." Hans winked in reply to his friend's jest.

Rose said, "Children, help me clear the table." As they did, the men got up and walked into the sitting room. Rose and Sarah began washing the dishes that the young boys brought him.

In the meantime, the men's voices could be heard from the sitting room as they began to discuss current events. They had all seated themselves comfortably with tumblers of brandy while Jacob smoked a pipe.

Volker said, "Gentlemen, I wanted to inform you that I have applied for military service."

Hans said, "Congratulations! You will join the ranks of the brave."

Jacob asked curiously, "What prompted this?"

Volker said thoughtfully, "There is something about this new man, Hitler. He inspires me to see a better Germany, a strong nation once again. I can feel proud to call myself German."

Jacob asked, "You weren't proud before?"

Volker replied, "The shame of our last defeat still lingers. I can feel it lifting."

Solomon said, "He's just another politician full of empty promises."

Jacob replied, "Perhaps we should hear him out. Give him a chance. He does promise change for our nation."

Hans lit a cigar and spoke between puffs. "We will judge the man by his actions, not his words then. Agreed?"

Jacob nodded. "That sounds very equitable."

Volker also nodded. "I agree, though I have already chosen my course."

Solomon cautioned, "You won't like the actions he takes, even if you like the pretty words."

Jacob looked at his father. "How do you know so much, Father?"

Solomon grinned. "I can see the future, just like your pretty Gypsy woman."

Jacob looked embarrassed. At that moment, Rose entered with a tray of sweet cakes. She asked, "And what are we discussing tonight?"

"A Gyp-...." Hans started, but Jacob cut him off. "Hitler."

"I don't trust the man," Rose declared.

"Not you, too, Rose?" Jacob asked.

She shook her head. "I don't know what it is, but there's something wrong about him."

Everyone is quiet for a moment. Hans broke the silence. "Thank you for the cakes, Frau Baumann."

The Broken Rainbow: Mysterious Dark Karma

The room waited quietly for Rose to leave, and she took the hint. "Yes, of course." She got up and left.

As soon as she was gone, Solomon said, "I told you that Herr Hitler is no good."

Hans replied, "Rose may be a great cook, but that doesn't mean she knows about politics."

Jacob turned to Volker. "So, Volker—when will you know?"

"I should hear within the week."

Jacob smiled. "Well, then let us toast our brave new soldier!"

They raised their glasses for the toast, and Hans began. "To Volker Kiel!"

Solomon and Jacob said in unison, "Mazel tov."

They drank to Volker, and then Sarah entered the room. She smiled at Jacob. He said, "Ah, gentlemen, let us adjourn to the living room where we will be entertained by Sarah's skill on the harp."

Hans said, "Wunderbar!"

They walked into the living room, which had a few chairs scattered about on thick, comfortable rugs on the floor. The boys had already taken seats on one of the rugs. Sarah took her place at the harp while the men found seats with their drinks, having put their smokes away.

As Sarah began to play beautifully on the harp, Rose smiled and looked at her daughter adoringly. While Hans looked happy while he took sips from his glass, Volker looked intense, his thoughts clearly elsewhere, and Jacob appeared troubled and thoughtful. Livka also sat on the floor, holding Englebert's hand and smiling as she enjoyed her grandchildren. David smiled up at his sister affectionately, and she returned his smile as she played.

Chapter 2: The Rise of Evil

3 Hitler Becomes Chancellor

It was three years later, 1936, and the men were at work in the shop as they listened to the radio. David, now 20, sported a thin beard.

The broadcaster's voice said, "In response to the Franco-Soviet pact, our Führer announced that Germany will re-occupy the Rhineland. Military forces are already in place and the reconstruction of forts and strongholds has begun. Chancellor Hitler encourages his people to be strong in the face of this French and Soviet encirclement, proclaiming Germany a powerful and formidable rival. The Führer spoke today in Berlin about the National Socialist revolution."

A recording of Hitler then played. "Within a few weeks the social prejudices of a thousand years were swept away. So great was the Revolution that its spiritual foundations have not been understood even today by a superficial world. They speak of democracies and dictatorships and have not realized that in this country a Revolution has taken place that can be described as democratic in the highest sense of the word. Does a more glorious socialism or a truer democracy exist than that which enables a German boy to find his way to the head of the nation? The purpose of the Revolution was not to deprive the privileged, rich class of its rights, but to raise a class without rights to equality...."

Jacob turned the radio down. "That reminds me, have you heard from Herr Kiel?"

David continued working as he replied. "I got a letter from him last week. He has been promoted to lieutenant!"

Jacob paused in his work for a moment. "He has found favor, it seems."

"I miss Volker. He was a good friend."

"He still is. He's just away right now. Is he still in Stuttgart?"

"He could be. But that is close to the Rhineland. Do you think they sent him there?"

"It could be. We will have to wait for another letter."

A Nazi officer walked into the shop at that moment, looking around at the various shoes. Sarah ran in, dressed in her dancing leotard. The officer looked at her lustfully the whole time she was in the shop as she ran up to her father and kissed him on the cheek.

"Goodbye, Father!"

"Enjoy your dance class," Jacob replied. She hugged David and then ran out. The Nazi followed her movement out of the shop. Jacob cleared his throat. "Can I help you?"

"Ah, yes. I have a question about these shoes."

The Nazi asked a few inconsequential questions about Jacob's wares and then left the shop. Outside the villagers went out their business as usual, but now there were occasional Nazi soldiers in the streets. A pair of them walked by the storefront speaking to each other.

Around noon, David paused in his work and looked up at Jacob. "Father, may I go? I told Anna I would visit today if I could."

Jacob grunted in thought. "Very well, finish up what you are doing."

David finished quickly, eagerly, and ran out the door. Moments later, Rose entered the shop. "Where is David running to?" she asked. "I just made him some lunch."

"He's off to see his girl again, dear," Jacob replied. "He seems like a man in love."

"Why couldn't he find a nice Jewish girl?"

"Now, Rose...." Jacob said in an admonishing tone.

Rose walked over to the window, where David was getting ready to leave on his bicycle, a small bag in his hand. "Don't forget to walk your sister home after her dance class," she called to him.

"I won't, Mother," he called back. "Goodbye!"

Rose sat down on a stool in thought while Jacob worked. "Maybe it is better he likes a German girl."

"Oh?" Jacob replied, still focusing more on his work than the conversation.

"Herr Hitler is not too fond of us. I was right about him."

"Perhaps."

"Perhaps? You know about the new laws: no more Jewish doctors, lawyers...."

"We still have our shop," Jacob pointed out, "and food to eat."

"So we remain silent."

Jacob put down his tools. "Rose, this is our home. Our family is here. What else can we do? We survive, we keep our heads down, don't bring attention to ourselves."

"What happens when they come for *us*, Jacob? What then?"

Jacob got up and walked over to her and held her in his arms. He looked down at her. "They won't. We are well-respected in this town. We've been here for years! We have loyal friends, loyal customers. We'll be fine. You'll see."

Rose looked at him dubiously, rose to give him a quick peck on the cheek, and went back into the living area of their home. Jacob got back to work on a shoe, albeit distractedly. He hit one of his fingers with the hammer, cried out softly in pain, and held his hand where he had hit it. He knew what the trouble was; Sarah was now a beautiful teenaged girl, and she was away at her dance class. He had been by there before while they were practicing. There were about ten other young girls in the class, and they would practice ballet to music played on a record player. And there were no men around to prevent any mischief from happening. Rose's words had only added to his worry.

Meanwhile, David rode his bike up to the front fence of a small house and got off. As he walked up the path to the front door, and Anna, a blonde-haired German girl, ran out to greet him. She gave him a hug and then they sat on the front porch together.

They talked and flirted, happy and oblivious to anything else in the world but each other; not even to the setting sun.

Anna said, "My father likes you."

David replied, "Oh really? That is good, but not very important."

"What? How can you say that?"

"What is more important is what *you* think. Do *you* like me, Anna?" He started to tickle her. "Do you? Hmm? Do you like me?"

She laughed as he tickled her. "Yes!" she gasped, "Yes! Stop! Yes of course!"

"I like you, too." He leaned in and they kissed.

After a moment, Anna pushed him away. "You!"

David smiled. "Me?"

"Yes, you. You are very silly!"

"Because I like you?"

"Yes. No! Not that."

"Why then?"

"Because I say so!"

"Now *that* is silly!"

"Then we are both silly."

"Agreed!" He kissed her again and looked into her eyes. Then, suddenly, he noticed the darkening sky and remembered his sister. "Oh, no!"

"What?" Anna asked, startled at his sudden change. "What is it?"

"I forgot!" He got up and ran to his bicycle. Anna stood up in confusion. He called over his shoulder, "I have to get my sister! Goodbye!"

Anna ran up to the fence as David rode off. She called after him, "Come back soon!" Anna walked back to the porch and notices that David left his keys behind. "Oh, he must have forgotten them in his rush." She went over to the side of the house where her bicycle leaned against the wall, got on, and rode off after David.

It was twilight as David rode hard down the narrow village streets to make it to Sarah's class. A few people walked on the side as he pedaled rapidly by them.

At that moment at Sarah's dance class, the music finished as the girls struck their final poses for the dance. Their instructor was a wrinkled but otherwise pretty woman in her fifties. She ended the rehearsal by saying, "Very well, that is enough for today."

The girls all ran to get their gear while Sarah wiped her face with a towel. Then she left the building along with some other students. They got into waiting carriages or met family outside. She looked up and down the street and saw no one waiting for her, so she sat down on the stair with her bag to await the arrival of her brother, figuring he must have been delayed.

It was by now fully dark. Sarah stood up, looked around again and saw that no one was coming to find her, so she started to walk home alone. The Nazi officer from the store earlier was on the other side of the street, watching her. Seeing her alone, he crossed the street and walked towards her.

"Going home to the shoe store?" he asked by way of greeting.

"Oh," she said, slightly started. 'Yes. I'm waiting for my brother."

The Nazi looked around. "He seems to be late. Perhaps I could give you a ride?"

"No, it's fine...."

The Broken Rainbow: Mysterious Dark Karma

The Nazi interrupted her by grabbing her arm. "I insist." He forced her to walk toward his car, parked a block away.

Back at the store, Jacob was back at work on the shoes, methodically working a piece of leather into shape. When he was down, he walked back into the kitchen to wash his hands. As he was wiping them dry, Rose walked in. "Almost time to eat?" he asked her.

"Yes, as soon as Sarah and David come back."

"What?" Jacob asked in shock. "They should have been back an hour ago." He went and grabbed his coat.

"Where are you going?" Rose asked.

"To find them, of course," he replied as he strode out the door.

Rose called after him, "Be careful!"

David was riding his bicycle towards the dance studio and saw Sarah being forced into a car by the Nazi. He shouted, "Hey!"

The officer did not hear him, or pretended not to, as he got in his car and drove off. David began to follow him on his bicycle, pedaling furiously as he strove to keep up.

At that moment, Jacob, driving his old car slowly down the street as he looked for his two children, saw David on his bicycle turn into the alley.

Sarah sat in the front seat, terrified, as the officer drove off. He glanced at her and said, "Your house isn't too far away."

"Not too far, no," she replied as she looked nervously at the door handle.

"Good. We have time to take a little detour first." He made a turn down a side street.

Though David had fallen behind, he was still around a hundred yards back and saw the car turn in the distance. He pumped even harder, straining to catch up.

The officer turned down a dark alleyway and parked. He looked at Sarah lustfully as he drew his gun and turned it on her. "Get out," he commanded.

"What?"

"Get out. Now."

Sarah got out of the car.

David came around the corner and saw Sarah taking off her blouse at gunpoint. Angrily, he pedaled even faster. The Nazi, filled with his lust for Sarah, didn't even notice David's approach. He licked his lips as Sarah put her blouse into the open door of the back seat.

"And the rest," the officer said. "Take them off."

David leapt from his bicycle just as he reached the soldier, crashing into him at full speed.

"David!" Sarah exclaimed.

At the same time, Jacob's car pulled to an abrupt halt with a slight squeak of protest from the tires, the nose of the car poking into the alley.

He got out of the car and ran towards David and the Nazi. "David!" David and the officer struggled on the ground. Sarah watched in terror, clinging to her blouse. The two men wrestled for the pistol. A shot rang out, followed by another. Sarah screamed. Jacob yelled in horror, "*David!*"

Jacob ran over to the two men on the ground. David wrests the pistol away from the Nazi for a moment, but the officer grabbed hold again. They roll over with the gun between them. Finally, there is a third shot and they stopped struggling. Jacob pulled David from on top of the officer.

"Father!" David gasped, utterly out of breath.

They both looked down and saw blood welling from the gunshot wound in the Nazi's chest. He clearly didn't have long to live. Jacob took the gun from David's hand and started to look around.

Two cars pulled up at that moment, blocking the way out. Four Nazi soldiers got out and converged on the scene. Sarah knelt on the ground crying as Jacob dropped the gun and raised his hands in surrender.

A Nazi lieutenant came up and evaluated the scene. He turned to speak over his shoulder to his soldiers. "Take them." As the soldiers kicked Jacob and David to the ground, he added, "Damn Jews!" He then noticed Sarah, who now was hiding in the back seat of the car. "And you, my dear—we have a special place for Jew whores."

Anna rode up to the street entrance and got off her bike. She saw what happened and hid, watching around the corner.

Chapter 3: The Messenger

4 Gypsy woman

    The next day, Anna was at the Baumann's house comforting Rose. As she held Rose, tears streamed freely from both women's eyes. "I will try to come again tomorrow," Anna promised Rose.
    "Thank you." Rose fell back sadly into the chair she was standing in front of as Anna left. She looked out the window where a light rain beat against the windowpane. "Lord, why?" A determination suddenly showed in her

eyes as a thought struck her. "That Gypsy woman." She stood up, pulled on her coat, grabbed an umbrella by the door, and left.

Later that night, the Gypsy woman was again on the street outside the tavern, soliciting the people walking by to tell them their fortunes. A middle-aged, surly black-haired man walked by wearing a hat and a long coat. She grabbed his arm. "Do you want to know your fortune?"

"Get away from me, woman," the man growled.

"It will only take a moment," she persisted.

He yanked his arm away; as he did, she accidentally stripped off his glove, now held in her hand. "I said..." he started to say but broke off as he saw her staring in fear at his hand, which had six fingers.

Her eyes narrowed. "I know..." she started to say, but he interrupted her.

"Yes, let's get my fortune read," he said abruptly. He grabbed her roughly by the arm and took her down the street to her parlor.

Once there, he threw her to the floor next to her table. He pulled out a straight razor, opened it, and stalked towards her.

"No!" she yelled as she grabbed the crystal ball off the table and threw it at him. He grunted as it hit his torso. He kicked the table out of the way and slashed her face, blood splattering on the floor.

Outside, the rain pelted down as Rose walked along the sidewalk with her umbrella. She passed the beer house where Jacob liked to go. She paused to looked at the front, just as she had at every storefront along the way. She continued on and came to another door and heard a scream behind it. She opened it to see the Gypsy woman screaming as blood ran down her face from a nasty slice. A man was ruthlessly attacking her and lashed out, slashing the woman's arm.

She screamed in pain again. Seeing Rose, she yelled, "Help!"

The man looked up from where he was struggling with the Gypsy woman as Rose entered. She took the scene in with one glance and said, "My God!" She turned and bolted out the door, calling out, "Police! Help, police!"

After a moment, Rose heard a police whistle and footsteps running towards her. "This way!" she called out and then ran back inside the parlor.

As she came back inside, she saw the man's alert face; clearly, he had heard the police whistle. He turned quickly back to the Gypsy woman and shoved her hard into the wall. He slashed her gut, blood spurting on his hands, the razor glistening red in the light. Some of the blood splattered on Rose. She wiped the blood from her face in shock and looked up into his eyes, which reflected cat-like in the low light. He turned and ran out the door. She ran outside after him.

As he burst out the door into the street and ran away, a policeman that was running up saw him and began to give chase. Rose called out, "Wait! No!" Without waiting to see if the policeman was going to pause, she ran back inside.

She found the Gypsy woman on the floor next to many of her trinkets which had been knocked over by the fight, trying to hold the blood back from spilling out of her stomach. Rose went over to the lady, took out her handkerchief, and cleaned the blood from her face as best she could. "It will be all right now," she said as soothingly as she could.

The Broken Rainbow: Mysterious Dark Karma

She took the handkerchief and put it underneath the woman's hand to press against the dreadful wound. The Gypsy said very weakly, "Thank you."

"I'm Rose, I'm..." Rose began.

"I know who you are. Sarah's mother. Has it happened yet?"

"You know? Yes, yes, it's happened. Oh, my God."

"I cannot change the future; I only see it. I am sorry."

"How do you know these things?" Rose demanded.

"I know what I know. That is why the Dark Guardian tried to kill me. I knew who he was."

"Dark Guardian?" Rose asked in confusion.

"Yes. They guard...the Dark Angels."

"The Dark Angels. Like you told Jacob."

"Yes. Jacob. They have six fingers, you see...." The Gypsy woman passed out.

The policeman entered the room at that point. "What happened?" he asked.

Rose turned to him. "Get a doctor! Quick!"

The policeman ran out. Rose turned back to the Gypsy, only to see her suddenly wake up, her eyes staring at whatever vision she was having. "Your seed, a light in the darkness. You must hide! Soon! They are...."

The woman fell over dead, her eyes still open. Rose gently closed them and held the woman to her as she cried.

A while later, Rose was returning home where she saw a group of men outside the cobbler's, some wearing armbands with swastikas, smashing the window of the shop. They didn't see her.

One man yelled, "Go home, Jew!"

Another man yelled, "Take your dirty business elsewhere!"

Rose snuck around to the back door of the house, hoping the men wouldn't see her. As soon as she could tell they didn't, she ran inside.

As she ran in, she saw her sons huddled together in the darkness. Engelbert was crying quietly. Solomon Jr looked up and said to her, "We have to go now, Mother."

"I know." They sat together in the dark and helplessly watched the men outside vandalize and set the shop on fire.

The next day, Sarah was sitting in a Nazi prisoner processing center in a room full of metal chairs with several other Jewish women. All of them shared a defeated look. Armed guards secure the doors into the room. One of them opened and a gruff-looking sergeant strode into the room.

He looked around and barked, "Heinrich. Heinrich!" A lady looked up sadly. "This way."

She walked along limply, and the sergeant pulled her more quickly to the front desk, grabbed some paperwork off the desk, and took her out through a back door.

Volker Kiel entered, now wearing the uniform of a Captain in the SS. He tried not to look at the women as he strode up to the clerk who sat behind the desk. Sarah watched him, but since his back was turned to her the entire time, she did not recognize him. The desk clerk looks up, anticipating Volker's order. "I'm here for the prisoner research information. Yes, that folder."

The clerk handed it to him. "Will there be anything else, Captain?"

"That is all. Heil Hitler."

The Broken Rainbow: Mysterious Dark Karma

"Heil Hitler."

Volker turned to walk out and saw Sarah. He recognized her, but his shocked expression quickly disappeared as he regained his composure. He strode purposefully to her. "You!" Sarah looked up at him with a start and saw the quick wink Volker gave her. "You thought you could get away with it, did you?"

Sarah looked frightened and did not respond. Volker turned back to the desk clerk. "Clerk! Get me this prisoner's paperwork! I will handle this one personally."

The clerk looked nervous and dug through some paperwork, finally producing a file. Volker strode up and snatched it. "Very well." He went back and grabbed Sarah roughly by the arm. "Shameful woman! The whore camps are too good for you! Maybe if you are alive after my interrogation, we will see what they do with you."

He marched her out the door as the guards saluted him. He put Sarah in the back seat of his car and drove off. As he started off, he tossed the prisoner file onto Sarah's lap. "So, your brother and father, too?" he asked her.

"Yes," she replied timidly.

"You're lucky I found you. You know where they were sending you?" Sarah nodded fearfully. "I will do what I can to protect you and help your family. It may take some time."

"Thank you, Volker," she said gratefully, now that he had expressed his intentions.

"Captain Kiel from now on, Sarah. Remember that."

It was evening when the car pulled up to a modest but well-tended house. Volker drove around to the back door, and they quickly got out to enter the house.

Volker took her into the sitting room where he had her take a seat. "You seem unharmed," he said. "I will keep you here, but you must remain out of sight."

"Oh, thank you, Volk—Captain Kiel," Sarah said gratefully.

He looked at her kindly. "There is nothing I can do for your father and brother, yet. However, I have been most favored by men high in the Nazi organization, as you can see." He gestured around at the house. "It's not a good time to be a Jew in Germany, Sarah. I have tried to find the rest of your family. It appears they've gone into hiding. I imagine they're at the cottage; I will try to contact them, discretely." He paused for a moment as he looked at her. He gently removed her Star of David necklace. "This will have to go, for now. You don't look like a Jew, and the less people realize that you are, the better."

"Volker," she started. Then she sprang up and clung to him as she began to cry.

He stiffened for a second, but then relaxed and began to pat her on the back comfortingly. "Remember now, girl, in this house, I am Captain Kiel. If anyone asks, you are a servant. Stay out of sight. We never knew each other before. Understand?"

She nodded into his chest as she continued to cry, the tension of the past several hours finally found its release.

The Broken Rainbow: Mysterious Dark Karma

Chapter 4: Sadness, Death, and Exile

5 Jewish Refugees Arrive in Barcelona

Rose stopped the carriage outside the cottage with Solomon Jr. sitting next to her. As they stepped to the ground, Englebert and Jacob Jr. exited the carriage. All the boys were somber, lacking their usual energy. The family begins to unpack the carriage; they only brought with them those belongings which they could carry. As Rose unloads a bundle, the Kiddish cup falls onto the grass. As Rose straightens up from picking it up, Grandmother Livka comes out of the house. She gives Rose a hug and then starts to help with the unpacking.

Wordlessly, Livka and Rose left the boys in the living room and went up to the bedroom, where Grandfather Solomon was gravely ill. They stood by his bedside, listening to his raspy breathing. They spoke to each other quietly to avoid disturbing him.

Livka said, "We dare not take him to the doctor now."

Rose replied, "They made Dr. Goldberg stop practicing. Thank goodness Dr. Emilio del Marmol is still allowed to practice, or we wouldn't have any medical help! Is he eating?"

Livka began to say, "Well…" when Solomon opened his eyes.

"Woman, stop talking about me like I'm not here," he grumbled testily.

Livka smiled. "He's not too bad, I suppose."

Rose and Livka tucked him back in and went downstairs to begin cooking dinner. Rose observed, "It's the Sabbath tomorrow."

"We can make enough of this for two meals, I think," Livka replied.

They finished their meal preparations and set the table. Making sure the boys washed up, they all sat down for dinner, save for Solomon, who remained in his bedroom, too ill to attend.

While they were eating, Englebert asked, "Can we play outside?"

"Finish your dinner, Englebert," Rose reproved him. "You know better."

Englebert turned back to his plate. Livka was pouring a glass of wine, but her trembling hands knocked over the glass. Wine spilled all over the table and onto the floor. Livka snatched a napkin off the table and got onto her knees to wipe the mess up off the floor. She lost her composure and started to weep, her tears falling into the wine on the floor.

Rose took one startled look at her mother-in-law and said, "Boys, go now, go out and play." The boys ran quickly outside as Rose went to comfort Livka. "It's all right, Livka, it will be fine."

"No, Rose—it won't," she sobbed. "He's dying." There was nothing else to say, and Rose held Livka as she cried.

Volker was seated at a table in the sitting room, his back to the door as Sarah entered. He was holding a letter that he had just finished reading. Without turning, he said, "Sarah, sit down."

She sat down wordlessly and watched as Volker turned to face her. He said, "I'm sorry to have to tell you this. I received word from Dr. Emilio del Marmol—your grandfather has died."

Sarah started to cry. Volker threw the letter away in disgust. He looked at Sarah, her head bowed as she wept, and took a step towards her to comfort her. He realized that she might want to endure her initial grief alone, and so changed his mind to instead step out of the room and leave her to it.

It was now 1938; two years had passed. Sarah sat in a chair in the small room that had become her own in Volker's house doing some knitting. She looked like a grown woman now, wearing makeup, and thanks to Volker's protection appeared healthy and strong.

Volker appeared in the doorway. "Sarah, when you are finished, come to my sitting room."

"Yes, Captain Kiel." Volker left, and Sarah hurried to reach a stopping point with her knitting. There was some urgency to his voice; he must have had something important to tell her.

When she entered the sitting room, Volker was standing, and she could see in his face a barely controlled nervous excitement.

"Sit," Volker said. Sarah sat in the chair he pointed to. "I have found a way to free your father and your brother." Sarah gasped. "You must be ready to leave at a moment's notice. Discreetly pack your things tomorrow."

"Yes, Captain Kiel." She went to the door and paused with her hand on the doorframe. "Thank you."

Jacob and David had been imprisoned at the Buchenwald Concentration camp for around a year. The closed gates bore the grim words in wrought iron *Jedem das Seine*.[5] The gates opened to let a Nazi staff car inside. Emaciated prisoners were hard at work in the yard, some digging and some setting posts for a fence.

David was digging with a shovel, covered in dirt and shirtless, his father Jacob not far away. They glanced at each other for a moment, weary, and then continued their exhausting work.

Inside the Commandant's office, Karl-Otto Koch, a balding, middle-aged man, sat at his desk in the well-apportioned office. A bottle of brandy and a cigar box sat on the surface. A soldier bearing a package entered the office, saluted, and extended the package.

"On the desk, Sergeant," Koch said. "Dismissed."

The soldier put the package down, saluted once more as he clicked his heels together with military precision, spun about, and left the office.

---

[5] "To each what he deserves"

Koch opened the package lazily. A stack of German Marks fell onto the desktop. He reached into the package, pulled out the rest of the money, and put it on the table. He read the note that came with the money. After a moment, he nodded and smiled before summoning his aide-de-camp.

"Lieutenant Weiss!"

The young lieutenant entered the room and stood at attention. "Ja, Herr Commandant!"

"Let me see the guard patrol schedule for this week."

"*Jawohl!*[6]" Weiss clicked his heels as he saluted and left the room.

Koch smiled as he took the money and put it in one of the drawers of his desk. He picked out a cigar from the box and a lighter, leaned back in his chair, and lit the cigar as he propped up his feet on the desk.

As evening fell on the concentration camp, a loud whistle sounded to signal the end of the workday. The prisoners started to put away their shovels and equipment under the watchful eyes of the guards. David and Jacob, exhausted, walked next to each other toward the barracks.

Lieutenant Weiss strode across the yard towards them. "You two!" They looked up at him, startled. "Extra duty tonight in the yard." He pointed to an area near the fence. "Keep digging over there."

"Yes, Herr Weiss," David said as Jacob nodded wearily.

---

[6] Yes, sir!

As they walked toward the fence, they looked at each other warily. "There is no rest for us, my son," Jacob said.

"Maybe it is better to give up and die," David said glumly.

"No, David—don't give them what they want."

David sighed wearily as they picked up their tools to continue working.

A few hours later, under the watchful eye of a guard they had come to know named Klaus, they continued to dig despite their extreme exhaustion. A pile of tools lay nearby. Then they heard the voice of Lieutenant Weiss.

"Klaus! *Kommst du hier!*[7]"

Klaus hesitated. "But—" he started to say.

Weiss barked, "*Komm hier jetzt!*[8]"

"Of course, Herr Weiss!" In spite of his reservations, Klaus left to go see what his officer wanted.

David and Jacob were left alone in the darkness. They exchanged suspicious looks, shrugged, and then threw down their shovels to dig through the piles of tools. Jacob finds a pair of wire cutters and started to cut through the fence while David kept watch.

There were strangely no guards in sight. David found himself watching his father more than keeping watch, and so neither man noticed a military jeep slowly and quietly approaching.

Jacob finished cutting free the bottom of the fence and lifted it up for David. "Go."

"No," David protested, "you go first."

"Be silent and go, boy!" Jacob commanded quietly.

---

[7] Come here!
[8] Come here now!

David crawled under the fence. The jeep started to drive towards the hole in the fence as David turned to hold the fence up for his father.

Jacob started to climb under but got caught on the fence. The jeep came around the corner and shone its lights on David and Jacob. David looked up into the lights.

"No!" he exclaimed.

Jacob was still struggling and stuck. The car came closer and stopped suddenly. A door opened and the dark silhouette of a camp guard in a helmet could be seen. "Halt!" the guard yelled. "Halt!"

David panicked and ran towards the guard as he screamed his defiance. Shots were heard, and David went down lifelessly. Jacob finally freed himself of the fence just in time to see David drop. "No!" he yelled. His yell turned into a scream as he was riddled with bullets.

The next day, as prisoners were forced to dig graves for Jacob and David, unceremoniously tossed into the pits and covered with dirt, Commandant Koch summoned Lieutenant Weiss to his office.

"And what was that commotion last night?" Koch asked.

"Two prisoners were killed in an escape attempt," Weiss replied.

"Oh, I see. How unfortunate." Koch took a sip from his glass of brandy. "Who were they?"

"Does it matter, Herr Commandant?"

"No. No, I suppose not. Double the guard tonight, Weiss. Dismissed."

Volker ran up the stairs of his house in his uniform and coat. He threw open the door to Sarah's small room. Sarah was in there, knitting as usual.

"You must go, now!" Volker said. He strode in and picked up the bags she had packed earlier. "Get your coat."

Sarah wordlessly threw her knitting into her travel back and picked up her coat. The two of them rapidly went downstairs to get into Volker's car.

The day was overcast as the car sped along. Sarah sat in the passenger seat as Volker drove. Without looking at her, he said, "I don't know how to tell you this."

Sarah asked, "What is it?"

"The escape attempt failed. Your father and your brother…." He turned to look at her. "They're dead."

"No!" she exclaimed in shock.

"Dr. Emilio del Marmol has made arrangements. The rest of your family is meeting us at the station. You will be leaving for Spain." Sarah began to weep. "You must be strong. Hold yourself together until you get to Spain. Do you understand?" She continued to cry. "I said, hold yourself together! Do not show that anything is wrong! Do you understand?" Sarah sniffled and nodded.

A short while later, Volker pulled into the train station. There they saw Emilio walking rapidly towards them holding an envelope. He came up to Volker and said, "I just received word. The Gestapo are on your tail, Volker. The time has come for us to retreat and leave Germany." He handed the envelope to Sarah. "The papers inside are for you and your family. You should be able to board a ship for Barcelona without any trouble."

Volker and Sarah got out with the bags and walked quickly out onto the platform where they found Rose, Livka, and the three Baumann boys waiting for the train. They were all carrying travel bags and train tickets.

Englebert watched in amazement as the train pulled in. "Wow, mother! Look at that train!"

The Broken Rainbow: Mysterious Dark Karma

Rose saw Sarah and was overcome with emotion. Sarah ran to her, and they embraced. "My sweet girl," Rose said as the boys all tugged on Sarah's skirt to get her attention.

Volker said, "No time for this now. You must go. Quickly, here are your papers! Get on the train!"

Sarah stepped away from Rose, and all of them looked at Volker. Sarah said, "Captain...Volker—thank you so much."

Volker handed her the Star of David necklace. "Here, take this. It's yours." Sarah took it and gave him a kiss on the cheek. Volker grew emotional as well. "Go. Go!"

They turned and hurriedly boarded the train. Volker watched them leave, his hands behind his back. After a few moments, the train pulled away, and he saw Sarah watching him out of a window.

Volker turned and got into his car. As he drove back home, he continually checked his rearview mirror nervously. There was no need; when he arrived at his house there were two Nazi staff cars waiting for him, a Gestapo major standing on the steps with four guards around him. When Volker got out of his car, the guards trained their rifles at him. He surrendered peacefully and got into the staff car.

Dr. Julio Antonio del Marmol

Chapter 5: No Escape from Evil

6 *Francisco Franco, Fascist Dictator of Spain*

By 1939, the family had relocated to the small town of Torreblanca, Spain. Small houses were crowded together along the street of this community on the Mediterranean coast. A few trees decorated the street; people walked by with hats to block the sun, and an occasional car drove by. Sarah entered their house carrying a basket of vegetables.

She walked through the clay house to the back room where her entire family now lived. A small window allowed light into the room, bedrolls laid against one wall, and a small table and dresser against the other. The table was covered by a simple tablecloth and the Kiddish cup sat in the center, the only piece of silver left to the family. Livka sat in a small chair in the corner, looking old and weary. The boys were playing a game with sticks on the beds. Rose looked up from her sewing as Sarah entered the room.

"It is war, Mother," Sarah told her.

Rose looked sad at that news. "More people will die."

Sarah put the vegetables on the small table. "We are safe from it here."

"For now, child."

Sarah looked at her mother thoughtfully. "I found some more work, down at the bakery."

"How much will they pay?" Rose asked.

"They don't pay in money," Sarah answered, "but I will get bread to bring home."

"The Lord knows we need it." Rose looked at the boys playing in their cheap clothing.

Sarah left the house with her empty basket to run some more errands. A Spanish inspector with the secret police stopped her. "Do you live in this house?"

"Yes," she replied, "with my family."

"I need to see your papers."

"I don't have them right now," Sarah protested.

"If you don't have your papers, you will have to pay me a...special tax. It will cost you fifty pesetas."

Sarah looked around for some support, but everyone assiduously minded their own business or seemed inclined to help. "But I don't have that."

The inspector looked at her greedily and lustfully. "There is also another way you could pay me." Sarah shook her head emphatically. "It's either that or the money. You have three days. Now go!"

That night, the family gathered together for dinner. Rose and Sarah were making a simple meal, while the boys remained unhappily quiet and Livka sat quietly in her chair.

Rose looked at the boys. "Boys, wash your hands for dinner." The boys acknowledged her and ran off to wash.

A second later, the window shattered as a brick was thrown through it. It landed on the table, knocking over some food. Livka screamed, Sarah was frozen in shock, but Rose angrily picked up the brick. It had a note wrapped around it which read, *Vete a casa judíos*[9] and had a Star of David with a red swastika drawn over the top of it.

The boys ran in. Englebert exclaimed, "What happened?"

Sarah looked at the boys and gathered them together. "Nothing. It's OK. Go finish washing up." The boys looked unsure, but Sarah shuffled them out of the room.

Rose took the note and crumpled it up. "They're after us, even here."

"No, mother," Sarah disagreed, "it's not many. Most people here do not believe this way."

"Then why doesn't someone stop them?"

---

[9] Go home Jews

"The police are corrupt. They don't care." Sarah took the note from her mother's hands and threw it away. "It will be all right, Mother."

"Will it, Sarah? Will it ever be all right again?"

Sarah held Rose while Livka got up and began to sweep up the broken glass.

The next day, as Sarah left with her basket to go to work, the owner of the house, Mrs. Cortez stopped her. She looked sympathetic and troubled. "Sarah."

"Oh, yes. Hello, Mrs. Cortez."

"Sarah, I'm sorry. It's not my fault."

"What isn't your fault?"

"You're going to have to leave my house. I'm sorry."

"Why? What have we done?"

"It's nothing you've done, gentle Sarah. It's just...." She glanced out into the street at the people walking by. The inspector stood across the street, giving them an evil look.

"I see," Sarah said in resignation. "I'll go tell my family."

"No, Sarah, I'll go do that. Go to work, make your money. You'll need it."

Sarah looked back at the house and then ran off to work. The policeman watched her go with a satisfied look.

That evening, Sarah returned home with her basket. As she approached the house, a dark-skinned man with curly black hair wearing the clothes of a sailor and carrying a small bag left the house. He looked at her for a moment and then continued on his way. Sarah watched in curiosity as he left and then entered the house. From a place of concealment, the inspector also watched the man leave.

Sarah entered the small room where the family lived. Rose, looking sad and determined, sat at the table which no longer was adorned by the Kiddish cup.

Sarah asked, "Mother, who was that man?"

"Sit down, Sarah," Rose said. Sarah put the basket away and sat down. "We are going on a ship."

"What?" Sarah asked. "Where?"

Englebert ran in at that moment. "Sarah!" he said excitedly. "We're leaving on a ship! We're going to Cuba!"

"Cuba?" Sarah asked.

"I wonder how big the ship is?" Englebert said. Then he ran off to look for his brothers. "Hey, Jacob—did you hear about the ship?"

Sarah looked at the empty spot on the table. "The cup?" she asked her mother. Rose nodded. "When are we leaving?"

"Two days."

"I'll start the preparations.

Rose said very quietly as Sarah got up, "I'll get you a harp."

"What?"

"After we get there. I'll get you a harp so you can play for us again."

"That will be nice, Mother." Sarah smiled weakly.

Two days later, the family left the house under cover of darkness, each of them carrying small bags. They walked quickly into town towards the port, keeping to the shadows on their trek through the night. An occasional drunk or vagrant walked by them, and in the shadows the figure of the inspector followed them.

As the family approached the docks, they headed towards one of the ships. As soon as he saw the ships, the inspector realized what they were planning to do and blew his police whistle. "*Alto en nombre de la ley!*[10]"

The family started to run and ducked into a nearby warehouse. Livka slumped to the ground, breathing heavily. The inspector ran up and stopped when he saw no one in sight.

He called out loudly, "I know you are close by! You can't have gotten too far!" He looked around at the nearby buildings. "I should have arrested you all from the start, but I am generous!"

He walked toward the building they were hiding in and tried to see through the windows in the dark. The family ducked down. "Let me make a deal with you: give me the girl, and I will let the rest of you escape."

Sarah started to get up, but Rose pushed her back down, emphatically shaking her head no. They could see the inspector outside in the dim light.

"This is your last chance," he called out. "I get the girl; you get your freedom."

They watched him in fear. Suddenly there was a crashing noise from a building on the other side of the street. The inspector turned and ran towards it.

"Run!" Rose urged them. "Run!"

The family started running toward a rear door they had spotted in the warehouse. Unnoticed by the family in their haste, Engelbert was missing.

The inspector ran to the building the crash had come from and burst through the door. He looked around as he tried to see in the darkness. As he did so, Engelbert slipped out a side window and ran towards the docks.

---

[10] Halt in the name of the law!

The Baumann family ran around the corner as the ship's whistle blew and saw the sailor starting to board her. Jacob Jr. called out, "Hey!"

The sailor turned around and waved frantically to them as they boarded the ship. It was only as they arranged themselves by the rail that Rose noticed Engelbert's absence.

"Engelbert!" she exclaimed. "Where is Engelbert?"

The family looked around in shock. He was nowhere to be seen, and the ship's crew were pulling the gangplank aboard.

Engelbert came running around a corner as fast as he could. He waved at the ship and shouted. Solomon Jr. said as he saw him, "Look! It's Engelbert!"

The family shouted encouragement to Engelbert as the ship began to pull away from the pier. He reached the edge and didn't stop, using his momentum to jump for it. His hands grabbed the side rails, and he managed to pull himself up. The inspector rounded the corner, out of breath, far too late to stop the family. He stood on the shore, his chest heaving, as he helplessly watched the ship leave.

The family watched the ocean as the ship hit open water. Engelbert held Livka's hand while Rose spoke with the sailor.

He said, "You will be in the cargo area, below decks." Rose nodded. The boys looked around the ship. "I'll bring you food from the galley when I can. Let's get below."

Rose looked at her sons. "Time to go, boys."

The boys were clearly excited, and Sarah smiled at them. Engelbert looked quite pleased with himself; Livka, however, looked nervous.

The sailor showed them the area of the cargo hold they would occupy during the voyage. They were a little crowded in the small area, but they managed to set up some crates to use as seats and spread blankets out on the deck. The area was lit by a single oil lantern.

"Is the ship fast?" Engelbert asked.

Sarah replied, "Yes, Engelbert. Can't you feel it."

Engelbert was still for a moment as he concentrated. "Yes! Yes, I can! I can feel it moving!"

Solomon Jr. said, "I can, too!"

Livka leaned against a crate, coughed weakly, and closed her eyes.

A few days passed, as the ship ploughed through the open sea, the sailor arrived with two trays of food for the family. It was simple sailor's fare, just bread and beans. "This is all I could get," he said apologetically.

"We are grateful," Rose said. The sailor nodded and left.

The boys gathered around to eat. Jacob Jr. moaned, "Not beans again!"

"Jacob!" Rose said sharply. "Be thankful to God for our food."

"I like beans," Engelbert said.

Sarah brought some bread to Livka. "Here, Grandmother, eat."

Livka sat up and looked wearily at the bread. "I'm not hungry."

"You must eat," Sarah urged.

"Later, my dear." Livka sank back down, looking pale.

Sarah went over to Rose. "I think Grandmother is sick."

"I know," Rose replied. "I think she is too old for all our hardships. Just pray to God that she can hold on." Sarah looked at Livka sadly.

The sun set several days later as the ship continued on her voyage to Cuba. The lantern lit the hold again. The three boys were all crying as Sarah and Rose ceremonially washed the body of the deceased Livka.

They wrapped her in a white sheet, and the sailor came down to collect it. Rose sat on a crate, a veil over her head as she prayed. "Blessed are you, oh Lord our God, Ruler of the universe, the true Judge." Sarah comforted the boys as they cried, and Rose continued to pray.

The sailor brought his bundle up on deck to the edge of the rail and paused for a moment to rest. He looked at the bundle and then the dark waves of the ocean in confusion. He felt he needed to do something but didn't know what. He crossed himself in Catholic fashion, picked up the body, and threw it overboard.

Finally, the sun rose to herald a beautiful day off the Cuban coast that the ship slowly cruised towards. The family stood on deck, looking at the view quietly, awed by the beauty of the landscape. The sailor approached them solemnly.

"Here," he said as he placed some money in Rose's hand.

"What?" she asked. "Why?"

"You paid me for six. I—this is the least I can do."

Rose bowed her head sadly. "Thank you."

Chapter 6: A Short-Lived Paradise

7 Immigrants Arriving in Havana

The family left the ship with their meager possessions. The sailor disembarked after them, looked back at the family for a moment, and then walked of toward the town of Havana. The family watched the people walking by and then at the city.

Sarah said, "A new life, once again."

Rose answered, "I think we should go back to our old life, Sarah."

"What do you mean?"

Rose said, "Let's make shoes. What do you think, my sons? Do you remember how?"

"I remember!" Engelbert exclaimed.

"I was the best," asserted Jacob Jr.

"No, I was the best," Solomon Jr. disagreed.

Jacob Jr. looked at Solomon Jr. "*We* are the best!"

Engelbert, not to be left out, said, "I'm the best, too!"

Sarah said with an amused smile at the boys, "I think the answer must be yes, Mother." The family made their way to begin their new life in Havana.

As the Baumanns began their new life, events in the world outside Cuba quickened pace. They read of the British Royal Air Force launching its first strike against Germany's fleet, the shockingly fast invasion and conquest of Poland, the seemingly abject surrenders of Belgium and then France, the Battle of Britain, and then listened in horror to radio accounts of the Japanese attack on the United States at their naval base in Pearl Harbor. Two days later, as they expected, Cuba declared war on Japan and then shortly afterwards against Germany and Italy.

It was now 1942, and Hitler was giving a speech in Berlin. "One the first day of September, 1939, we made two pronouncements in the Reichstag session of that date: first, that now that they have forced this war upon us no amount of military force and no length of time will ever be able to conquer us; and second, if the Jewry is starting an international world war to eliminate the Aryan nations of Europe, then it won't be the Aryan nation which will be wiped out but Jewry.

"They have drawn nation after nation into this war. The men who pull the strings of this demented man in the White House have managed actually to draw one nation after the other into this war. But to just the same degree a wave of anti-Semitism has swept over nation after nation. And it will move on farther. State after state that enters this war will one day become anti-Semitic. In Germany, too, the Jews once laughed at my prophecies. I don't know whether they are still laughing, or whether they have lost the inclination to laugh, but I can assure you that everywhere they will stop laughing. With these prophecies, I shall prove to be right, and history will absolve me."

I discovered later on how profound an impact this speech had on a teenaged Fidel Castro. I caught him practicing in his office one day to a recording of this speech, and he told me the following story.
He had been standing in front of a mirror in his bedroom, initially to admire how his first beard was growing in. The mirror was attached to his dresser, and on top of the dresser was a copy of *Mein Kampf*. He saw it and began to imitate Hitler's mannerisms and vocal cadence patterns as he recited the speech he had memorized. "I don't know whether they are still laughing, or whether they have the inclination to laugh, but I can assure you that everywhere they will stop laughing. With these prophecies, I shall prove to be right, and history will absolve me."
He said he would have continued to do it again from the start, but at that moment his mother called out to him that it was time to go to school. He posed in the mirror one last time before turning away to leave.

It was now 1943, and the Baumanns had moved to the capital of the same name as the Pinar del Rio Province on the occidental side of Cuba. They had set up a house next to a small shoemaking shop in that beautiful city of Pinar del Rio. The shop proclaimed to all who walked by in the street that it was "Baumann, Shoemaker" in Spanish.

Solomon Jr., now a teenager like both his brothers, walked from the house into the shop. He found Jacob Jr. already at work as he walked up to a table to prepare his tools. Jacob Jr. finished up with a shoe set on a special stand for the work.

As Solomon Jr. began to measure some pieces of leather, Engelbert came running in with his usual energy. "I've got some new leather," he announced as he dumped the material on the table.

"Oh, thank you, Engelbert," Solomon Jr. said.

"Do you need anything else?" Engelbert asked.

"No, thank you," Solomon Jr. replied. "Go see if Sarah needs any help in the house."

"Right!" Engelbert replied as he turned and ran into the house.

"He still has all the energy of a child," Jacob Jr. remarked.

"I wish I still did," Solomon Jr. replied with a gentle smile as both of them got back to work.

Sarah, now a grown woman, was helping her mother in the kitchen while they listened to music on the radio. The song ended, and the announcer came on with a news bulletin.

"Here is the latest news for the hour. With the success of Allied forces landing in Reggio de Calabria, Italy has surrendered. Significant advances are being made on many fronts as the Allies are pushing the Germans back, while they still occupy the capital of Rome. Stay tuned to this station for more updates."

Rose was kneading some bread and paused for a moment. "It is almost over."

"Do you think?" Sarah asked dubiously. "Hitler is crafty; he might still find a way to win."

"Let us pray he does not. For everyone's sake." There was a knock at the door, and Rose smiled. "That would be your young pilot, I believe, Sarah."

"Oh!" Sarah exclaimed. She wiped her hands off and tried to fix her hair. "Do I look all right?"

Rose smiled. "You'd better not leave him waiting too long."

"Right!" Sarah replied. She went to the door and opened it. As her mother predicted, it was Ramon, a young Cuban man who was nicely dressed, clean-shaven, with curly hair and a friendly smile.

"Sarah!" he exclaimed.

"Yes," she answered, "what is it, Ramon?"

He looked excited, but then he paused. "Well, may I come in first?"

"Of course!" Sarah replied as she stepped back and opened the door wider to allow him in. He gave Sarah a big hug. "Well? What has you so happy?"

"They gave us planes, Sarah! The United States! I'm going to fly one!"

"Well, that is good news for you, my handsome pilot. Will you stay for dinner?"

Ramon poked his head into the kitchen. "If that is all right with Mrs. Baumann?"

Rose replied, "Of course it is, dear."

Jacob Jr. and Solomon Jr. came in from the shop at that moment. Both youths greeted Ramon warmly, and he replied, "Greetings! Finished with work for today? Where is Engelbert?"

Jacob Jr. looked behind and shrugged. "He's still in the shop, cleaning up. He will come soon if he is hungry."

Back in the shop, Engelbert had indeed finished cleaning up and left. Outside, he paused and looked up into the sky as he took a deep breath of air before entering the house. He entered the dining room where he found Sarah, Jacob Jr., Solomon Jr., and Ramon already seated as Rose finished dinner preparations.

Ramon said, "There you are, Engelbert!"

Engelbert replied, "Here you are, Ramon! It's good to see you!"

"And you as well!"

Engelbert looked at Rose. "I'm hungry. Is it time to eat?"

"Just about ready, dear," Rose replied. "Sit down. Did you wash your hands?"

"Right, mother." Engelbert rushed off to wash his hands.

Rose finished setting out the meal while the rest of the table chatted politely. A new silver Kiddush cup adorned the center of the table. Engelbert returned and took his seat.

Solomon Jr. stood to begin the prayer as the eldest male in the family. Ramon and the rest bowed their heads in reverence. "Blessed are you, Lord our God, King of the universe, who brings forth bread from the earth."

Solomon Jr. passed the bread around and they began to eat. As the Baumann family and Ramon enjoyed their dinner together, a warm glow emanated from the window outside.

As dinner finished, Rose and Sarah rose to take the plates to the kitchen. Ramon asked, "Solomon, how is the shoemaking business?"

"Shoes?" Solomon Jr. asked with a chuckle. "All I make now are boots for the army! But it is good. Plenty of work to do."

"I am glad you have so much work!" Ramon smiled. Sarah walked in behind Ramon. As she passed him, he took her hand, causing her a little embarrassment. "And you, beautiful flower. Can you play for us on your harp?"

Sarah smiled sweetly, and the rest of the family took a seat as she took her place at the harp. As they settled in, Rose looked at the old, framed picture of Livka and Solomon on the mantel next to a painting of Old Jerusalem on the wall. Ramon watched Sarah with evident delight. Engelbert held his mother's hand, Solomon Jr. watched Sarah play, while Jacob Jr. listened intently with his eyes closed. Rose smiled at her daughter and looked at Engelbert.

Chapter 7: Sarah's Brief Happiness

8 Jewish Wedding

The green field with a gazebo was decorated with white ribbons and flowers for a wedding. There were a few tables scattered around and people were eating as they celebrated the wedding feast of Sarah and Ramon.

A Chuppah[11] was positioned at one end as Rose and Ramon's mother stood before the guests holding plates. They smashed the plates onto the ground together, and then laughed and clapped together.

---

[11] A white canopy held up by four poles and decorated with flowers used in Jewish weddings

The Broken Rainbow: Mysterious Dark Karma

The guests cheered and applauded and then started to eat. Everyone grew quiet as Sarah, the beautiful bride, arrived. Ramon appeared on the other side of the field and strode towards her and pulled the veil down over her face. He was then escorted by two of his friends to the Chuppah to wait for Sarah.

Rose and Ramon's mother got on each side of Sarah to escort her to Ramon. The local rabbi stood at the Chuppah waiting for the couple as Sarah arrived. Englebert brought an ornate box to Ramon, who opened it and took out the wedding ring. Shyly, Sarah extended the forefinger of her left hand so that he could place the ring on it.

Solomon Jr. brought a copy of the ketubah[12] to the rabbi, who read it out loud. "On the first day of the week, the eighteenth day of the month of September in the year nineteen hundred and forty-three, here in Pinar del Rio, in the presence of family and friends, the beloveds Sarah Baumann and Ramon Famosa entered into the covenant of marriage.

Ramon and Sarah smiled at each other as he continued, "As we embark on life's journey, we promise to love, cherish, encourage, and inspire one another. May we continue to grow together, maintaining the courage and determination to pursue our desired paths. As life partners, we shall endeavor to build a home with love, peace, tolerance, and charity. Through each other's eyes, we will see the world in a new way and be better together."

Jacob Jr. brought a tray with two golden wine goblets for the bride and groom. The rabbi said a

---

[12] Marriage contract

blessing over them, and they drank. A young girl handed a glass to Sarah, who then handed it to Ramon; he put it on the ground and broke it by stepping on it. The ceremony was finished, and the party began. Everyone celebrated; a small group of local townspeople played music on violins and other instruments, people danced, and Sarah and Ramon danced together happily.

Three months later, Sarah and Ramon had established their own home. Sarah sat in a chair as she happily knitted, and her harp sat in one corner of the room. The door flew open, and Ramon burst in, full of happiness and excitement.

"Sarah, my darling," he said, "you won't believe it!"

She stood up. "What is it?"

"They've asked me to fly, I'm going to fly for the Allies!"

"What?"

"They need more pilots, Sarah. I'm going to Europe!"

Sarah was torn by that news, and it showed. "But we were just married three months ago!"

"Oh, Sarah, we can't be selfish. There is a war on! Remember all the other Jews that didn't escape the Nazis."

Her face took on a determined look. "You're right, Ramon. Of course."

"I'm going to go tell everyone else! I'll be back in a little while." He started to run out, stopped, and came back to kiss her on the cheek. Sarah smiled at him. He left then, and she sat back down to return to her knitting. She stopped, lost in thought for a moment, and then started knitting again.

It was mid-June of 1944. Sarah sat in her chair, now visibly pregnant. Her mother was visiting her, cleaning the

The Broken Rainbow: Mysterious Dark Karma

house as an assistance for her expectant daughter. They listened to the radio as Rose worked.

The radio newsman said, "The historic landing of the Allies at Normandy has accomplished the breaking of the Atlantic defense of the Axis powers. Over one hundred thousand Allied troops have successfully landed and are advancing towards Germany. Significant gains in Italy for the Allies are reported as well, after Rome was taken by Allied Forces."

That September, Sarah, now six months pregnant, answered the door to receive a bundle of letters from the mail carrier. She sat down next to a table to sort through the mail. One of the letters caught her eye—it was from the Cuban military. She opened it fearfully and the first lines broke her heart. *We regret to inform you….*

She began to cry as she sat there, sobbing quietly as she absorbed the news. Rose walked in and saw her daughter's distressed state. "Sarah, what is it?" Sarah weakly held out the letter as she continued to cry. Rose quickly snatched it and read. "Oh, no. Oh, no! Poor Sarah!" Rose knelt down to comfort her, and they cried together.

It was a December night when the baby came. Rose and a midwife helped Sarah as she gave birth. The midwife waited for the baby near the cloth covering Sarah's legs while Rose held her hand.

Sarah's face strained as she pushed with all her might. Her face clenched and then relaxed. A moment later she heard the baby's cry as the midwife cleaned it off. The midwife said, "It's a boy, Sarah." Sarah smiled tiredly, happy in spite of her exhaustion.

A few days later, rain was pouring down outside Sarah's home as she rocked her son, Miguel Angel, in her chair. Rose was visiting again; she stared out into the rain as they listened to the radio news: "The war is still not over, but Hitler is dead. It has been confirmed that Hitler and his wife, Eva Braun, died by suicide in his bunker in Berlin. It has been reported in recent weeks that Hitler became troubled and unstable amidst reports of German losses...." The rain stopped suddenly, and Rose walked outside.

The wet ground outside the house sparkled as the sun broke through from behind a cloud. Rose stared off into the sky. A rainbow formed for a moment, then parts of it faded away, leaving broken segments of the rainbow in the sky before fading away altogether when the sun reappeared fully. Rose covered her mouth with her hand in astonishment.

Outside the house of his wealthy family, Fidel Castro saw the same broken rainbow. As he held his copy of *Mein Kampf*, he said, "Farewell, Comandante Hitler."

The years rolled by, and Miguel Angel was now a teenager. He had stopped by a bakery to get some bread from a friendly, chubby baker with a mustache. The baker rang up the order and gave Miguel his change. "There you are."

Miguel looked over and saw some sweet bread. "Oh! I forgot the sweet bread!"

The baker looked at it and back at the teen boy with a smile. "Take one, no charge. I've known your family for years."

Miguel took it and put it in the bag. As he ran out the door, he called over his shoulder, "Gracias!"

It was the night of December 31, 1958. There was mass rioting and celebration in Pinar del Rio as the news of

The Broken Rainbow: Mysterious Dark Karma

Castro's victory spread. People were smashing windows, mobs attacked people suspected of supporting Batista, some of whom wore red and black 26th of July bracelets. There were screams and more sounds of property being damaged. Rioters yelled, "Castro is victorious! Batista is no more!"

Some rioters overturned a car and set it on fire. People ran screaming through the streets and in the darkness, faces were lit by a hellish orange-red glow from the fires. Rose, Sarah, and Miguel Angel were walking home from a New Year's party in the middle of the chaos. Miguel observed, "Maybe we should have stayed home tonight."

A group of rioters were cornering a man; among them was a dark man with six fingers—the same one who had killed the Gypsy woman. One of the rioters accused, "You! You worked for Batista!"

"No," the poor man protested. "No! I'm just a baker!"

Another rioter said, "I remember you! You were in his police!"

"No! Not me!"

The dark man took the same razor he had used on the Gypsy out of his coat. He lunged in swiftly and precisely as he slit the baker's throat.

Miguel and the two women walked by at that moment and saw it happen. The crowd scattered save for the dark man. Miguel ran over to the baker and cradled the man in his arms. "Oh, no!" he sobbed.

The dark man turned towards Rose and Sarah; his eyes had an unearthly glow. He flicked his razor back open, and blood dripped from the blade. Rose screamed, and Miguel looked up just in time to see the man slash at Sarah and his mother's blood splatter on his grandmother's face.

Rose screamed, "No!"

Later that night, a cheap black and white television set in the Baumann house was on, though the room was empty. The screen showed Fidel Castro speaking from Havana. "The revolution cannot be completed in a single day, but you may be sure that we will carry the revolution through to the full. You may be sure that for the first time the Republic will be truly and entirely free and the people will have their just recompense.

"What exists is goodwill and we shall do everything necessary. However, I will repeat here what I have already said, and history will absolve me, that we shall insure the maintenance, assistance, and education shall not be lacking for the children. We have a free country here. We have no censorship, and the press is free. The people can gather freely if they want to. There is no tormenting of political prisoners, no murders, no terror. America needs an example like this in all its nations. It needs for the millionaires who have become rich by stealing the people's money to lose everything they have stolen, to have it stolen back from them.

"Today, on behalf of all the Cuban people and in the name of the revolution, I want to say this: thank you."

The sound of applause came from the television audience. Rose had come into the room to see the end of the speech. She shook her head. "Oh, no. Not again."

The Broken Rainbow: Mysterious Dark Karma

Chapter 8: The Love of My Youth and the First Connection

9 The Cuban Lightning at 17

Pinar del Rio, Cuba
1959
The beginning of the revolution's triumph

I had recently had that meeting with Castro and received my appointment as a Commander and the Commander-in-Chief of the Juvenile Commandos in the Rius Rivera military compound. The next day I was proud to be invited on a scuba diving excursion with my best friend Joaquin, the fiancée to my sister Disa, who were to be married the next year.

In the early hours of the morning, Joaquin picked me up in front of my house with his younger sister, Sonya. After we greeted each other, Joaquin drove towards the beach of Las Canas in his father's jeep. As we arrived at the yacht Joaquin's three friends, who comprised the team of the scuba diving club Joachin had formed, started our first lessons as the first class they would have. We learned how to use the aqualung and regulators, as well many techniques how to preserve the oxygen in the tanks and how to inspect the equipment meticulously before any expedition, so that no one's life would be put at risk.

I was nearly twelve and Sonya eleven. We were both fascinated and followed to the letter the instruction of not only Joaquin's friends but Joaquin himself as the leader of the scuba diving team. Joaquin had been a role model that I had looked up to with great respect. And as the fiancé of my favorite sister, even though I didn't know how to swim yet I trusted Joaquin so much to accept the challenge to become one more member of the team for the scuba diving club. I had delayed learning out to swim because I had a very bad experience with the water a few years previously. Joaquin had assured me that I didn't even need to know how to swim. Once you put on the fins and mask with the snorkel on, you basically floated. Joachin's younger brother was unable to participate in the fishing trip due to a case of measles. The rest of our group comprised Joachin's three friends: El Gallego, a tall, skinny guy nearly 6'6" with olive skin and little education; Olerio, 5'1, athletic, red haired with freckles on his cheeks and forehead, and an explosive personality; and Pancho the Skinny, the joker of the group

The Broken Rainbow: Mysterious Dark Karma

Joaquin and Disa had not anticipated the radical change the revolution would cause in the world of politics. Unfortunately, the destiny of everyone was altered and changed forever with that broken rainbow in the sky in that morning of January of 1959 and the dark karma this event unfortunately brought to everyone and the persecution of the Baumann family of Miguel Angel.

After we received our basic training for a few hours and made sure that everything was fine, we went down the stairs of the yacht to enter the water. We swam with the team for about an hour or two and returned to the yacht. Shoving our masks up onto our faces, we climbed over the rail and onto the deck. Sonya, who had gone ahead of me, grabbed at her mask and snorkel which was about to fall off her head. The weight of the mask, combined with that of the tanks, fell off her head before she could grab them. We could see mask and tanks sink rapidly to the bottom of the sea floor in the clear water, the sun glinting off the stainless-steel edge of the mask as it sank.

Sonya looked down, tremendous frustration on her face as she sorrowfully watched her mask and tank lying on top of the algae on the sea floor. Joaquin, full of indignation, yelled with all the strength of his lungs from the deck, "That happens only to the people who are stupid and don't pay any attention to their training! I should never have brought you with us because I know you're a spoiled brat."

Sonya looked at him angrily, her ears and cheeks as red as tomatoes in her rage. "No, you're wrong. This could happen to anyone, and that has a name: accident. But to those like you abusers and bullies with superiority complexes, the rest of us are stupid." She looked at me in complete shame with tears in her eyes.

I shook my head in disgust. Every one of Joaquin's friends looked at Joaquin reproachfully, but none of them dared to say anything, looking at each other wordlessly.

Joaquin, extremely upset and angry, replied to Sonya as he opened both arms expressively, "Well, what are you waiting for? Jump into the water and bring that back up!"

If looks could kill, he would have been struck down that moment. She replied, "You know very well that neither Julio Antonio nor I know how to swim. You promised us that in this sport of scuba diving that it's not necessary to know how to swim because all we needed to do is kick with our legs to use the fins to move, that this technique was more than sufficient to keep yourself afloat and maintain control. Today was my first time that I've come to learn this sport from you, and now you want me to jump in the water without any supervision to save your stupid mask and snorkel? You must be kidding! Are you?"

She shook her head in disgust. She added, "You really are a jerk, my brother. The only one who is really stupid right here, unfortunately. Probably, I am after all stupid to believe you and come with you to be abused once more by you. Never again will I go anywhere with you to do anything. My big sister told me that I was crazy to go with my narcissist brother who has no love or respect for anyone but loves himself so much that he has no room in his heart for anyone else."

She looked at me as she finished. "You wouldn't know, Julio Antonio, that I feel sorry for your sister. Please tell her what happened here today when you go home. If he treats me, his youngest sister, this way, what can she expect from her future husband?"

The Broken Rainbow: Mysterious Dark Karma

I nodded my head silently. I looked into her eyes and clearly saw her frustration. This didn't go over well with Joaquin, who grew more enraged and this time he yelled at me. "What—you're going to be on the side of this spoiled brat?" I made no reply. I only shrugged my shoulders and began to pick my equipment up off the deck. I started to put my equipment back on. He looked at me and smiled sarcastically. He yelled at me, "What, you're going to be the hero to rescue my sister's equipment from the bottom of the ocean?" I didn't reply and continued to get into my equipment.

I walked to the railing of the yacht and leaned back to fall into the ocean with the intention of retrieving Sonya's mask and snorkel right before the eyes of Joaquin, Sonya, and his friends. The last thing I heard was from El Gallego was, "I like this kid. He has the testicles of an elephant."

I smiled and looked at all of them gathered at the railing. I took a deep breath and went down at the same time, like I did the first time with Joaquin and his friends. One of the first things he had said was to never go into the water alone, because it was a sport activity and to watch out for each other, so no one wound up in the mouth of a fish. After all, I started to think, I might not like very much being under the command of this bullying leader. As I descended, I saw by the light of the sun the sheen from the mask shimmering in the water on top of the aquatic plants. Without any fear and proud of being so lucky as to see it right there, I grabbed the mask from its resting place on the marine plant. Before the eyes of everyone looking down at me from the railing, I started to head back to the surface, but something strange happened that nearly cost me my life.

The elastic band of my mask suddenly grew soft, and water flooded into my mask. When I realized what was happening, I reached up and realized the old rubber had broken over my right ear. The pressure of the water forced its way into my mask. Thinking quickly, I thought to replace my mask with Sonya's, but I realized to my surprise that Sonya's band was also broken.

This was why she had lost her gear. It appeared that, after all, everything was Joaquin's fault, since he was the team leader who should have supervised and checked all the equipment before he gave it to us. It was his negligence caused by his rush, and he had overlooked that the rubber straps of both masks were old and cracked, ready to break, and should have been replaced. In the midst of my agony, I was completely outraged at how everything he had accused his sister of being was actually his own fault, and how he had behaved so poorly towards his younger sister, yelling at her in front of us and embarrassing her.

I shook my head in my upset state and looked towards the surface. I was perhaps fifty feet down. In complete frustration, I could see that unless I moved my legs to continue go up, I was going to run out of air. My legs practically came to be paralyzed through fear and panic, like two concrete columns that didn't respond to me at all. I found I was being dragged down to the bottom once more. I felt a strong current of electricity running through my legs to my spine that kept them immobile and without strength. I looked up once more to beg God for help. As I saw at that moment I started to swallow the salty water in my throat; it looked like I was beginning to drown, right beneath the yacht and before the eyes of these supposed

The Broken Rainbow: Mysterious Dark Karma

friends who either didn't understand the gravity of the situation I was going through or, as I got to know later, were held back by Joaquin who wanted to give me a lesson for defending his sister and trying to be, from his point of view, a hero. I thought for a minute all I was trying to do was be fair. Look at what I got instead!

From where I was in the water, I saw only one person that showed any distress and hitting Joaquin's shoulder agitatedly and telling him that I was drowning and needed help. I don't know if it was from lack of oxygen or panic, but I saw in the sky as I looked through the clear waters the clear images of my two guardian angels that had been watching out for me all my life since the moment of my birth, protecting me.

They both fought in the sky with Satan's disciples with swords in their hands. It looked like they were fighting for my life against those diabolic beings that wanted to take me to Hell with them out of the world. I saw as if I were watching a television with interference. It looked like my life was escaping my small body and now my weak body that continued to sink to the bottom, slowly drinking more and more seawater, right in front of the eyes of everyone along the rails of the yacht as they watched me sink.

Suddenly, an enormous, fat multicolored rainbow, cut in two pieces, appeared in the sky under that powerful, majestic sun. The surface of the water was dimpled by a drizzle of water, but the sun remained like a powerful spotlight shining on the situation. It looked like it shone directly into the eyes of the disciples of Satan.

In the beginning, it looked like they were winning the battle against my angels, forcing them to back up. Now that extraordinary, powerful beam of bright light blinded them, and they started to get killed one at a time by the swords of my angels, falling to the water one at a time, dissolving seconds after hitting the bottom like magic. Maybe they were returning to the Hell they had come from. Another beam of light like a bolt of lightning hit the ocean, cutting the broken rainbow into multiple pieces.

I discovered later that Sonya, filled with rage and indignation, pushed Joaquin over the rails of the yacht with all her strength. "Bully, coward—get him out of the water! Are you blind? He is drowning!"

At the same time this happened, the lightning, more powerful this time, cut through the drizzle, striking the water near me at the bottom. As it hit the water, Joaquin easily leaped ten feet above the surface, shocked by that electrical discharge. The strong electrical current shook his body, causing to convulse as he was moved by the electricity as if an extraordinary and superhuman force wanted to teach him a lesson for his conduct.

Under the water, where I was still trying to move my legs, I felt the electrical shock from that last bolt of lightning near me. Instead of having an adverse result to me, it was more like a battery in my legs got recharged, penetrating my legs to my spine and moving my legs back to normal. I felt the energy surge up to my head, making me vomit out the seawater I had already swallowed. With tremendous speed, that energy brought me to the surface, where I coughed and spluttered, expelling the rest of the water, right next to the unconscious Joaquin who was floating face down in the water. I turned him over so that his face was in the air to save him. As I did so, he coughed and spat water out of his mouth and nose.

The Broken Rainbow: Mysterious Dark Karma

I looked up at the sky with gratitude. I was sure that between the clouds and the light rain that was growing stronger that I could see the smiling faces of my two angels, smiling in triumph at once more saving me from a certain death. I dragged Joaquin's body under my left arm around his neck and helped myself with the fins by kicking like an outboard motor with the unbelievable power which now functioned properly for me.

Helping myself with my right hand, I tried to get close to the yacht. El Gallego, Joaquin's best friend, came to help me and get Joaquin out of my hands. He said to me, "What irony! The supposed team lead has been rescued by the youngest student." He said that with a little ironic smile.

Joaquin, only semi-conscious, said, "What? What? What's up? What did you say, Gallego?"

"Brother, not much. You owe your life to our young friend here. There's no doubt in my mind after what I saw today that he is one protected by God. He gave all of us today a very strong lesson in generosity and humility."

Joaquin, with a disgusted smirk, said, "Yeah, yeah. Yeah, yeah."

After we all got back on board the yacht, Joaquin still dizzy and recovering, was very frustrated and angry. He yelled, "Where's that little brat that pushed me overboard?"

He grabbed the rails. He looked like he was feeling better and returning to his original bullying attitude, not digesting what his friend had just said to him. He yelled at Sonya as he slapped her violently across her face, "Everything that happened here today is your fault. Stupid brat! We should never have brought you on this excursion with us."

Gallego tried to restrain him. "Calm down, brother, calm down. You're still not yourself. Don't do anything you'll regret later."

Ignoring him, he grabbed Sonya and yelled into her face, "Why did you shove me into the water without any warning? You proved to be very stupid. I could have hit my head against the metal of the ladder or against the hull! You didn't realize that you could kill someone doing that?"

I observed everything a short distance away. I realized that Joaquin was growing more and more upset, probably remembering the incident before. Now, with his left hand on the rail and his right on Sonya's throat, his intention was clearly to throw her overboard. "How would you like if it I did the same to you?"

I very clearly saw and read his intentions in his mind. As I heard his voice and saw his movements, I knew he was going to do it. Without thinking twice, in a rapid move I grabbed a harpoon rifle from the pile on top of the storage cabinets and pointed it at him. I shot, not to wound him or kill him, but in an effort to restrain him in his evil intention to drop his sister overboard.

Before I could pull the trigger, I could clearly read his mind. The moment he decided to do it is when I squeezed the shot off. The long iron harpoon shot from the rifle and flew through the air, the spear tip of the harpoon driving deep into the wood, the shaft vibrating rapidly. As if guided by divine hands, the tip of the spear struck between two of Joachim's fingers on his left hand, taking only a little piece of his skin from both fingers with it. It panicked him more than it did any real damage, which is exactly what I wanted to do with him. Terrified, he looked at the trickle of blood between his fingers without knowing what kind of damage he had actually sustained. He removed his hand from the spear, his eyes bulging out of their sockets.

He yelled, "Have you gone crazy?" He examined his hand, which was bleeding profusely. It was really only a micro cut, and he took a couple of steps back from the rail. Sonya used this opportunity to rapidly take the offensive to get the upper hand.

She yelled, "I don't want to be on your yacht one single minute more. Tell your guys to turn the yacht around, I want to go home. The only crazy person here, maybe possessed by Satan, is you. I warn you that you should be prepared for the worst consequences for that tiny wound you have on your fingers when I tell Mom and Dad all that happened here today!"

Joaquin looked into her eyes with a desire to slap her again, but he held himself back this time. He turned around and maintaining a lousy attitude as he saw the reproachful looks of everyone else mixed with indignation in their eyes, including me.

I pointed a different rifle at him I had just scooped up. He looked at me in confusion. I yelled, "Don't push me. This time, I will not aim at your hand. I'm in complete agreement with your sister. I also want to go home. You've completely defrauded and disappointed me by showing your true colors today with your irrational attitude. You owe every single one of us an enormous apology. Those two elastic bands on the masks that Sonya and I wore were nothing more than the result of your intrinsic negligence. You blamed your sister unfairly of being negligent and stupid, humiliating her with your arrogant attitude in front of everyone with no reason at all to justify what you said. The true stupidity, after all, came from you and your macho attitude. You lost your best qualities that until today I had admired in you and considered you to be my role model and best friend."

I shook my head in completely disgusted deception. "I believe there's a very strong possibility that Sonya has every reason to believe you're possessed by Satan based on your irrational behavior. You took a complete turnaround in your personality today and took all of us by surprise."

Joaquin shook his head in disagreement, but he looked demoralized as he hung his head. He looked like my words affected him to utterly demoralize him. He turned around and, raising his right hand high and looking at Gallego who had the steering wheel in his hand and gestured for the yacht to be turned around and head for home. Gallego obeyed his signals and turned the vessel around and we navigated back towards Playa Las Canas.

As Joaquin walked toward the cabinets along the deck, he examined the small wounds he had on his left hand. Sonya shot him a dirty look and walked far away from him to sit down next to me. She put her right hand on my shoulder and said with a small smile, "Thank you very much, Julio Antonio, for saving my life. I have to be honest with you—my brother scared the daylights out of me. He's scared me before a couple of times, but not this way. I saw in his eyes the hatred and evil intentions of throwing me into the water. He doesn't even realize it, in his mental irritation and incoherent demented desire for revenge, that when he threw me overboard would be a sure death."

She looked around her to make sure no one was watching us. She gave me a small but significant kiss on my cheek. Even though it only lasted a few seconds, it remained impregnated in my memory for the rest of my life. She whispered in my ear, "You are a true gentleman. Thank you again for defending me from that bully and evilly possessed brother." She gave me a small, innocent yet mischievous smile. "I would like it very much if you would be in the future the one that destiny elects to be by my side the rest of my life."

I smiled in great satisfaction and pride. I felt the same attraction towards her, not only for her physical beauty but also for her extremely great personality and loyalty to the point of being in my heart a divine nobility. I replied with conviction, "For me, this is not only would be a great honor but always it would give me a great happiness."

She smiled again with even greater satisfaction. Her eyes shone as she replied, "You are the best." She took my face between both hands and this time kissed me on the lips in gratitude. This one was more prolonged as she mashed her lips against mine. I felt as if my lips were welded to hers with gratitude and love in compensation for my words.

This particular kiss is the one which really sparked a very great flame of love in my heart that I never was able to completely suffocate or turn off. Every time I think that I was no longer feeling it any longer, no matter how much time passed, each time I think of her my heart accelerates and gives me butterflies in my stomach, even though I would have several other relationships in my future at that point. This particular sensation I felt with her managed to make my hands moist with a cold sweat that I felt at that particular moment, bringing back once more every single time that marvelous, precious love from my infancy.

Sonya asked me to tell my sister Disa what had happened that day on the yacht, but I never did for a long while. I considered doing so would be gossip and disloyalty to Joaquin, who once was my friend and role model. On top of that, I didn't want to break Disa's heart; she would eventually discover the truth about him. I decided to wait and not be the bearer of bad news. I gave it more time and pillow to that particular incident; if there is anything I really despise, it's feeling hatred and being involved in intrigue.

But from that day on, I kept my distance from Joaquin to the point that when he came to visit my sister at our house, in order to avoid passing in front of him, I would leave the house through the back door. It reached the point as well that my sister, a woman after all with feminine instincts, noticed my withdrawal from her fiancé would ask me on several occasions what had happened on the excursion with Joaquin on the yacht. "After that, I've never seen you friendly with him again," she observed.

I always found an excuse, telling her, "I'm very busy organizing my Juvenile Commandos. That's the only reason. Nothing happened."

Of course, she never believed what I told her, as I corroborated months later. She kept that thorn of curiosity in her heart until many months later when she discovered that Joaquin's last name as well as his father's and another member of his family appeared in the official newspaper by the new revolutionary government as corrupt individuals who had sucked money from the dictator Batista in payroll as informants.

It had taken time for them to dig through all the papers and corruption the previous administration had conducted and found a list of those working with him and published it. The dictator had been to the Cuban people in general, killing hundreds of thousands of young students and members of the opposition. Even if Joaquin was only pretending to work with these criminals, cashing monthly checks that were called *botelleros*[13] like silent spies pretending to be against the dictator, the reality was that they were on his payroll, who secretly paid them for their collaboration in keeping him in power with their loyal work. It was a huge shame for every citizen who had decency, principals, and morals, regardless of their political affiliation. All these people were leeches sucking off the public treasury.

    As I came into my house that afternoon, I found Disa crying her eyes out with her heart broken. Then, and only then, did I reveal to her what had transpired on that scuba diving excursion on the yacht after Mima had shown me the list in the newspaper with Joaquin and his family's name published. Mima said, "Why didn't you tell your sister that before?"

    "I didn't want to break her heart. I realized that she would eventually learn the truth; whoever would do that to you will do the same to someone else."

---

[13] Empty bottles.

Chapter 9: Disappointments in Abundance

10 Las Canas Fishing Boat

　　Needless to say, the wedding was off, the informal compromise was dissolved, and a few months later I left my house feeling completely deceived by the ideology and the direction the new revolutionary government was taking towards "moderate" socialism. The leaders of the Cuban revolution hid the truth by disguising the real Marxist communism as a "moderate" socialist and humanitarian revolution.

　　As I left my house, I found my good friend and neighbor Miguel Angel Baumann. He told me that day, after we greeted each other, that he was leaving the next day to Pico Turquino to work as a teacher in political indoctrination under the revolutionary government. I was not at all surprised, because everyone at that time was fanatic about the revolution.

What surprised me was when he told me that Joaquin has been arrested by the government together with his father and other members of his family. That really filled my heart with sorrow and distress, even though Joaquin had defrauded me completely. They were accused of being counterrevolutionaries, taken before the military tribunal, and sentenced to between ten and twenty years, every one of them. They were now in political prison for their acts of insurrection.

This saddened and depressed me in my heart. Only murders with multiple crimes had been sentenced for such a prolonged incarceration. I wondered why it had to be a military tribunal and not a civil court. It didn't sound right to me at all; I realized later that these were all kangaroo courts created by the government and the military, in which the defense attorney, prosecutor, and the judge were all members of the military. In the worst scenarios, they of course wound up before the firing squad.

We finished talking and said goodbye, and I jumped into my military jeep. Even though I had not seen Sonya all those months since that trip in Las Canas, I drove towards her house. Joaquin was not her preferred brother, but he was still her blood. And of course, her father and other members of her family were involved, and I considered it only proper, even though she had never tried to contact me and only glimpsed me a couple of times in the street, pretending not to see me. I thought that the decent thing to do was to talk to her and alleviate her sorrow by giving my condolences for the tragedy she was going through.

As I drove to her house, I thought how so many people who were as politically ignorant as Miguel Angel would tell me they liked moderate socialism. He unfortunately was blinded by the false promises of the new leaders of the revolution.

Little did he know that the philosophy didn't exist. Moderate socialism was only a fantasy that in the end only led towards Marxist-Leninism as a totalitarian regime, exactly the way my uncle Emilio had shown me in history books. Now, unfortunately, that history was repeating in our beautiful island of Cuba.

As I arrived at her house and stopped the jeep in front of it, I looked at my watch, noting it was around nine p.m. on a hot summer day in the month of June. The house was completely darkened. Even the porch light was off. For a moment I thought that the rest of the family was probably at the beach house in Las Canas, trying to stay away from the city and the shameful scandal of what had happened to them. They didn't' want to see the ugly, unfriendly faces of their curious neighbors who, for the most part, were completely fanatics for the revolution and its leaders to the point of being capable of yelling for a firing squad, including those who had been before their best friends. It brought all these distressed and crazy memories of what I had read about the French Revolution.

I rang the doorbell several times, but nobody answered. I was about ready to leave, and when I had half-turned, I could hear the metal locks inside the door moving. Someone was unlocking the door, sliding aside the double security locks. The door opened, and I saw the beautiful figure of Sonya lit by dim lights inside. She was

The Broken Rainbow: Mysterious Dark Karma

yawning hugely, covering her mouth with her hand. She was dressed in white shorts and white T-shirt, her hair mussed as if she had been half asleep.

In the few months since I had last seen her, she had reached puberty between her breasts and height. She was now a beautiful young woman. She recognized me at once and her face lit up with joy. "Julio Antonio!" She opened her arms and said, "I'm sorry. I fell asleep in the living room and didn't hear the doorbell. Please come in. Where have you been? Why didn't you come to visit me? What happened? You disappeared!" She gestured with her right hand for me to come into the house.

I hesitated for a few seconds. "No, I'm just here for a few minutes. I don't mean to bother or inconvenience you—sorry to wake you up...."

She put her left hand over my mouth to prevent me from finishing. She took my elbow by her right hand and gently pulled me inside. "The people, come in, come in," she said as she gestured around. Once inside, she closed the door and engaged several locks. "The people are crazy. They're keeping their eyes on us constantly and report to the government who comes in and out of the house. I figured you hadn't come to visit me because of that."

"You know me. I'm not scared of anyone and don't care about anybody. Whatever they want to believe or not believe is their own business."

She gave me a huge smile. "Boy, you look so handsome in that uniform!"

I smiled and shook my head modestly. "Thank you. I don't think this uniform will last for too long. Get your fill of it."

She looked at me in surprise, not understanding what I was saying. "I saw you on TV with Fidel, Che, and all these people. What are you talking about?"

"Never mind. I'll give you more details later on. Let's sit down and talk for a bit."

She raised her right hand high in embarrassment at her curiously. "You have nothing to worry about. My family doesn't like this government. But your family likes it! I don't know why you're saying you're not going to stay in uniform for too long. That doesn't mean we can't be friends."

I replied, "Remember, not everything is the way it appears to be. Remember also that not all that shines is gold."

She shook her head, her confusion even greater. We walked through the living room and sat down on a small loveseat across from the white baby grand piano that rested on one of the sides of the living room. She said, "I have fresh lemonade. Do you want some? I have lemonade, lemonade, and lemonade with ice."

I smiled. "Well, I think I'll take the last one, the lemonade with ice. That sounds to me, since you said it with more emphasis, more refreshing."

We both laughed. Sonya stood up and said, "I've been waiting for all these months and missing you. You haven't visited me, called me, or anything. It's been almost half a year! I started to believe that I did or said something that offended you. After the excursion and the friction with my brother from Hell, you never contacted me again. I never knew what happened to you." She squeezed my right shoulder. "I feel extremely happy that you've come to visit me today."

She left to the back of the house to get our drinks. I followed her with my eyes, admiring her beautiful legs and curvaceous, sculpted body until she disappeared from view. A little while later she returned with a tray, two glasses, and a jar of lemonade with ice. She said, "Your favorite beverage: lemonade with ice, made by these hands only a few hours ago before I fell asleep on that sofa." She pointed to a long sofa on one side of the living room. I could see a couple of red satin sheets and two pillows in the same color decorated with embroidery in pink borders.

Sonya rested the tray on the center table and then proceeded to pour the lemonade into the glasses, handing one of them to me. "Let's toast with the last thing I told you on the yacht when we saw each other last." She gave me a mischievous smile. "If you remember what I said."

I smiled, a little embarrassed, and nodding. I already had my glass close to my lips. "Are you sure you want me to repeat your words here and at this moment?"

She shook her head ambivalently. "Why not?" She smiled and looked me in the eyes. "If you remember, why not? My family isn't here. They're in the city, in the capital of Havana. Tomorrow is the assigned day for the visit with my brother in La Cabaña prison. Next week we have to go back again to visit my father. They're staying there together for the next two weeks. We have this large house all to ourselves. I believe God sent you to me today to give me support and alleviate the pain of my tragedy with my family. But I repeat, if you don't remember what I said to you, don't feel guilty. But this means that you didn't take my words seriously. I know you men aren't as romantic as we women are. At least, that is what my mother and older sister have told me. But I always replied to both of them that you are a different gentleman, distinct from every other man I've met so far except for my father, who I love very much."

"That are some big shoes for me to fill—your father's!"

"Yes, I know. You're not at all like my brother, that's for sure. Probably he is the man that both my mother and sister refer to, the common, vulgar, and ungentlemanly individual. Not my knight in shining armor, Julio Antonio del Marmol. What do you say to all this?"

I smiled. "You caught me by surprise, girl. I didn't think you held me in such high standard. I'll try not to disappoint you like your brother did." I raised my glass to my lips. She did the same, and our eyes held each other. With the sensuality of an adult woman, she put her lips to the glass and took a tiny sip. We looked at each other deeply and in silence, both enjoying the drink of that delicious lemonade. I took a little piece of ice in my mouth and swirled it around inside my mouth, sticking my tongue out periodically as I did. Then I started to chew on the ice slowly.

I swallowed and said, "I would like it very much myself that you could be selected by destiny to be by my side for the rest of my life." She took a deep sigh.

Then she jumped up out of her seat as if by a spring and came to my side joyfully. I nearly dropped my glass of lemonade when she hugged me fiercely as she had months before on the yacht. She put both hands on my face and gave me a crushed her lips against mine emotionally and joyously. At first, it was just a happy, strong kiss, but then we started kissing in ever-increasing sexual intensity. We parted, looking at each other, and then began kissing again tenderly that grew more and more prolonged until she placed her right hand on my chest and pushed me gently away. "You know I'm a virgin. Have you had any sexual experiences before?"

I shook my head. "No. I'm a virgin, like you."

She smiled with tremendous satisfaction with some kind of mischievous joy. She said, "Don't worry and relax. I bought a textbook on human sexuality after scuba diving trip. I've been preparing myself for this moment all these past months because I don't want just to be your first experience but also mine own as well. I don't care if destiny will separate us and keep us united or far away in the future, but this incredible memory will be for us unforgettable."

She rose up from the love seat. "Are you OK to follow the lead that I've acquired in this fabulous book?"

I shook my head and with a vague gesture of agreement, I replied, "I always have an open mind to acquire new knowledge and like Socrates the Greek philosopher said, the only thing I know for certain is that I know nothing. I add to that my own words, my version is I only know that my doors in my mind and spirit are always open, prepared, and at the disposition each day to teach, dialogue and learn from everyone."

Sonya smiled. "Well, you will have to prepare yourself to learn today." She turned all the lights off, leaving the place in near darkness. Then she lit some scented candles. After she had finished, she gave me a pleasant, large smile. "I have no doubts in my mind that you will one day become a great writer. I like your saying better than that of Socrates." I smiled and she nodded. "I will be back in a few seconds. I want to change my clothing for something more appropriate, as the book suggests."

"You look magnificent in what you have on, but as an obedient disciple, if that is your wish, go ahead." I took a little sip of my lemonade, observing her and her beautiful body disappear into the interior of the house.

A few minutes later, Sonya returned wrapped in a bathrobe that was completely see through. It showed in the dim light of the candles her magnificent young, tender body. She grinned broadly. In one hand she held a bottle of liquid Vaseline; in the other the book on human sexuality she had mentioned earlier. She put it down on a table next on one side of the sofa. Still beautifully smiling, she asked, "Do you need help to remove your clothing, or do you prefer to do it yourself?"

I smiled mischievously. "Even though I'm very independent some of the time, a small help can be welcomed, especially when it comes to remove these very high military boots I'm wearing right now."

She continued smiling as she bent over in front of me to help me remove my boots. As she innocently did that, nearly kneeling on the floor right before my eyes, she unconsciously exposed her beautiful breasts which looked like peaches with their pink nipples that appeared to dangle from her chest. It crossed my immature mind with that comparison that they were ripe peaches ready to eat. As I smiled in satisfaction.

This act of exposure was spontaneous, arising out of her intention to help me, not out of her ultimate desire. It took me by complete surprise, and my body reacted to the pleasure it gave me. She noticed my erection and looked at the bulge in my pants with surprised pleasure. She waggled her eyebrows suggestively and smiled in satisfaction.

I asked, "What is the Vaseline for?"

As she removed my boots, she replied, "According to my book, lubrication is the most important key in order to be able to prevent irritation and be able to enjoy the sex in plenitude. We should not forget that we both are virgins."

I grinned broadly as I lay down on the sofa. I took the bottle of Vaseline as I did. "I had a substitution in mind, something that I believe will have better results and better flavor." I said no other word. I stood up and walked over to the refrigerator near the dining room. I opened it, found what I was looking for, and without saying what it was picked it out and returned to Sonya. I held my right hand up, showing her a bar of butter. "I don't know if you know this or were able to learn it from your book, but the most important thing in sex is foreplay. The emotional and physical stimulation between two people creates the greatest sexual arousal and excitement in a couple."

I smiled again as I put the butter bar on a plate next to the sofa and pushed away the Vaseline jar. I started to remove my clothes. "I don't know if you prefer the flavor of Vaseline in your mouth, but I like the taste of butter better. It's also more nutritious and delicious." I grinned at her mischievously and waggled my eyebrows at her as well.

She shook her head. "Are you sure you haven't done this before? It's hard to believe that you haven't."

I shook my head. "I swear to you that, as I said before, I've never done this." I dropped all jocularity and looked at her with conviction. "I've had a great sexual education from one of the best teachers—of course, only in the theory—from my older half-brother. You never have the pleasure of knowing him, because he hasn't lived with us for a long time now. He was the first sexual encounter my father had with a lady of the night, long before my father ever met my mother. My half-brother had become a pimp for his mother when he was only fifteen years old. As my mother said, he was a chip off the old block."

Sonya's eyes widened in surprise, and she grinned broadly. "Now I comprehend your knowledge to switch the Vaseline for butter. Your brother probably taught you about foreplay. In this case, I'm the bread that you put the butter on to eat with pleasure before the penetration. That way we'll make our experience a very exquisite and memorable time. In this case," she added as she took the book from my hand and put it back on the table, "I love very much the advice you obtained from your older brother. In my mind, I've already imagined it, and now I will forget about that book. I will invite you as you take the initiative to allow you in my heart to be whose leads this momentum. As we all should follow those who have more experience than we do."

She picked up the bar of butter and handed it to me as she lay back on the sofa. She said with anticipatory excitement, "We should follow your brother's advice to the teeth. Our satisfaction depends on that. I trust you will put into practice all the theory you've learned to the best of your ability."

She closed her eyes and gave a long sigh of satisfaction as I knelt and put my head in between her legs. She uttered guttural moans of satisfaction. She said brokenly, "Oh, Julio Antonio, bless the knowledge of your big brother!"

That extraordinary first sexual experience with someone very special would be very difficult to ever forget even if you live a few lifetimes, not only for her

The Broken Rainbow: Mysterious Dark Karma

extraordinary qualities but also for the spiritual and physical beauty that left a lasting impression in my mind.

A few hours later, we said goodbye with profound sadness, both feeling in our hearts that we might never see other again for a long time, if ever. The uncertain political unrest that existed in Cuba at that time certainly offered no guarantee that we would see each other again. Unrest such as this was spread by the Cuban communists all over the rest of the free world, financed by Russia and China had one single objective in mind: the subjugation and asphyxiation of all liberty for the rest of humanity.

A few weeks later I stopped by Sonya's house again to find to my sadness that she and her family had moved to the capital of Havana, trying to shorten the distance and so be able to be closer to the political prison of La Cabaña, where her father and brother were serving their long sentences as conspirators against the revolutionary Cuban government.

I tried to find the address to where they had moved, they evidently wanted to hide from not only neighbors but people who knew them. Even those people who had the address never shared it with me. These circumstances kept us apart until 1963. I continued my military assignment that had been allotted to me by the Commander-in-Chief to the revolution, Fidel Castro—to create a new youth army, the Commandos at the Service to the Revolution.

My proximity to the leaders of the revolution also allowed me to discover before anyone else what the leaders really had planned for the future of Cuba. As the youngest Commander of the revolution, I learned the many dark secrets of every single one of the leaders I dealt with. I discovered from the lips of Ernesto "Che" Guevara, also an agent for the Soviet KGB, what the true ideological route they wanted to implant in Cuba.

This, of course, not only broke my heart but brought me to the verge of wanting to abandon the island illegally and made me very close to my uncle Emilio, my father's brother, who to my surprise revealed that he had been a master spy for the West for decades. During World War 2, he supervised South and Central America as well as the Caribbean Islands to prevent the Nazis from taking over on the continent. As my uncle revealed this secret to me, he also proposed something to me I never expected to be— the youngest spy in history, recruited and trained by my uncle, and became a very sophisticated, dangerous spy, all to further my effort to stop the imposition of that despicable totalitarian regime in Cuba that the leaders wanted to press onto my beautiful island.

The Broken Rainbow: Mysterious Dark Karma

Chapter 10: Conception of the Crime and a Deceptive Plot

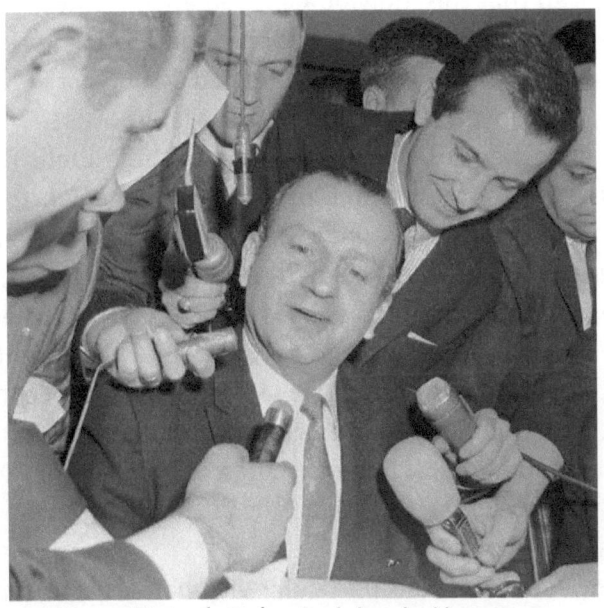

11 Jack Ruby Arriving in Havana

The next morning following that memorable night I was back in the Cuban capital, the beautiful and picturesque city of Havana. Che had asked me to please go and pick his guest Jack Ruby up from the airport. He was supposed to meet that day and was allowing me to use his three luxury Oldsmobile automobiles and use the men of his escort to bring his associate in crime from the Rancho Boyeros airport.

I knew Ruby quite well by now because of his multiple visits to Havana. Che considered him one of his most important international connections. Mr. Jacob Ruby, better known as Jack Ruby, was chubby and well-dressed with a mafioso look. This was also not the first time I had picked up him from the airport. His visits to Havana normally were quite short, but Che always made certain that they were pleasant and luxurious.

I figured that this individual played an extremely important role in Che's plans of global conquest. He always showered him with presents and Tropicana dancers, the most beautiful women available. These dancers lived a double life: in addition to their public role as entertainers, they served Che as MQ-1 agents who were international assassins, capable of performing whatever intelligence mission was assigned to them. In this case, Che used these women to keep Ruby extremely satisfied sexually as well as keeping Che fully informed whether his associate continued to remain loyal. Since Che didn't trust anyone, he needed continual assurance that whoever worked with him didn't have a change of heart. Like the old dog trained by the KGB that he was, he didn't even trust his own shadow.

It appeared that this particular visit had a specific and important objective. Even though the previous ones had been short, they needed to meet face to face when they needed to communicate something of extraordinary importance without concerns of being intercepted or recorded and so avoid any risk at all of their conversation to end up in the ears of their enemies.

We continued onto Calzada de Rancho Boyeros with our precious cargo en route to the luxury cabaret nightclub, the famous Tropicana, where Che had asked me to bring Ruby. A little later, as I heard from Che's lips, I learned that this was part of the plot of the assassination of the President of United States, John F. Kennedy.

This particular visit was to fully detail what Ruby had compromised with Che in order to seal the fate of Lee Harvey Oswald. They were to completely dissociate after that last visit of this gangster to Havana. Che wanted to make certain no trace would exist of the master plan they had developed so meticulously. Ruby was to be the trigger that had would permanently seal the lips of the only one who knew the real truth behind this conspiracy. This would maintain wrapped the enigma of that assassination with impunity as Che had repeated several times to me for over a hundred years without anyone at all ever being able to figure out who was the brain behind this operation.

I sat next to Ruby in the backseat of the center Oldsmobile, with the escort traveling in the one in front and behind us, like Che was accustomed to travel. Ruby felt extremely comfortable since he now knew me so well and tried to start a conversation with me, possibly in an attempt to earn my confidence.

"Do you know why I'm here in Havana today?" he asked.

I shook my head and shrugged, a vague expression on my face, like I always did not only with him but with all those associated with anyone involved with the leaders of the revolution. My Uncle Emilio was very careful to warn me to take extreme care in whatever I said to these individuals. They would always try to earn merit by obtaining your trust and pretending to be your friend. Like all communists are accustomed to do, they would use among them any information they could get against me to better their own positions. Because I knew this, I limited myself to only listen and reply only with small talk, without giving any elaboration in any answer to his questions.

In his attempt to promote conversation between us, he continually talked, and I learned pretty much his life story. According to him, he was born of Polish immigrants and raised in the Jewish faith. His nickname among his friends was Sparky, which he absolutely had hated. He continued to brag about things that were supposed to be classified, such as that he had several FBI and Secret Service agents on his payroll. His organization, the Mafia, even had federal judges in their pocket. Either he was trying to impress me or intimidate me by showing his power and how much importance he had. He even went so far as to tell me that when he was about my age, he cut the tongue out of one the associates of his Cosa Nostra because he had betrayed one of the family bosses by providing information to the DA in Dallas about his activities, offering himself as a witness to the family business. Of course, the DA was never able to bring him to testify against them. After the tongue was cut out, then they cut off his head.

I observed him carefully and smiled a little. I took my beret off and put it on top of my left knee. I ran my fingers through my hair with my right hand and nodded a little, smiling in approval in order to please him and let him believe I was impressed by his tales. Ruby didn't have the

The Broken Rainbow: Mysterious Dark Karma

slightest idea, of course, who I really was and what I did in my other life as a professional spy. My uncle and his team had put me through hell, readying me for any possibility of being captured and tortured, but also putting me through the worst physical and psychological tests to be able to endure any interrogation without talking. Now more experienced after three years, they had also trained me to detect the psychological condition of my enemies; and Ruby was not exactly my friend.

This particular skill I had learned showed me that Ruby not only tried to impress me but also that he felt intimidated and uncomfortable by my presence and personality. I was sitting so close to him, so I noticed that the fact that I was so young and was so close to the revolution's leaders instilled in him a terrible fear and insecurity of whatever I might say to Che, Fidel, and the others. I was able to confirm this, because even though the air conditioning was on full blast in the Oldsmobile, I could see drops of sweat glistening on his forehead as he talked to me non-stop, and I continued in my vague gestures and slight smiles.

In a desperate attempt to make me part of his conversation, he started to tell me in great detail how he tricked some federal agents before he left Dallas that evidently had been following him for weeks. Apparently, Internal Affairs had gotten involved in some kind of investigation into his activities, so his buddies in law enforcement had warned him to watch his back. They had told him even at the airport as he was getting ready to leave for Cuba and complete the plans that he and Che had which, according to him, would make history and change the rest of the world for a long, long time.

A flower shop was located on the corner of Avenue One Hundred. As we passed by it, I saw several cars with the flags of the Russian embassy on their front bumpers which caught my attention. I knew the ambassador and all his entourage, since their embassy took up an entire level of the Hilton Hotel (now the Havana Libre), but what I had never seen before in his entourage was a tall, beautiful young woman. She was elegantly dressed and looked like a Greek goddess. As I looked into her face my ESP clicked in my memory and I knew that face from somewhere. She was picking beautiful, long-stemmed roses, blood red in color. I looked at her face more closely and said excitedly to my driver Daniel, "Stop, please! Pull over!"

Daniel pulled over a little more than twenty feet past the flower shop's parking spaces, and my mind confirmed absolutely that the face of that woman was my Sonya. She was already leaving the flower shop beside the Russian ambassador, surrounded by bodyguards, and walking towards the cars in the parking lot not far away. Thousands of questions floated around my mind at that moment, but my memory stopped and focused instead on one of the most beautiful and unique memories I had of her a few years previous. I rapidly walked towards them and tried to reach her before she left in those cars if she might not even recognize me.

I saw her getting close to the car as the bodyguards opened the doors, and I yelled, "Sonya! Is that you?"

The smallest of the bodyguards, who looked like a kid with straight, greasy blond hair, a high hairline, and small eyes—he reminded me of cartoon fleas—was the first one to become aware of my presence. He touched the man in charge of the escort to attract his attention. They both reached inside the white guayaberas they wore. The ambassador, however, recognized not just me but also

Che's escort cars and raised his arms high. He yelled, "No, no, Vladimir. This is the Commandantico, one of Che's most trusted people."

Sonya immediately looked up in complete surprise. She looked at me from head to toe, still hesitantly for a few seconds. She quickly recovered herself and with still the roses in her hands and a huge smile on her face now walked a few steps towards me at first and then began to run to me. She gave me a bear hug and said in my ear, "My God, you don't know how much I've missed you, Julio Antonio del Marmol."

I smiled happily at her recognition and expression of missing me. I replied in her ear with a joke. "You've been missing me? Or the butter?"

She stepped back and slapped me jokingly on the shoulder with her right hand. She gave me that mischievous smile. "Both, because I haven't seen you for three years, and because in that same time the butter disappeared from the market among so many other products!"

We both laughed, and the ambassador and his escort, uncomprehending our amusement but knew from our demeanor that either we knew each other well or were family. The ambassador raised his right hand high to wave at me, and I waved back at him. Sonya said, "I have to go. The ambassador has a very important meeting and only stopped here to get flowers for the people from North America coming to visit him here. He asked me what flowers I thought would be good."

"OK, when can we see each other later?"

She took a card out of the small purse that hung from her shoulder. It bore the logo of the Russian Embassy indicating she was a diplomatic attaché. She handed the roses to me, and I held them as she wrote a telephone number and address on the back of the card. She hugged me again and said in my ear, "I'll be waiting for you with anticipation."

I replied with a small, mischievous smile, "A lot sooner than you can imagine. Probably tonight."

She let go of my hand, squeezing it before she detached. "I'm very happy to see you again."

I returned to our cars while she returned to the Russian ambassador's entourage, and we continued on our separate ways. Not long afterwards, as we arrived at the Tropicana, we realized we were going to the same place. They were parking just as we were arriving.

As the ambassador walked through the Tropicana gardens with Sonya and his bodyguard, they saw us arriving, laughed, and waved at us. Everyone thought at that moment that it was an extraordinary coincidence; but as I always say, everything has a reason and little that happens is coincidence. The Supreme Architect of the Universe makes us all encounter each other. At the same time a strange rainbow formed in the tropical sun, the mists, and a couple clouds. It was broken in two. It was exactly six days before John F. Kennedy was killed.

The Broken Rainbow: Mysterious Dark Karma

Chapter 11: Che's Deadly Amazon and Partners in Crime

12 Che's "Amazons" at the Tropicana

As we walked into the reception area, we met up with Che and the rest of his entourage. Che was smiling ear to ear happily and surrounded by several dancers from the Tropicana including their leader, Tanya. No one knew or imagined that these beautiful cabaret ballerinas were in reality Che's most powerful weapons as well-trained assassins. He used them not just to entertain both adversaries and friends but also for missions with international ramifications.

They all stood up as we entered the banquet room. There was a long table filled with exquisite, elaborate high cuisine dishes and by the side of every chair at the table I noticed a complete bar of butter and in the middle several baskets of bread and croissants, something the common people of Cuba hadn't seen for years.

Three suckling pigs were on the table, roasted golden to perfection with yucca around them, decorated with tropical fruits and plantain bananas and a red apple in each, making it look like the capitalist pigs had died with the red communist symbol in their mouths.

I looked at the bars of butter; at the same time Sonya did as well, and we exchanged mischievous smiles of a shared secret as we waggled our eyebrows at each other. We thought we had done this without anyone seeing us, but as I looked to the left, I noticed that the youngest kid with the dirty blond hair was watching the two of us. I looked him up and down. He looked like he was no more than 12, around 5'6" or 5'7" and reminded me of myself when I at the beginning of the revolution went everywhere with Fidel Castro and the others on television and other public places. I thought this young man might have been brought to Cuba with the ambassador by the KGB to train him and later incorporate him into the diplomatic circles of espionage.

Something I observed immediately corroborated what I had suspected. There was a man with six fingers, dressed in civilian clothes who accompanied Che everywhere. He not only shook the hand of this boy but also gave him a bear hug and a kiss on each cheek. I never seen him do this before; it appeared they had known each other for a while or had a special relationship between them. The man with six fingers had never before held a long conversation with anyone, and the most peculiar aspect about him wasn't just the number of fingers but he had the exact same pestilent odor of sulfur as was well-known to be exuded by Che.

The most significant part of the whole thing in the end was that no one knew where the six-fingered man had come from. I had asked Che on one occasion where he had known the man from, and Che said he was an old friend from his infancy in Argentina. On another occasion, in a conversation with the rest of the group he said that the man had known him in Mexico when they were preparing the yacht *Granma* for the guerilla expedition that began historic revolution in Cuba. Like typical liars who normally forget the stories they already said before and wind up contradicting themselves.

In the end, we all knew that either Che or Fidel evidently had no interest at all in any of us knowing the true identity and origin of this strange character. What completely convinced me that something strange existed that was sinister and diabolic between this individual was when the young man, came over to me and extended his hand.

He said, "It's been a long time since I've wanted to know you personally. I've never had the opportunity. My name is Vladimir Putin." When he looked at you his eyes had the emptiness of an individual with no soul lost in the universe. I hesitated for a second, looking deeply into his little eyes. He pushed his hand forward a little aggressively. "It will be an extremely great honor to be your friend, Commandantico."

I felt obliged now to take his hand. As I did, I felt a strange chill that went all through my body from my neck to my toes. I saw, as on a TV screen, future disasters for humanity like I had seen in the movies from the Second World War now projected many years ahead, where children, women, and old men get killed by bombs and high caliber weapons. Their mutilated bodies which lay strewn in the streets fed the wild dogs.

At that moment, the ambassador's voice broke in on my thoughts loudly. "Vladimir! Vladimir!" I let go of his hand suddenly. At the same time, out of respect for the ambassador, Putin released my hand as abruptly. This might have distracted from my reaction a little bit, serving as a cover for my poor manners. From what I could see and read in his mind of those horrible images that he would be solely and directly responsible for that future genocide.

The ambassador pointed with his finger to Sonya and said, "Vladimir, bring me the roses."

After Vladimir replied, "OK," he turned back to me and said a little nervously, "It's been a great honor to meet you."

I replied with a little nod of my head and a small half-smile. My stomach was turning upside down, groaning, after the images I had seen while shaking that young boy's hand. The ambassador, surrounded by Che's Amazons, took the red roses and handed them to Tanya, who rewarded him with a kiss on the mouth as well as a kiss on each cheek, followed by a big hug.

After a while, everyone had eaten all the delicious food and Che leaned over to Jack Ruby's ear to say something. Both men stood up, and Che leaned over to speak to the ambassador in a very low voice. The ambassador stood up and said to the one who looked like the leader, "You guys can go back to the embassy. Vladimir will remain here. Take Sonya with you and resume your routines."

The Broken Rainbow: Mysterious Dark Karma

The men nodded, and Che led the way into the conference room in the further recesses of the banquet room, followed by Ruby, the ambassador, the six-fingered man, and two Amazons that looked like Tanya's assistance. The rest of us remained. Sonya waved to me as they were leaving, and I returned the wave. Before they entered the conference room, Che looked back and noticed I hadn't left my chair. He raised his right hand high and gestured for me to join them.

I nodded and stood up to follow the group into the conference room. I could see that Ruby, already inside the room, was seated at the conference table, proceeding to remove a black briefcase that was attached to his right hand all this time with stainless steel handcuffs. He opened it at the same time Che brought another, identical briefcase and opened it by punching the combination into the lock of the case.

Finally, we could all see in plain view the mystery of the contents in Che's case. It was completely full of bundles of $10,000 in hundred-dollar bills; but I was surprised to see in Ruby's briefcase nothing but long lists on IBM printout computer sheets.

Ruby spoke to Che and the Russian ambassador in a boastful manner, "These are all the names of agents from the Secret Service, FBI, and other agencies with details and positions in their respective departments, along with the amounts of money we paid each of them in cash for their services in the operation we're about to execute in a few days when we eclipse that young and inexperienced President who now believes is omnipotent and cannot be touched. He's convinced himself that he can send assassins to eliminate any leader in the world without suffering any consequence to himself or his family."

After they went over everything with each other, Ruby removed from a compartment of his briefcase two badges, one from the FBI and the other from the Secret Service. He handed them to Che.

Che asked with a cynical smile, "Are these originals?"

With the same cynicism Ruby replied, "Of course, my friend. Why else do you think it cost us so much money?"

Che turned and asked, "Can I keep them?"

Ruby shrugged. "Of course. You paid for them! There are a few I kept for you so you can have faith that when the event takes place our people will be completely secure. This a reassurance to keep others away who might prevent our men from leaving the perimeter of operation, which will immediately be sealed by the local authorities."

Che handed the badges to the Russian ambassador with a satisfied smile. "I will return them to you later, but I need to take these to Moscow, where they can be perfectly duplicated. We might even be able to have our master spies use them in certain situations. It might save their lives."

"Don't forget to send them back to me," said Che. "We also have a good use for them. We have several agents infiltrated in the USA, and I bet my life that they will have moments where these badges could be a key element to get out of a hot situation."

"Of course, my friend," the ambassador replied. "This is a very great accomplishment." He turned to Ruby. "Good job. We don't have any of this, Comrade Ruby."

Ruby grinned broadly in satisfaction and nodded. "Thank you, Mr. Ambassador. Always at your service and to the Global Socialist Revolution."

At that moment, the door to the conference room opened suddenly, taking everyone by surprise. The arrogant figures of a group of bodyguards entered the place, followed by the Commander-in-Chief of the revolution, Fidel Castro. Everyone froze at the interruption and the undeniable charisma of that leader. With his usual Havana cigar in his mouth and a huge smile on his face, he nearly yelled, "Down with the Imperialist Yankee and the Donkey President!"

Everyone stood up to cheer and applaud. Che hesitated for a few seconds, knowing that Fidel's presence completely overshadowed him. In the end, his common sense prevailed and be also began to applaud. I had no doubt that Fidel took the spotlight entirely from Che and left him in the dark on purpose. Very gently, Fidel pushed Che out of the way to get to the head of the table and patted Ruby's shoulder. Then he shook Jack's hand and hugged him.

Ruby rushed to return the cordial greetings with tremendous joy in his face, especially when Fidel said loudly, "I want to apologize for interrupting your meeting. I only came to shake the hand of a true altruistic internationalist revolutionary like this man, who is willing to offer everything, including his own freedom and life, for our cause."

Jack Ruby's eyes brimmed with emotion at the compliments he had heard from the top leader of the revolution. Ruby patted Fidel's shoulder in clear display of affection and gratitude. He replied, "For me, it is a great honor, my commander in chief." Everyone had returned to their seats, but now they stood to applaud Ruby as Fidel held the man's arm up like he was a boxing champion.

After a few seconds of applause, I could clearly see Che clenching jaw as he tried to contain his frustration. Che told me the next day that all the cheering and applause recognizing Ruby was nothing more than a very unnecessary display from Fidel. Castro knew very well that all the adulation should have been directed towards Che, who had recruited Ruby into *his* plan. Ruby was merely another Yankee Imperialist that had been converted by Che into a mercenary in the favor of the internationalist cause, far from being a proletariat and true revolutionary as Fidel had claimed.

A little smile of satisfaction escaped my control and showed on my face at Che's discontent at Fidel's extreme attention showered on Ruby. It was clear that Che considered it undeserved. I had been a spy already for three years and had observed the game these two men played with each other and felt certain that Fidel had done this intentionally, which also explained the unexpected nature of the visit. Fidel wanted to suffocate Che's ego just a little bit; it bothered Fidel that his closest friend had a Napoleonic complex. They never stopped being in competition with each other and their egos all the way down the line to the end of their relationship.

Fidel took the podium. We all knew that when he took the microphone it was like candy with kid—you weren't going to get it away from him for a while, and no one would say much more the rest of the evening. He spoke plainly about "his" plan which would not only decapitate the North American donkey but also the most important mega-plan that he had already put in motion with hundreds of thousands of plants pretending to be political exiles from Cuba, disaffected by the communist government.

The Broken Rainbow: Mysterious Dark Karma

They had penetrated every single institution, even law enforcement, and these individuals were working to destroy the beautiful democracy of not just the USA but also were double-edged knives as they were working for the Ministry of the Interior's G-2 as spies. They called this operation the Thirteenth of March. It had been initiated by the extreme Left in North America in order to take the White House and the Capitol Building in DC in a very-well planned anti-capitalist revolution. In consequence they would penetrate the structure of the North American government, supported by the religious leader and pastor Malcolm X and the formation of a group called Black Panther Party.

He held his index finger high. "We have many civil rights leaders in the USA at the level of Angela Davis and many others who have been waiting for this moment to take the reins of power and convert the nation into a new USA: the United Socialists of America." He pointed at Ruby and said to him, "Remember, every single thing Che said here is in your hands." He shook his head. "You cannot fail. OK, Jack?"

Jack's face was very serious as he replied. "I will not fail, Commander-in-Chief."

We all stood up again and applauded. Fidel smiled from ear to ear and nodded. "That is what I want to hear from you. Homeland or Death, we will conquer!"

We said goodbye to everyone, and Fidel came over to me. "I don't think Che needs you here anymore. Why don't you come with us? I want to discuss a few things with you, and I saw you left your jeep at my office. You need a ride back."

"Yes. Che picked me up from there."

Fidel turned to Che. "Do you need the Commandantico anymore?"

"No, that's fine. He did what I needed him to do and did a great job." Che didn't dare to contradict Fidel in front of everyone and said goodbye to me, since Fidel had been very clear about taking me back with him.

We left the conference room followed by Fidel's escort. We walked through the Tropicana gardens. As we walked towards the cars, Fidel asked, "Commandantico, answer me straight—what do you think about this gangster friend of Che's? Do you think he will fulfill his mission, or is there a possibility he might betray us to the CIA for more money than we've paid him?"

I tilted my head down with an uncertain expression. "I don't know, my Comandante. It all depends on what you expect of him. If what you expect involves a lot of personal risk and sacrifice, there's a strong possibility he'll get cold feet and maybe try to find an exit from whatever compromise he made with you. A good alternative, of course, would be going to the CIA, taking into consideration he might receive twice what you've paid him, since they have more money than you do. In this case, he not only will make more money, but he won't have to move a single finger and take any risk at all."

Fidel scratched at his neck nervously with his left hand. "Exactly what I said to Che and our friends the Russians! Imagine if this happens, what is next is the complete ruination of our reputation with the Russians and our plans will be incomplete. Lee Oswald represents tremendous danger while he's alive; he could expose the whole plan. We all know he's a double agent for the CIA. Logically, he'll expose all of us in the assassination plot.

The Broken Rainbow: Mysterious Dark Karma

This is assuming that our men don't fail in killing that donkey imbecile President."

We got into the cars and left the club, heading towards the Prime Minister's offices in Vedado. I very carefully used Che's name and said, "I'm sorry, Comandante. I might not have all the information necessary to express an opinion, but Che expressed in absolute confidentiality that the donkey will be dead very soon. It doesn't matter which route he takes or who is protecting his back. Everyone has been bought. My question is what difference would it make if Oswald remains alive or not, if it's already a done deal with no escape route?"

Fidel looked me straight in the eyes with his tiny eyes which always reminded me of a comic book flea, trying to penetrate my brain. After a few seconds, he said, "Yes, what Che told you is true. The problem, though, is that with Oswald dead all of us will be exonerated of all suspicion. He is our decoy. With him alive, he could blow the whistle and it makes sense that whatever he'll say would create an investigation which will, in the end, implicate us."

I smiled with slight sarcasm. "In this case, Comandante, with something of such vital importance, I won't sleep in peace if all this depends on and is in the hands of someone without scruples and conviction like Jack Ruby. As you know, gangsters have no loyalty to anyone. They are mercenaries. In general, the men who embrace this kind of work care only about money. Unless you have a very thick chain of steel around his neck, or he knows that his betrayal will cause him to pay the high price of his own head."

Fidel nodded, deeply worried by what I had said. He patted me on the knee. "That is exactly what I told

Che. You think very similar to me. That is why I like to exchange ideas with you. Even though you are so young, you have a very great mind."

"Thank you, Comandante."

Fidel shook his head. "This stupid Argentinian, Che, thinks he knows everything, and he assures me that he will shave his beard if Ruby fails us. I know for a fact that he will put down Oswald immediately after our men put down Kennedy."

I smiled. And shrugged. "What is the tremendous sacrifice in shaving his beard?"

Fidel grinned and gesticulated broadly. "Oh, ho! For Che's ego? That would be the end of the world! It would be worse than asking him to take a shower every day!" He laughed at his own joke. "I believe that he probably would renounce his 'Comandante' and get on the first plane to Argentina to finish the medical degree he bought."

I limited myself to smile because I didn't know what Fidel's intentions were behind all the derogatory comments about Che, worse than anything he had said to me before. "He's not a bad guy. You're right, though, Comandante, you have to hold your nose to walk behind him." Fidel laughed again.

We arrived at the Prime Minister's office. Fidel turned to me and said once more before I got out of the car, "Be very careful with Che. His ego is his worst enemy. I don't want him to get you into any trouble, OK?"

"Of course, Comandante. I'll keep my eyes open and keep you informed as always."

Fidel nodded. "Good man! Keep me proud of you." He gestured his gratitude for my supportive comments.

"Of course, my Commander. Thank you very much for your advice."

The Broken Rainbow: Mysterious Dark Karma

He nodded again and gave me a small pat on the shoulder as I got out. I walked to the Soviet UAZ I had left behind in the parking lot. I got into the vehicle and turned the engine on. I sat in thought for a few seconds before putting it in gear to leave, trying to put in order what I would do first.

Dr. Julio Antonio del Marmol

Chapter 12: Putin's Diabolic Circle

13 The Russian Embassy at the Havana Libre

I watched Fidel walk into his private office followed by his escort. A few seconds later, Che arrived in his three Oldsmobiles. The mysterious six-fingered man was with him as the two of them walked inside, leaving the escort by the cars. They saw my vehicle about fifty feet away, and Che raised his right hand unhappily and gave me a salute with a long face. My psychic reading told me he was thinking how I could dare leave him behind and go with Fidel. It crossed my mind that it had to be more than my leaving him behind that was bothering him so badly.

I heard a short time later Che and Castro screaming obscenities at each other, every word clearly heard throughout the compound. Che yelled, the noise echoing along the streets, "How the hell did you dare to practically ignore me in front of my own friends and associates in such a way, right in front of the Russian ambassador?"

I realized the egotistical nature of these two men had been repressed for so long that evidently the cup was overflowing. Both of them, without holding back, used this moment for not the first time to insult each other, without caring at all who was listening to vent their frustrations with each other. Che accused Fidel of being insensitive, arrogant, and reckless as he showed very little respect to Che in front of the others, not giving a good example for anyone in the future to show him any respect in the future, especially Jack Ruby, who had become Che's exclusive contact in the USA and the key subject to the plan that he himself had molded.

Fidel didn't even bother in his long rambling speech, so concerned was he with his glorification and glorifying the imbecile gangster Ruby to acknowledge Che and that Fidel knew better than anyone that he didn't have any sympathy or trust in that individual. Che went farther to accuse Fidel of glorifying someone not in their circle and ignoring Che and all the members of his team. Not content with all this, Che went further back in time to accuse Fidel of getting him out of the Sierra Maestra and sending him with Camilo Cienfuegos to go to the other end of the island to get rid of not just Camilo but both of them at the same time, hoping they would get killed by the Dictator's army. To Fidel's egotistic way of thinking, in getting rid of the two of them he would shine more and at the same time be able to turn both of them into martyrs.

That last part was the final drop of water to overflow Fidel's cup. He replied that if that's what Che thinks of him, there's no reason for the two of them to be together anymore and if Che didn't like the way Fidel conducted and led his revolution, he could go to hell and form his own revolution in another part of the world where he wouldn't have to see him or smell his horrible, pestilent body odor. "I don't even know how you can live with yourself and sleep at night smelling like a pig," Fidel concluded.

Che yelled, "Fuck you, motherfucker! I don't ever want to see you again for the rest of my life!"

There was a pause and then a very loud sound which concerned us, as it sounded like they had started to shoot at each other. We later discovered that Che had slammed the glass door of Fidel's office on his way out that it had shattered.

A few seconds later Che left the office with his mysterious friend who followed him wherever he went like a puppy dog. When he left the building, he didn't even acknowledge me and jumped into his Oldsmobile and yelled at the lead driver to go. Their tires screeching on the pavement, they left the compound as if someone had lit their tails on fire.

I shook my head after what I had heard, simply sitting in the jeep and thought that Che's future, right at that moment, had been sealed. Even though they had frequently argued many times before, it had never sunk to this level of disrespect. Knowing Fidel as well as I did, I felt that Che had signed his own death warrant without even knowing it. Unwanted, he had given Fidel what the Supreme Leader had wanted and had been looking to do for a long time now—to turn the diabolic, stinking Argentinian into an international martyr for his cause and be able to continue to fool all the younger generations with the new name of "Marxist Progressive."

After all that scandal, I drove to the hotel where I had been staying, the Havana Libre. I waved, my right hand high, to the chief attendant, Carlos. He waved back with a smile. I entered the lobby and walked through the reception area. One of the girls at the desk knew me well and held a phone message note for me. I took it, thanked her, and continued toward the back of the building and the public restrooms, looking at the note as I walked. It was from my Uncle Emilio. I went to the pay phones outside the restrooms, opened one of the cabinets to ensure privacy, and dialed the number I had memorized.

The note read, *Julio Antonio del Marmol from Dr. Emilio del Marmol. You have a package at my house with clean clothes and other personal items. Call me please.*

When he answered, we exchanged greetings and I indicated that if he was available, I would stop by in a little while to pick up the package if it wouldn't be inconvenient.

He replied that he would be waiting for me with love and affection. We said goodbye and I hung up after telling him that I would be there in twenty minutes. I pulled the business card Sonya had given me from the pocket of my military shirt. I turned it over and dialed the number she had written on the back.

After a few rings I heard her beautiful, musical voice which to my surprise came to the phone saying, "Julio Antonio, is it you?"

"How did you know it was me? Have you become a psychic now, one more virtue in your box of beautiful attributes and gifts God gave you?"

She laughed. "I love you. You're always so gentle and gallant."

"I'm just being truthful. You're not just physically beautiful but spiritually."

"Really?"

"Yes, really. And after seeing you today, you've grown up to be an even bigger peach."

She laughed in a genuine manner. "No, no, no—none of that psychic craziness or medium stuff. I wish! I believe you are the psychic here, but you told me not to share that, and I only ever told my mother."

"You see? The secret's no longer a secret since you told your mother."

"Don't worry. My mother doesn't live with me; I live by myself. She never talks to anyone; she's dedicated her life to my father and brother."

"How are they doing?"

"Imagine it! In prison for so long."

"Have they told anyone at the embassy?"

"No. This is our secret, please. My mother only calls me once a month, late at night, so she doesn't call attention to me. That's why I knew it had to be you, since no one calls me here and she's not due to make her call yet. I've been waiting for your call since I left the embassy this afternoon."

I looked at my Japanese wristwatch that my brother-in-law Canen had given me: a Seiko NH36A on his last trip to Tokyo to keep his promise. He said he hadn't paid more than $100 for it, but it looked so wonderful that it looked like a $20,000 watch. It was a two-toned watch of blue and gold. I smiled, remembering what had motivated it[14]. I was silent for a moment, thinking about that. It was 7:30 pm.

My prolonged silence prompted Sonya. "Hello? Are you still there?"

"Yes. I had one of those moments of distraction, thinking of the past."

"With me?"

"That never went away. This is something unimportant. But you never went away. If you have no plans for the rest of the evening, I'd like to take you to dinner and a surprise at a very fancy nightclub, the Capri."

"The Capri! Oh, my God—can you take me to that fancy place? I don't have any appropriate clothes."

"Honey, I can take you anyplace. Remember, Papa Fidel's paying."

"You called me at exactly the right moment. I was about to take a bath and then get something to eat before bed. I have no plans at all."

"OK. I have to make a brief visit to my Uncle Emilio in Miramar, and I see your address is there, as well." I checked my watch again. "How about I pick you up between 8:30 and 9?"

"That's perfect. I can get ready and maybe even run out to a store to get appropriate clothes to wear."

"OK, I want you to be the most beautiful woman tonight at the Capri."

---

[14] As related in *Black Tears: The Havana Syndrome*

She replied enthusiastically. "Very well! I can't wait to see you! Thanks for your invitation."

"Sonya, for me it's more than a great pleasure. You don't know how long I've been waiting for this opportunity."

We said goodbye and I left the Hilton to go to Miramar, where I knew for certain that my uncle was waiting with great eagerness. He only called me at the hotel in a great emergency. I had been at his house only the day before, not even twelve hours ago, so something important had prompted the call.

When I arrived at the Nautico, he was at his accustomed place at one of the tables on the beach beneath an umbrella. I could see clearly as I walked to the table the garment bag hanging beneath the umbrella. Through the transparent plastic cover, I could see the elegant tuxedo that Mima had mentioned before during a phone call that she tailored for me for the very near wedding between my sister Disa and Canen, like I had asked her for. She needed me to try it on to see if any alterations were needed. I smiled when I saw the tuxedo. I knew my mother was an excellent tailor, having been the cornerstone for my father's business, and that it would fit me like a glove, like everything else Mima had made for me since my earliest years. My smile grew bigger because I had been thinking how opportune that the tuxedo had arrived on the day I was to reunite with Sonya. It had not been sent by Mima—this had been sent by God!

Even though the sun had been warm that day in November, it had grown dark, leaving a very faint light on the horizon. The black clouds were running rapidly, and a light sprinkle of rain began, with lightning in the distance illuminating the horizon occasionally in the dark night coming to replace the beautiful day that was dying.

My uncle received me with a big smile and offered me a cup of hot chocolate with the *biscocios* he had brought on a small tray from his house. I sat next to him, and he asked, "How much time do we have?"

"Only six days, unfortunately. Things have accelerated, and the man that has been selected to eliminate the decoy for them arrived today. I personally picked him up from the airport. I don't believe the time, velocity, and intensity of these events will allow us to do much to prevent this assassination. I believe it will go down in history as Che predicted and remain a large enigma in silence for over a hundred years without anyone knowing or have exact knowledge of who the brain behind this extraordinary and beyond imagination assassination."

My uncle let me know that even though he knew the intelligence activities in North America involved a long process to have anything serious measures in place, due to the regulations and bureaucratic rules inside the systems of the various agencies, there was a good majority who had great intentions to protect the democracy. They frequently worked against each other, blocking our best efforts and benefit, handicapping our leaders and freedom in the process of protecting freedom itself.

He assured me he would do everything possible and impossible and would give the highest priority classifications as extremely urgent with the new information I had put into his hands as he had done with all my previous information relating to this operation as I had delivered to him previously in the past months to his contact in the Navy base at Guantanamo. The individual who was in charge of receiving specifically this intel did not work with any other intelligence sources but delivered it directly to Langley and then to the President. This individual had been assigned by intelligence with the designation of 24. He and his contact at the base had been extremely worried about the past packages that I had put into my uncle's hands. It was so bad that even though he knew it was breaking protocol that he had asked for a personal interview with me.

My uncle said he declined the request very strongly, even though they had a long and cordial relationship, refusing to divulge to him my identity as it would incur a tremendous risk that could put in danger the future of the whole line of information. He could make no exceptions for him or anyone else. He finished, "As I had told my contact before from the very beginning, that is one of the conditions, that I was going to be the channel for the information from this particular spy. Never, never before had this been breached. This would remain so unless the life of the contact himself came to be in imminent danger and it became necessary to reveal the identity of the spy known as the Lightning because the highest intelligence officers in the Navy base would need to have an ID in order to receive him into the base. This protocol was never to be violated for anyone, because that could not only cost the life of the contact but also the many high officers and high-level ministers in the Cuban government who directly or indirectly work with the Lightning.

My uncle looked me deeply in the eyes. "Of course, I only follow the protocol. It's up to you and only you if you want to accept that meeting with Agent 24. Even in spite of my refusal he's asked me again if I could consult with you one last time. A single record of Fidel and Che or Che and any other person while they're talking about the assassination of Kennedy will be extremely important and a decisive way to convince the President to not go to Dallas, Texas. It will not only facilitate protecting the President, but it would create a justification for a direct military invasion by the Navy and other Armed Forces of the United States into Cuba."

I smiled. "Yes, I agree 100% with Agent 24. But if something goes wrong, they will leave me like the crazy man painting the ceiling of the nut house without a ladder and tell me to hold myself up there by the brush. The only difference between this joke and that of the crazy guy is that my brush will be full of red paint, and it won't be precisely paint—it will be my blood when I fall down because there won't be anyone there to hold or catch me."

Uncle Emilio smiled and nodded. "You are 100% right. That is why I've repeatedly denied this interview with you. Even though I have absolute trust in this particular individual, because he's not only worked with the CIA at the highest levels, but he works with a very, very old organization, the one I started in back in the old days during our fight against the Nazis—the League. To be a member of this organization you have to be bulletproof. We jokingly say that an elephant would go through the eye of a needle before a double agent would get through the net in any attempt to infiltrate this sophisticated agency. That's how tight this organization is."

I smiled slightly. "Say hello to your friend, Agent 24. I want to send a message to him through you. Tell him that, with all my respect, I'm declining that meeting. I consider it unnecessary, and I don't believe will change much at all for me to take such a high risk for his President. This doesn't take into consideration that I don't believe this President deserves it. He didn't play clean with the lives of my compatriots in the Brigade 2506. So many of those young kids died because of his cowardly negligence. Do me a favor, Uncle: ask Agent 24 if, were he in my shoes, he would be capable of exposing not only his life but also blow his cover for a man of that caliber."

"OK. I believe that's a fair question. Knowing him, he'll laugh and say that he knows I trained you." My uncle reclined in his chair with a grave and exasperated expression in his eyes. He grimaced in distaste and squeezed his chin. With irony in his voice he added, "You should never forget your friends, but also never forget your enemies and their betrayals. The Kennedys have never shown to us a microscopic gesture of being our friends. To me they are mercenaries, and if we're sincere with ourselves, as Agent 24 will know, we can say without fear of being wrong that they are a little bit worse than our enemies.

"In his hypocrisy, President Kennedy never backed up the invasion and was never shy about expressing it in public as necessary for Cubans to recover their freedom. On the contrary, he tried to block every single effort and even sabotage it to take off his shoulders the obligation that he inherited from his predecessor, Dwight D. Eisenhower. But he doesn't possess a smidgeon of integrity or the courage to say it publicly. All he had to do as an honorable man would be to cancel the agreement contracted by the previous President. Instead, like a corrupt politician does, he took the conniving and deceitful way in order to escape from the moral ideological compromise the United States government and the prior President had with the youngest Cubans who had been trained with the hope of bringing freedom to their country. Little did they know that they were being lied to and misled, because even as he gave that speech Kennedy already knew that he would be sending them to an assured death.

"Not only would they not return freedom to the Cuban people, but he was going to condemn the entire American continent and serve it on a silver platter for the expansion and intervention of Russia and China and their despised totalitarian ideologies of Marxist-Leninist that has cost so much innocent lives around the world. Not just Russian and Chinese lives but all the other countries in South and Central America will be condemned in the future to this barbarous lie that this young President of the United States was committing."

I understood the frustration and indignation my uncle felt. His face was red, and his jaw was clenched. I replied in a very calm voice to soften his emotional state. "My uncle, you have to remember, as you've told me many times, all politicians are the same—unscrupulous mercenaries who only look out for their own interests and not those of the majority."

He smiled ant took a dip of his hot chocolate. A little calmer now, he said, "No doubt that you've come to be my best student. You've gotten to understand the ins and outs of this game very well. You're right. But the only difference between the other politicians and the Kennedys is that Kennedy has a choice of doing a great thing to be remembered by in history for several generations ahead by behaving like a man who loves his country and the continent. But in order to take the responsibility from his shoulder he decided to change the point of embarkation from Trinidad to the Bay of Pigs. One day history will bring to light this malicious and arbitrary decision made at the last minute with the intention of frustrating that military operation and cause its failure. They will know that this not only brought nefarious consequences for the whole continent, including his beautiful USA. I believe that history will be just, that the Kennedy brothers will be remembered for the highest cowardice and crimes that any President of America ever committed, that history will leave a big black spot on his legacy as a President and all the memory of the youngest men who left their lives on the beaches of the Bay of Pigs in vain, and as their leader, President Kennedy, remembered as a coward and a traitor to the idea of a free Cuba and American continent."

He paused for a moment. "When you go back to your vehicle, you'll find in the passenger seat a folder with significant details of supreme importance about your old friend and new contact who has appeared in your life. She's extremely valuable for your work in international espionage. I have received a debriefing today before you arrived from those who are guarding your back day and night that destiny has brought you on the same road as her. Now it's your mission to try and recruit her and include her in our cause; of course, assuming she hasn't already been recruited by another agency, either friendly or enemy. Her position in the Russian embassy as an assistant attaché to the Russian ambassador makes her an extremely rare jewel and a great fountain of information for every single agency."

I smiled. "Do you think we can trust her?"

He smiled back at me. "Using your common sense and your great natural gifts, I have no doubt in my mind with what you've learned with us in these past years you've not just turned into a regular spy but into a master spy in this game; don't ever have any doubts that you are the master in this game. If not, you would never have been able to make a fool out of one of the greatest master spies ever to exist: Ernesto Che Guevara, along with many others at an international level like Lee Harvey Oswald."

He reclined in his chair and took another sip from his hot chocolate with a large smile of satisfaction. "I can assure you that in all my years of experience I've never seen done the things that have been done by you in less than three years." He raised his eyebrows in wonderment. "I only can imagine what you're going to be able to do in ten years from now. Only those who have been close to you like we've been for the last three or four years could comprehend and have an idea of what you'll become."

I smiled and thanked him for his reassurance. I could not deny that I felt extremely proud to hear that from his lips. We stood up and embraced as we said our goodbyes. I walked toward the UAZ. As I opened the door and entered. Like he had said, there was a folder on the passenger's seat with a little note which read, *Burn this after you've read it and put it in the drawers of your mind. Love, Chandee.* She had even drawn a little heart, and I smiled as I returned to my memories of that Chinese-Cuban girl who had become my first student and assistant. I repeated to myself and mumbled, "*Chinita, chinita, cubanita.* You've learned more than what I ever taught you."

Chapter 13: A Week Filled with Surprises

14 *Mansion in Miramar, around 5th Avenue*

    I examined the folder meticulously for a little while as I sat there. When I was done, I put it under the driver's seat. I checked my watch, knowing that I had limited time to do what needed to be done and still be able to pick Sonya up when we agreed. Realizing my tight schedule, I got out of there as fast as I could, heading towards to Boca Ciega, the mansion Che used where I intended to change my clothing and take my pick from the elaborate collection of luxury cars in the underground garage that he maintained for himself. These cars had been confiscated not just from the wealthy and super rich people who had left the country but also those who had left the island after becoming disaffected with the system.

Che had frequently offered me the use of any of those cars anytime I wanted. I knew the guards watching the place well, and they knew me. I also knew the entire layout and security protocols. I had entertained the idea of replacing the Russian UAZ for something more appropriate to the occasion. I wanted to impress my childhood friend and love. With a big smile on my face, after I arrived at the mansion, I went down to the garage. Without hesitation, I selected a 1957 red Corvette convertible with white stripes along the side and a white interior.

When I left the place, very happy with my selection, I returned to Havana to look for Sonya's address in Miramar. As I drove along the La Via Blanca, a large multilane freeway, I checked my wristwatch and saw that my time was running out, given the distance I needed to drive to pick her up on time. I accelerated to around 120 miles per hour in order to get there on time without giving her a bad first impression.

Fortunately, I had no accidents or impediments, and I arrived at her address a few minutes early. As I drove through the front gate onto the driveway of the large mansion, I stopped, doubting as to whether this was the right place or not. The gates which served as the entry to the drive hung on both sides from rusty hinges, ready to collapse, and stood completely open. I looked at the number on the column of the gate, and it matched what Sonya had written on the back of the embassy business card.

Carefully, navigating around the debris that had fallen from the trees onto the drive as well as some large potholes to avoid damaging the undercarriage of this car, it crossed my mind that this mansion without doubt previously was absolutely breathtaking. Now, however, it was completely in ruins. It looked abandoned and uninhabited. For a few minutes I doubted that anyone could live there in those conditions. Unaccustomed to retreating under any circumstances, as I had learned from my training, I continued carefully along the driveway.

Though the community of Miramar had been in the past an area of prosperity and a status symbol to everyone in Havana both before and after the revolution, many of these luxury mansions had been vandalized by mobs. Those who feared retribution amidst the political disturbance had abandoned the country, leaving behind these beautiful mansions, cars, yachts, and everything else they possessed in order to save their lives and those of their families on the night of December 31, 1958. It was difficult to believe that, after only three years after the Marxist socialist revolution had declared Fidel Castro as Supreme Leader, that this radical political change had clearly destroyed and depopulated properties, parks, even the national zoo with the lack of maintenance and care one had seen clearly everywhere.

I stopped the Corvette before what appeared to be the entryway of this gigantic estate beneath an overhang. I had to avoid the overhang because of the debris there and parked a little distance away across from a gigantic fountain which still functioned that was filled with water lilies and weeds in poor maintenance.

I got out and started to walk to the entryway. A large black German shepherd bounded out of one side of the mansion, barking and growling loudly. It ran towards me

The Broken Rainbow: Mysterious Dark Karma

with an unfriendly welcome, baring its fangs to clearly indicate that I was trespassing there. From its attitude, it wanted a piece of me as I walked fearlessly towards the front door. He caught me by surprise; in the condition the mansion appeared to be in, I didn't think anyone would be there, especially a loose dog.

I rapidly recovered from my surprise and prepared for the worst like I had learned in the past years. I picked up a pair of large chunks of concrete, I raised both hands high, my eyes staring into the aggressive dog's eyes. I yelled, "Stop! If you don't want to die by my hand, you shut up!"

I spoke with such fierceness with my aggressive stance, the dog, as if understanding me, stopped a few feet away. He still growled and bared his fangs at me, but he stopped barking. He continued to look at me. I yelled, "Bad dog! Bad dog! Go away!" I raised my right hand higher as if I were about to throw the rock at him.

To my surprise, the dog stopped growling and retreated a little. He looked at me in my eyes still, unmoving, one paw ready to either run or charge. At that moment, the enormous front doors of the villa opened and the tall, beautiful figure of Sonya, very well-dressed in a long black and white gown with a beautiful red rose on the left side of her breast, wearing a white hat with a black bandana, emerged. She yelled at the dog in a commanding voice, "Lucifer! Stop! Stop now! Go back!" She pointed towards the house. The dog obeyed and walked very slowly back to where it had come from.

I thought to myself, *Boy! Aha! Lucifer—what a name for that dog!* Lucifer, evidently, was not a bad dog and obeyed his mistress.

Sonya smiled and gestured to me to come closer. "There's no doubt in my mind that the dog doesn't scare a wolf."

I smiled slightly as I walked over to her. We hugged and a small kiss on each other's lips. "What kind of name is that for a dog? Even though he may really honor that name."

She smiled wider. "He's not really that aggressive, only with strangers. And that's good; believe it or not, that's my father's idea, being an atheist and a little communist. He sent it as a puppy as a gift through one of his political prisoner friends who was released early. According to Father's theory, that kind of name will impress anyone, and even if he turns out to be a sissy, and everyone will be afraid of him. The idea was for them to grow up together and form a bond, so he would be a guardian for my little boy."

I raised an eyebrow in surprise at the mention of a son. Sonya saw and smiled again. With the back of her right hand, she caressed my cheek, "You have to remember, it's been three years since the last time we saw each other. In all that time, which has passed so quickly, many things have happened." She grinned a little mischievously. "I hope that you like surprises, because I have quite a few of them in the drawers of my memory. Some I want to share with you before we even go to our dinner reunion so we can start fresh without any secrets the beautiful relationship we began many years ago before destiny played a nasty game with us, frustrating with unbearable cruelty us without any alternative."

As I walked into that enormous mansion which had looked from the outside to be in ruins, my surprise grew as I saw the beauty and luxury the interior displayed so extravagantly. Even the furniture looked like it had been created by a famous designer, with impeccable, exquisite taste and maintained in immaculate cleanliness. There was even an indoor pool with marble statues of lions and other animals. I looked around, my admiration and surprise clearly reflected in my face.

Sonya smiled and linked her arm with mine. She asked, "Do you like all that you see?"

I smiled. "Who wouldn't like what I see? Everything is beautiful."

"I want you to consider this home to be yours from now on, if you like it." She pulled out of her pocket a key on a keychain with a golden heart.

I took it in my hand, completely taken by surprise. I could only say, "Thank you very much. Are you sure? As you said yourself before, it's been many years that have passed. Maybe I'm involved in things in my life that you might find far away from your tastes or ability to accept."

She replied, looking intensely into my eyes and a loving smile, "Never could I be more certain in my life than I am now. I've been waiting for this moment for the past three long years without resting a single night. Every time I lay in my bed by myself to wake up by myself, I've been thinking of you. I never stopped asking God to find you in my path the same way we found each other today, in a very casual manner without compromising the dignity that I've saved like a treasure and kept intact all these three years. I don't care who you've been with in the past or the present romantically. The only fact that you're here with me tonight, dressed so elegantly in that beautiful tailor-made tuxedo leaves me in no doubt that total bonding of our hearts three years ago in that beautiful hot summer day, when our bodies and spirits united with the blessing of the Supreme Architect of the Universe forever."

Two tears rolled down her cheek; they looked like tears of happiness, but I asked, "Why are you crying?"

"Because I found you again."

I kissed her passionately and deeply. Something deep within my feelings stirred to feel and hear those beautiful words expressing Sonya's deepest feelings. We had stopped by the vast swimming pool lit by colorful lights and the three marble lions which were at one angle of the swimming pool. Our silhouettes reflected in the water by the light as we kissed. We stayed there for a while, contemplating each other and kissing once more.

Then the automatic pump of the pool started up, and water issued from the mouths of the three lions into the pool. We awoke from our romantic sublime moment. We slowly parted, both smiling as we watched the water flowing into the pool. I caressed her cheek with the back of my hand. I said softly, "You never left my heart and memories. And no, I'm not involved with anyone romantically at this moment."

She caressed my cheek in the same manner. We were about to kiss again, but a lady with long, wavy hair brushed to one side of her face, who resembled an Indian mystic with large eyes and olive skin entered from one of the doors leading into the room with the swimming pool. She said, "I'm sorry to interrupt, my lady, but your boy is already asleep. You can leave anytime you want if you wish to."

Sonya nodded and gestured with her right hand to beckon her. "Come here, Marina. I want you to meet the love of my life, the one I've been telling and bragging about for so many years."

Marina was middle-aged and smiled from ear to ear upon hearing that. With an expression of surprised pleasure, she raised a hand to her mouth. She said joyfully, "Finally! The father of Julius Christian."

Sonya looked at my face. I looked at her and she nodded. She said in a low voice, "This is another of my surprises."

Marina, as she walked around the pool towards us, noticed the surprise in my face and Sonya's reaction, tried to explain. She raised her left hand to her mouth. "I'm sorry. Did I say something indiscrete?"

Sonya put her hand on Marina's shoulder. "Thank you. You actually saved me the effort and facilitated my new surprise to him."

I extended my hand to Marina and said, "My name is Julio Antonio del Marmol. Thank you for your indiscretion. This is really the best surprise Sonya has for me." She looked at me in gratitude and affection in her eyes. Timidly at first, she stepped towards me and gave me a strong hug.

She turned slightly. "It's a very, very great pleasure to meet you, Julio Antonio. Now I will go back to my duties in the house. I wish you a beautiful and unforgettable night." She left us to our privacy.

We returned to kiss each other, more passionately than before, until Sonya gently pushed me away. "I'd better stop, or we won't be able to have our first reunion dinner. I don't want to frustrate due to our internal passionate fire of love. I don't want to be responsible for ruining our first reencounter with this precious moment, because my intention and lovely internal fire. This momentum should become one of our best memories for our future. The best thing is to postpone our passion that's built over the last three years until later, OK?"

"OK. I only want to ask you a little thing before we leave."

"OK. What is it?"

"Will you let me see my son for a few seconds before we leave, if you don't mind, please?"

She smiled. "Love, if you hadn't asked me to do so, maybe this would have disappointed me a little."

I bent down a little and she kissed my cheek. She said, "Thank you for completing my beautiful and happy night. Also, thank you for continuing to be the gallant, generous, and extraordinary man that you used to be still three years later. Julio Antonio del Marmol, don't ever change, please."

She took my hand. Holding hands, we walked up some marble stairs to the second level of the mansion and stopped by the little boy's room next to the master bedroom. When we arrived at his bedroom where he was in a profound sleep, I realized that this room was actually connected to the master bedroom.

Sonya went over to the bed and pulled the sheet away from his face and little head. At that moment, my heart stopped. I looked at the little boy of around three years of age, white-skinned like coconut meat and very bright, wavy, red hair. If before this moment I had any doubts about what Sonya had said, when I saw of this boy who so resembled my own baby pictures and was still held in my memory wiped all uncertainties away completely, especially when I saw the long hair, so unusual in baby boys in that time.

Full of curiosity, I wondered at that moment why she left him with the long hair. But then I remembered how my Mima had always called me her carrot cake at that age, and even heard her voice saying it at that moment. In a soft voice, trying to avoid waking the boy, I asked Sonya, "Why haven't you cut his hair? He almost looks like a girl with that long hair."

Sonya put a finger to her lips and signaled for us to leave the room. She took me by my right arm and gently guided me out. Once we were in the hall near the stairs, she said, "As you know, I'm a Catholic. The reason that I haven't cut his hair is because when he was born, he was so sick that he almost died. As a Christian, I got on my knees one night when I didn't think he was going to make it and made a promise to Jesus Christ that if He saved my boy, I would not cut his hair for eight years so that he grows up in resembling Him. I don't care about anyone's criticism, and I know he'll receive some, and even my family went to the extent that they felt I was converting my boy through my religious fanaticism into an effeminate sissy. I'm making my ears deaf and not paying any attention to them. I always reply to them that my boy will pick whatever sexuality he finds suitable for himself, and that's his decision, not ours. God will protect him from all the evil in this world and I will not allow any breach of the promise that I, his mother, made for him."

As I heard Sonya's conviction and faith, I could not hold myself from grinning broadly as I took her hand and squeezed it hard with mine in satisfaction. I remembered that Mima had done the same with me in similar circumstances. I asked, "What made you choose that name your boy?"

She said in quick conviction, "*Our* boy. The first name is yours; I just changed the 'o' in Julio to a 'u.'

That way, it wouldn't complicate things for you or create any guilt if it reached your ears. Until this day, I haven't revealed to anyone that you are the father of my boy. You are the only man I have ever had sexual relations before and after my baby boy."

I stopped for a few seconds on the bottom stairs on that long staircase and turned slightly. I looked straight into her eyes. "Why?"

She smiled. "Which of the two whys applies to your question? The first one, the why I haven't told anyone you are the father of your son, or the second one, why haven't I had any sex with any other man?"

I thought about it for a few seconds. "Well, in reality, if you don't have any objections, I just would like very much to know the answer to both those questions. Even though I can at least imagine the answer for the first one."

She smiled and squeezed my arm. "I understand your curiosity perfectly. And no, I don't have any objections or secrets with you. As I told you before, I would like very much to begin a new life, clean and with no secrets between you and I."

"I like that."

We continued to walk to the bottom of the stairs. Sonya said with another squeeze of my arm as she shook it gently. "I only ask you to not be so serious when you ask me anything at all. I'm in the disposition to satisfy every single question you have. I don't want to leave any curiosity in your mind. The same way I expect you to be of the disposition to satisfy my curiosity." She smiled mischievously.

I changed my demeanor from serious to a slight smile, looking now into her eyes. "Of course. With no integrity and reciprocity, love dies, and the exchange can avert discord and misery that eventually feeds and makes larger the distrust that will grow deep roots into your heart destroy all the beauty, noble, and good intentions without distinction of sex for all of humanity."

"Wow!" she exclaimed and stopped on the last step of the stairs. She hugged me close to her body and looked into my eyes with genuine joy. "Those words that came so spontaneously out of your heart I know come from the most profound depths of your soul and deserves a recompense, one of the most passionate kisses to you from my heart." She gave me a passionate, lingering kiss.

When we separated, she added, "What you just said you should write down. If one day you become somebody published these phrases from you can help future generations to maintain cordiality, peace, and fraternity."

I smiled. "Thank you very much. I'm glad my words reached deep into your heart. All I was doing was telling you what I felt in mine. I wasn't even expecting that kiss. That was the cherry on top. But you still haven't answered either of my questions. I'm not going not let you get away with that."

She grinned from ear to ear and said with a mischievous expression, "Oh, I'm sorry. Let's continue our previous conversation. It's very simple. As is logical, when we both decided to make love and let our passions and sexual desires manifest, we both were underage. I believed that revealing your name to my parents would only complicate things a lot more for you than they already were when they discovered I was pregnant. That's why I decided this would be my secret until I decided for myself to share this secret with you, when destiny brought us together again. I had the complete assurance and conviction that this would happen, as it has now by the Divine Power of the Supreme Architect, when the time was right."

I smiled in satisfaction for that truly extreme vow of loyalty that she had made to herself, knowing the morality and customs of that time, especially in our country. I could only imagine the psychological pressure and recriminations she suffered from her parents to compel her to confess who the father was. As that time the logical thing to do was to talk to the parents of the boy and ask them to assume the responsibility when the baby was born and make them when they reached an appropriate age marry to cover the family honor of the young girl in the face of society.

We looked at each other filled with love, admiration, and mutual respect at how similar our personalities were. She kissed me again, this time tenderly on my lips, taking my face between her hands. "And the second question is the easiest one. We women not only have sex to have it; we are more spiritual, not as physical as men are. Never, in the past three years, have I found anyone in my road that conquered my heart spiritually." She held up her pinky. "Never, even when I dated other boys, did I find one with this much," she added with a mischievous smile, "to being close to who you are. That's why the doors of my virginity closed after you. I think in order to open them we will need a lot of butter again."

I smiled. "Remind me, when we return from dinner tonight, OK?"

"Oh, no—don't worry about it. With the shortage in Cuba of everything, that's the first thing I took from the Russian embassy after my encounter with you today. I have it in the refrigerator in my room."

Chapter 14: The Ups and Downs of the Hotel Capri and Cabaret

15 *Julio Antonio's band, Los Gatos Negros*

We laughed as we left the house. I opened the passenger door of the Corvette for her. Once we were both seated, she said, "Beautiful car! Who did you steal it from?"

I gave her a small smile and shook my head. "I don't like to steal from anyone. It's not my car—it illegitimately belongs to Che. You have to ask him that question, though I don't think he'll be able to give you a proper answer to it. There are so many thousands of people who abandoned the country that

I don't think he even knows who, exactly, this car legitimately belongs to. I don't believe this Marxist Argentinian cares about that at all. Not only that, he has at least forty more, in his underground garage, locked and gathering dust. I don't believe that he ever dropped a single bead of sweat to acquire any of them."

Sonya looked at me with a small smile. "You don't like Che too much, eh?"

My smile turned into a grin. "Who I really like, very much is you. Of that, you should never have any doubt."

Sonya leaned in to kiss me on the cheek. "I like you very much, too. That's a very clever way of not responding to my answer."

I smiled again wordlessly. I held out my right hand to take her left hand and looked into her eyes. "Changing the conversation, you will make every man and woman jealous when we go into the Capri Cabaret. I don't think anyone there ever saw a woman as beautiful as you look tonight and with such a distinguished elegance and class in all their lives."

Sonya blushed furiously and put both hands to her face. "Be careful! If you continue to give me all these compliments and tell me all these beautiful things about myself, you will convince me and and then in the future you'll repent because you've converted me into a very conceited and vain creature."

I shook my head. Sonya smiled again. "You? No! You could never be like that. Not the mother of my child!"

She leaned over her seat to give me another tender kiss on the cheek. I noticed at that moment that we were being followed. It looked like some of her Russian friends from the embassy. I said nothing but kept my cool, pretending nonchalantly that nothing was happening.

The Broken Rainbow: Mysterious Dark Karma

I drove into the valet parking by the main entrance to the hotel. As I did, I saw the car that had been following, continuing in after us. It was being taken care of by the young valets—a red 1956 MG. It belonged to a producer and emcee for the Capri show, Fernando Arencibia. I had met Fernando at a *belada*[15] in the FOCSA building where the composer and director for the CMQ TV station, Maestro Carlos Anzas, had introduced us. I noticed that he continued stare at me with a great deal of attention as if he were trying to recognize me and couldn't remember, or perhaps he was captured by Sonya's beauty.

As I got out of the Corvette and gave the instructions to the valet to park it as close to the front door as possible for security reasons like I always did, and they knew I would take care of them properly when I left; they also knew me as the Commandantico and respected me. Fernando still had not taken his eyes off of us, watching all of our movements carefully. When he saw that my car was not taken into the underground garage like all the others but parked practically in the front door where all the VIP and dignitary's cars were left, he could no longer contain his curiosity. He raised his hand to attract our attention, taking the initiative. I gave him a big smile in reply to his greeting. "How are you doing, Fernando?"

He acknowledged and was taken by surprise by the cordial reply as he approached me. He took the arm of the tall, blonde beautiful lady with large green

---

[15] A private modern music gathering of the elite of Cuban intellectuals, similar to other performance parties seen in the Bohemian centers of the United States and Europe.

eyes by his side and came over to us. He said, "I'm sorry, I know I know you from someplace, but I can't remember where. Have I seen you on TV or at some artistic venue with my friends?"

I grinned. "Both."

He shook his head in confusion. "How is that?" He raised his eyebrows.

I held out my right hand to shake his hand. "My name is Julio Antonio del Marmol, el Commandantico. You've probably seen me next to Fidel and other leaders of the revolution many times. If you think back, not long ago you and I were introduced in the FOCSA building by Maestro Carlos Anzas..."

"Oh!" he interrupted, finally recognizing me. "Yes, yes. I'm sorry, I didn't fully recognize you because you looked like the French actor Alain Delon, but you cut your hair. You used to have long hair. With that fancy tuxedo you're wearing, probably the latest style from Paris and your beautiful brand-new Corvette, you definitely look more like a movie star." He opened his arms and kissed Sonya's hand with a bow. He added, "And with this beautiful woman by your side, probably the most beautiful one to ever enter this place, of course I didn't recognize you! You're in disguise, Commandantico!"

Sonya glanced at me with a small smile. "Thank you for your nice compliments."

"It's not a compliment, it comes from my heart. I'm going to steal you from him and make you the prima ballerina in my show!"

"My name is Sonya," she said.

He clapped his hand to his mouth and looked at me with greater attention this time and incredulity. "Oh, my God! You're the one you were singing that beautiful song that's been a hit all over the country in every single radio station! Isn't that true?" he asked excitedly.

"Yes, you're right again. She is the Sonya that inspired me to write that song. Thank you for saying it's a beautiful piece of music. Today we've been reunited after not seeing each other for three years."

"Oh, my God! We have to tell this beautiful story in my show!"

"But remember," I said, "this story is a lot more complicated than even I can imagine. The moment I sat down at my piano to write 'Sonya, the Love of my Infancy,' I expected to sit down again at the piano to compose its sequel to continue this story of love not too far in the future. Now I can do it out of the ordinary and completely extraordinary not just for me but for the public who received that song with so much love and care."

The beautiful woman with him, feeling a little neglected, held out her hand. "I'm Sylvia. Nice to meet you." I took her hand and kissed it respectfully with a small bow. As I was about to say my name to her, before I let her hand go, she raised her left hand high. "You don't have to tell me your name. You're famous, honey. You're Julio Antonio del Marmol, the Commandantico. I know you very well and the music of your musical group, The Black Cats, all week long all over the place. Congratulations, you're number 1 all over the country on Radio Progreso, CMQ, and all the other stations around the country." She held out her hand. "I hope that your reunion is permanent and full of happiness for both of you."

Sonya smiled in satisfaction. She said with conviction and optimism, "Thank you very much, Sylvia. Our future is already here with us. Our happiness won't wait and arrived just today to stay with us forever." She pointed at herself. "Today, we have been reunited."

Fernando took two tickets out of his jacket pocket and handed them to me. "After your dinner, I'll wait for you guys at my show. These are free tickets."

I pulled out the two tickets from my tuxedo and showed them to him. "Thank you very much, Fernando, but next time. We'll take a rain check, but this time I'm ahead of you."

Fernando looked at me in surprise. "Oh! You've already bought tickets for my show. But we're changing the program next week, so come then. I think you'll be delighted with it. I've been invited after next week's show to a *belada* with dancers, musicians, movie directors, and all the intellectuals for all the movies for every single actor and actress in this town."

"Very well," I replied. "Thank you very much. We'll do that."

We said goodbye and entered the hotel. Sonya and I walked to the cabaret where we sat down and had an exquisite dinner. Afterwards, we started to enjoy the magnificent Midnight Show. To honor its name, it started precisely a few minutes before twelve am. The lights turned off a few seconds before and the curtain went up. The orchestra played a beautiful introduction with massive tympany. It was a beautiful production, announcing Fernando dressed in a tuxedo in very much the same style as mine.

He announced the program of the night. Sonya took my hand with a smile of happiness. "Thank you for bringing me to this beautiful place. This is actually one of my greatest wishes before I die: coming to the Capri. And you made it possible tonight."

The Broken Rainbow: Mysterious Dark Karma

I whispered into her ear as the show started, "It's great that I've made you happy. That is the most important thing in life."

We continued to have a good time, enjoying the tragic play about an Indian slave, based on a musical composition of Ernesto Lecuona Siboney. After the play ended, they presented different musical groups famous at that time, one of which was Los Zafiros, the quartet of Meme Solis played a couple of pieces, then the act was closed with Meme Solis himself playing the piano in a very beautiful piece that was his own composition. After Meme finished his act, Fernando came on stage and approached the edge of the stage.

He said, "We have a special surprise tonight for us. We all have heard on our radios all over the country for over two weeks now, 'My Sonya,' and we have the honor to have with us tonight in the audience Julio Antonio del Marmol, the composer and singer of that song. And if that weren't enough, he's come with a great company that he reunited with tonight in an unbelievable play of destiny, the love of his infancy, after they've been separated for several years, Sonya Lazo, the inspiration for that beautiful song. Let's put our hands together for this brilliant composer and singer of modern tempo."

The audience gave us resounding applause for several minutes. I stood up, caught by surprise by that improvised introduction, but what surprised me most was that the audience stood up, asking that I sing for them.

Fernando, a man with great experience of directing this show for so many years, knew very well how to steer the audience to perfection, as it brough such value to his show. I had no doubt that he had been cooking this idea ever since he saw us in the parking lot, meticulously, to use us to close his show with the golden brush that night.

Fernando admitted it to me when I encountered him later. He said I had come like sent by God from the sky to raise the popularity of the show that night, which for the past few months had been declining enormously by every communist measurement the Cuban government had imposed on the island. Not only had they scared off the people with money, their primary clientele, but also the international tourists had reduced in numbers daily for the past three years. When he saw me there in the parking lot, he saw a great opportunity since my music had been playing at number one all over the island that this would spread from the capital to the rest of the country and expected it would create a new clientele that he so badly needed. He was afraid of losing his job.

When I finished singing that night, I had to admit that the tremendous and warm welcome I received was one of the greatest satisfactions in my life from that beautiful audience. I never received such a long and warm ovation anywhere else. People asked me for more and more after I already played several songs on the piano, I finished by singing in English an arrangement I had made on my own for the soundtrack for *La Dolce Vida*, the movie directed by Federico Fellini, and starring Marcello Mastroianni. It was a slow rock ballad that was inspired by the film's soundtrack. The public received it with tremendous enthusiasm and asked for yet more. I declined respectfully, using as my excuse that I needed to return to the side of my Sonya who had been waiting for me too long already.

The guilt got them to applaud and tell me to go with Sonya. Under the applause and adulation, we both stood up and quickly, politely got out of there and practically ran through the lobby to the parking lot. Fortunately for me, the car was right at the door. I gave a generous tip to the attendant, we rushed out of there, and I saw in the rearview mirror Fernando and Sylvia running behind us with documents in their hands with a very profitable contract for further appearances. I never did give him an answer to his offer, for obvious reasons.

    As we left the Capri that night, I saw our tail following us again, all the way to Sonya's residence in Miramar. Sonya either didn't care or didn't pay attention. She rested her head on my shoulder and said, "You can't imagine how proud I am of you, not just for your musical talents that God gave you but also for your class and poise, especially when you gave the public in a polite way such a brilliant excuse without offending anyone or trying to hurt anyone's feelings. You can't imagine what those words meant to me. Like I told you before, it's neither not your fault nor mine that I've gone to bed only in the company of my baby and in the morning getting out of bed with the same loneliness and praying to God that you would appear in my road, keeping my secret and my son by my side without being able to tell anyone anything for fear of complicating the things even more. All the miseries of the past three years have all been wiped out in a single night and replaced by a beautiful fountain of happiness that I never imagined would arrive in my life. Tonight will remain in my heart and mind all my life. Nobody can ever take that away from me. There is no doubt in my mind that this is a great gift from God."

I caressed her long hair and turned a little to kiss her head. We arrived at her place. As we entered the driveway, I saw the car that had been following us all night. We parked the car under the overhang, and Lucifer came out, barking furiously as he had before. Sonya immediately reprimanded him. "Bad dog! Go! Go to your house."

Lucifer whined as he recognized her voice. I said, "No, don't do that. Don't reprimand him when he's only doing his job and protecting your property. Call him. I want him to know me and be his friend."

She shook her head. "Really? You want to have Lucifer as a friend?"

"Why not? With God, everything is possible, even sitting Lucifer on his tail. Don't you believe so?"

She smiled. "You're incorrigible. You're right, though." She called Lucifer, who was walking slowly into his house in the back. "Come on, Lucifer!"

Hearing Sonya's voice in a different tempo of music to his ears, Lucifer stopped. "I have a surprise for you!" He dashed back to us, his tail wagging furiously. She opened the cover on a metal decorated urn and reached inside. She pulled out a handful of what appeared to be crackers but were pieces of beef jerky cut shaped like bones.

As soon as she showed them to Lucifer, he sat down before her on his tail, licking his chops. She gave me a handful. "Give him some and you'll see how quickly you make friends. Hold out your hand." She said, "Lucifer, Julio Antonio is a friend."

I held out my hand for him to sniff it. He looked me in the eyes, and I offered without fear some of those jerky chips that he liked so much. They smelled horrible, more like a Russian meat can, nothing very pleasant to human olfactory nerves. Evidently, however, to Lucifer they were a delicacy. I had no doubts that this had been manufactured in Russia; in Cuba, even food for human beings had disappeared. Animals had to be content with whatever was left over from the table. They were slowly growing feral as there was less and less coming from the tables of Cuban families.

After a few minutes of friendly contact with Lucifer, we went inside the residence. Sonya suggested we go up to the room of Julius Christian as she was very anxious to see him again. This was the first time in three years that she had left him alone at night only in the company of her caretaker, Marina.

I was surprised to see her when we came into the baby's room half-asleep in a comfortable chair next to the boy's crib like a guard dog. With a big smile on her face, she wiped her eyes in submissive respect, she got up to greet us. "I hope you've had an unforgettable and beautiful night and your beautiful reunion of your souls."

Sonya replied, "Yes, yes. It was really something unforgettable. He surpassed all my expectations."

Marina smiled from ear to ear when she heard that. "Oh, you don't know how much joy you gave me by saying that, Miss Sonya."

"Thank you, Marina. How has my baby been behaving in my absence?"

Marina smiled again. "Happy and sleeping. He hasn't woken up at all, like a little angel."

Sonya smiled. "Very well. Thank you very much. Now it's your turn to go get some sleep like the angel you are to me. Go and rest in your room downstairs. I'll take care of him the rest of the night."

Marina shook her head. "No, no, Miss Sonya. I'll stay here with him in case he wakes up later tonight, like I always do. Besides, tonight is a special night for you both. I've been thinking that you need some privacy, and the baby's room is too close to yours." She smiled mischievously. "I think it's a better idea if I take the baby to my room tonight. Downstairs he'll rest the same as he does here, and you won't have to worry about him the rest of the night."

Sonya looked unsure. We looked at each other without a word. She said to Marina, "I think your idea is a great one, Marina. Thank you for your suggestion." I remained silent but smiled.

I said, "Thank you very much, Marina."

She replied, "Mister, to me it is a pleasure. You're welcome." She gently picked the boy up, wrapped him in the same blanket he was sleeping on and said, "You both have a beautiful and romantic night."

Sonya gave the boy a tender kiss as Marina passed by before disappearing down the stairs. Sonya closed the door to the baby's room and held her right hand out to me with a huge smile on her face.

The Broken Rainbow: Mysterious Dark Karma

Chapter 15: The Deathtrap and Sophisticated Plate

16 Sonya

Sonya said, "Well, finally alone all to ourselves!" After a small, tender kiss on my lips, one on my nose, and one on each of my eyes, I initiated this time the passionate kiss which lasted for a little while. She separated gently and said in my ear, "Let's go to our room where I have the butter ready to go in the mini-refrigerator in the bar."

I smiled and entered into an enormous, luxurious master bedroom with her, dominated by a half-moon bed covered in black and white satin bedclothes that matched her outfit exactly. She removed the hat which had created such a sensation and put it on top of some pillows which lay on the bedroom bench at the end of the bed.

    Sonya walked towards a beautiful alpaca rug, also black and white but with some brown pieces, brought her hands up to the neck of a beautiful, elegant gown and pulled on some lacing there, allowing the entire dress to fall away, leaving her body completely naked save for her black underwear and bra covering her firm breasts. She dropped those and showed me her beautiful pink nipples. "Do you like what you see, even after the baby?"

    I took some deep breaths, observing her for a few seconds. I removed my tie from the tuxedo and began to walk towards her. I opened both arms and said, "You look now better than ever." I touched her face with both my hands. "You are like a good quality wine: the longer it has been bottled, the more exquisite it will taste."

    She smiled as we began to kiss passionately while she helped me slowly to remove my clothes, both consumed by the passion of that beautiful moment we had been waiting those three years for. After we made love on top of the alpaca rug, we made love again on top of that beautiful bed. After we were both completely satisfied, Sonya went to the refrigerator and brought out a bottle of champagne, some orange juice, and made mimosas in beautiful Baccarat glasses. She also brought out some hors d'oeuvres. We smiled, looking into each other's eyes, enjoying crackers with Russian beluga caviar and shrimp on top. We toasted to our future and she said, "This is the advantage of working with the Russians." She gestured around at the exotic food the Cuban people hadn't seen for three years.

"Yes, and maybe the disadvantage we have. I don't know if you've noticed, but those same Russians supplying the champagne and caviar have been following us around all night, from when we left here until we came back."

She smiled mischievously. "Yes, I know. You never know if they're doing it for our security or whatever it is. Who cares? I have nothing to worry about."

I looked doubtful. "Be very careful. That's the excuse that Satan uses to protect you and instead ends up stealing your soul."

She looked at me seriously. "What can they do if we don't do anything wrong? Whoever does nothing wrong has nothing to worry about. I don't care if they follow us the rest of our lives."

"I'm not too sure about that. I don't like people always sneaking around behind my back."

"Do you have anything to hide? Are you worried about something? Are you perhaps working as a spy for another country?"

"Whoa, wow! Three questions shot all at once! This means one single question for each year we haven't seen each other. I think the honeymoon has been very short."

Sonya understood that she had crossed the line a little into indiscretion and hurried to apologize and calm me down. She leaned in towards me and gave me a tender kiss on the cheek. "I'm sorry, love. Please. It's not my intention to upset you. I only worry that those who have been protecting me and our boy might think that you aren't what you appear to be and that you break bread with our enemies."

I smiled. "Of that you don't have to worry about at all, love. I have my ideology very well-defined. No one and nobody can ever buy me, bribe me with any type of material things, fame, or false glory. I have only one ideology, and that will die with me."

Our conversation was interrupted suddenly by some screaming from downstairs. It sounded like Marina. Sonya took her left hand to her mouth, put the glass of mimosa down on the nightstand next to her, jumped out the bed, and pulled a semi-automatic Makarov pistol from under the mattress. "Please, wait for me here. Don't do anything. Let me deal with this, whatever it is. I can deal with it myself. The last thing I want to happen tonight is you getting hurt."

She wrapped herself in a bathrobe and left the room in a rush. I tried to get dressed, but in my rush, I could not find my pants. I finally located them and hurriedly put them on. Without my shoes, I looked out the window of the master bedroom which looked out over the driveway. Though the light was poor, I could see a sedan that looked much like one of the ones the Russian ambassador used in Cuba. I had no weapon with me, as my pistol was in the glove compartment of the Corvette. I had to get out without being seen.

I rushed down the stairs very carefully, looking everywhere. I heard and saw nothing. Almost at the last step, I heard yells of protest from the boy. "No, no—leave me alone! You're bad guys!"

Two shots were heard. Sonya screamed. I rushed to the front door, got out onto the porch, and ducked into the alley, looking for the Corvette. I stepped on something in the darkness on the ground. Something sticky was on my feet, and I realized in that dim light that one of the bulbs by the front door that my hands were smeared with blood. The body of Lucifer lay at my feet in a pool of his blood, the head hanging only by a piece of flesh.

I wondered what sort of diabolic individuals would kill the dog in this fashion. I got up and tried to reach the Corvette. As I walked to the car, I heard voices. I ran to the back of the car and saw three tall men walking towards the Mercedes with the teenaged Vladimir Putin leaving the mansion. The tall muscular man had the young boy under one arm, his mouth gagged tightly. Julius was moving, fighting his captor. I was next to the driver's side, and I moved to keep the car between us so I could remain unseen. I had no doubts now that everything indicated the purpose of their being there was simply to take Julius Christian. From what Sonya had told me, nobody knew that the baby was my son.

From all the evidence she had shown me, I wondered what the reason was for kidnapping the boy unless Sonya was involved in the business of espionage and her enemies, whoever they might be, had done this in an act of vengeance or to use the little boy as a retaliation to take from her some kind of important information that they needed so badly.

I kept my cover and as they brought the boy to the car and shoved him into the back of the seat. I went around completely to the passenger door. I waited until they were all in their vehicle before opening the door and chance having the light reveal my position. I opened the glove compartment of the Corvette, and as fast as I could to save both my life and that of the little boy, I pulled out the pistol and cocked it. As they started to leave the driveway, I carefully aimed at the rear tires. I shot the left one followed by the right one. The car veered suddenly and then stopped.

Both men in the back seat left the sedan with submachine guns and sprayed the Corvette. I got down on my stomach and waited until the firing stopped. Aiming beneath the Corvette, I shot once more, this time aiming first at man on the left and then the one on the right, each in the leg. Both wounded, they jumped inside the sedan.

I thought they wouldn't be able to leave, but the tires were airless rubber ones, bullet proof, and they left at a high speed, leaving the driveway towards Fifth Avenue, which led into the city. I ran into the residence, fearing the worst for Sonya and Marina.

When I entered Marina's room, I found her dead in a large pool of blood. Like the dog, she was virtually decapitated, her glassy eyes staring right at me. Her expression was one of terror, as if she had seen the Devil himself just before she died.

Leaning against her body on the other side was Sonya, with bloody spot on the shoulder of her bathrobe as the blood pooled on the marble floor. She appeared at first dead and my heart stopped, filled with remorse from the conversation we had just had. I could not help two tears rolling down my cheeks. For a few seconds I maintained myself paralyzed in shock, full of confusion and rage, asking God why I could never have a little happiness for very long.

Something turned my heart back on with joy. Sonya groaned in pain and then moved her head a little. I rushed to her side. As I knelt next to her, I opened her robe to look at her wound. I saw a bullet hole under her left breast near her shoulder. That was the entry wound, and as I looked a little more closely, I saw the exit wound under her armpit. It was not an internal injury but more a flesh wound. In time she would be OK. The only problem was that I could tell that she had lost a lot of blood.

Without wasting any time, I pulled out a couple of handkerchiefs, folded them up, and put them against the injury, one in front and one in back, and tied them into place with the belt of her robe to improvise a bandage. She was still semi-conscious; I tried to lift her, but she was a little too heavy for me. I said in a strong, commanding voice, "If you want to live, I need your help. I cannot get you out of the house if you don't assist me." I tapped her cheeks lightly to bring her around. "I don't want to drag you to the car. That will make your wound worse and cause you to bleed more."

After a few seconds of repeating this, Sonya finally opened her eyes and looked me straight in my eyes. "Why are you hitting me? What did I do to you?"

I smiled. "There it goes—I got you back. Nothing. You're shot and you've lost a lot of blood. I need your help to get you up off the floor. I have to take you to a hospital at once. If not, you'll die for sure."

These last words shot into her brain, and she became alert at once. She put one arm around my right shoulder. Holding me, she managed to stand up off the floor. Very slowly, I dragged her with difficulty to the Corvette, opened the passenger door, cleaned the shattered glass off the seat, and got her seated comfortably. I went and sat on the driver's side and looked through the window, which resembled a strainer. I said, "If Che doesn't change the window of this car, the next one to use it won't need any air conditioning." I started the engine.

Sonya looked at me. "How do you still have the strength to make a joke at a moment like this?"

"Honey, precisely that is what we need right now—a little humor. And thank God that no bullet damaged the engine, which is running perfectly, or the radiator.

I drove away from the mansion and took her to the nearest hospital wearing only my tuxedo pants at a high speed, trying to save the life of my youngest love, Sonya.

A little while later, we arrived at the *Clinico Quirurgico*[16]. The surgeons in the emergency room immediately took Sonya and rolled her into the operating room. She was hooked up for a blood transfusion.

A couple of hours later, one of the doctors came out and reassured me that Sonya would be all right. "She's still under the effects of the anesthesia, but we had to replace some sections of the brachial artery. A few centimeters closer in, and that bullet would have gone into her heart. She's stable and out of all danger, but we should keep her in the hospital for the next several days for observation."

"Can I see her?"

"Yes." They took me into the recovery room, where she was still unconscious. She looked like a pale angel. I caressed her long hair and gave her a tender kiss on the forehead, thanking God at that moment that the bullet which was aimed for her heart had instead been deflected. Those assailants who apparently wanted her dead must have assumed that they had accomplished their mission and left her for dead. I decided that the main objective of the mission was to kidnap Julius Christian.

I left the hospital full of worries and questions. Why would they want to kidnap a child? If nobody knew he

---

[16] Surgical clinic

was my son, like Sonya said, what was the objective? I drove back to Miramar and Sonya's house to pick up the rest of my tuxedo and also to see if I could find any evidence or piece of that puzzle in the mansion which would answer the questions and doubts I had.

When I arrived, the sun was coming up. I found everything as I had left it before. I looked through Sonya's closet and found one of her jogging suits. I tried to put it on and realized that we were the same size, as it fit me quite well. I went down to the garage and looked for a pick and shovel in the utensils closet where they kept the garden tools.

I went to one side of the mansion and dug a hole deep enough to be able to bury the bodies of the dog and Marina. After I finished and brought both bodies, I proceeded to cover them in order to conceal completely what had happened there. It was all extremely strange. I didn't want whoever was behind all this to try to implicate me with the local authorities in that horrendous crime, especially knowing as I did that the men in the Russian embassy and perhaps the ambassador himself were involved in it all. Unfortunately for me, they were the ones running Cuba at that moment. Whoever had the power would have the law on their side.

After I finished my work and cleaned up the blood, I took the jogging suit I had borrowed, put it in a plastic bag, went into the master bathroom, and took a cold shower. I had not slept all night, added to the physical exercise I had first with Sonya and then what happened afterwards, my brain needed to be alert. So even though I was freezing, I took that cold shower, even though it was late November. I got dressed and began to check through the drawers of her dresser and search the bedroom. I found nothing that gave me any indication why these assailants had to do this.

I had almost given up and bent over to fix the cuff of my pants when I saw between the mattress and the box spring of the bed something shining and golden in the exact same place she had gotten her pistol from. It was an 8x10 picture frame. I pulled it out and saw a picture inside with Sonya and her son. I wondered why this was hidden beneath the mattress in the same place she had concealed a weapon. It didn't make any sense, which bothered me even more.

I looked at the picture for a while and saw that Lucifer was next to her son. It was a very recent picture. Something else caught my attention. The background did not match that of the images in the photo. Someone had doctored a different background behind the primary photo for reasons still unknown to me. Everything became more and more complicated by the second. I decided to get out of there at once.

I put the picture back where I had found it, walked out of the mansion, and double locked the door with the key Sonya gave me. I got into the Corvette and drove into the city, stopping at a coffee shop which had a public phone. I called my uncle Emilio to update him as to what had happened in the past twelve hours.

He informed me that we needed to meet that afternoon, because Canen had called an emergency meeting. I told him that I also had a matter I needed to discuss with the team. We set the meeting, I hung up, and I kept driving towards Boca Ciega. When I arrived, parked the car in the same place I had gotten it, and wrote a note for Che to leave on the windshield: *What you see here is another attempt on my life. I'll give you more details later.* I got into my UAZ and left to meet with my uncle.

The Broken Rainbow: Mysterious Dark Karma

We agreed to meet in what we called Blue 00; it was only used for extraordinary emergencies. Everything had happened so quickly: my reunion with Sonya, the news I had a son I never knew about, the men from the Russian embassy with the young man Vladimir Putin, and his strange, close relationship with the six-fingered man who had appeared out of nowhere and now was a nail in the flesh for Che, never leaving his side for a single moment. Everything was a little overwhelming for me. Very confused, even though I was accustomed to maintaining my equanimity, I felt a tremendous weight on my shoulders for the kidnapping of that boy and Marina's death as well as Sonya's near-death.

Chapter 16: The Miracle and First Contact with the League

17 Agent 24 Meets with the Gentleman of Paris

    I drove near a Catholic church on my way out of the city. I was not accustomed to entering churches, especially now when anyone that did so could identify themselves as an enemy to the socialist revolution. My uncle and his other advisors had recommended that I kept myself far away from such institutions. The bells in the tower were ringing for the morning prayers, and I felt an internal impulse to stop, perhaps needing to find some tranquility and peace in order to put my worries into order and refresh my foggy mind.

The Broken Rainbow: Mysterious Dark Karma

The music of the bells sounded like waves in the ocean, communicating with me. They called me to that place as if calling from Heaven. Forgetting completely about the security recommendations of all my advisors, I decided to take the risk of being seen by the government spies that attended religious services to record who came in and out, taking pictures of the people and later finding the names of the individuals to report them to the G-2 to add to what they called the blacklist of the revolution: worms or deplorables at the service of the Imperial Yankee. Of course, it was nothing more than demagogic communist propaganda. The "imperialist Yankees" never persecuted their citizens for the preference in religious ideas.

I took all necessary precautions to avoid anyone seeing me, especially in the UAZ, by driving around the church and parking behind a flower shop two or three buildings past the church. Since I was dressed in a tuxedo, I figured no one would be around that early in the morning of a cold November inside the church, unless someone had the same spiritual needs I had at that moment.

There was a small factory of glazed pipes used for drains and sewers next to the church. By going through the back yard of the factory, I could reach one of the side doors of the church. As I came inside that I realized my worries were unfounded. It looked like no one was there. I smiled, my worries evaporating. Additionally, it wasn't a weekend; this was the middle of the week.

I walked up the transept to the main altar which had a large image of Jesus Christ on a wooden cross, His crown of thorns on His head and the wound from the spear thrust in His right chest. The blood on His forehead was very vivid. I sank onto the comfortable red velvet-covered kneeler before the altar and crossed myself, put my hands together, and began to pray. I tried to communicate to Jesus all the tribulations I had encountered in the previous twenty-four hours and asked Him for guidance and strength, to be able to continue my work to destroy those evil forces that now had taken power in my country and their ambition to dominate the entire world.

I looked at the image of Jesus and the wound under His ribs and had nearly closed my eyes when something happened which made me open my eyes wide in shocked surprise. I don't know if it was my imagination or if I had gone back to that time, but the Body of Jesus began to bleed as if the wound was freshly opened. Blood, or something of that color, poured out over the rest of the image on the wall. Several drops fell and formed a pool on the white marble right before the altar. Surprised and thoroughly taken off guard, I thought first that this was not possible—it had to be an optical illusion. I rubbed my eyes with the knuckles of my hands and looked again, trying to determine if what my eyes were showing me was actually happening or if it was a product of my imagination.

Something even stranger happened. As I rubbed my eyes, an enormous bald eagle with eyes the blue color of the sky on a clear day flew through the front doors of the church. This vision came not from my point of view, since my back was to the front door, but through the eyes behind the altar. The eagle flew directly towards the altar, so close to my head that I felt the soft touch of the feathers brush my face and the wind of its passage. I closed my eyes instinctively, trying to protect them from any impact with that beautiful, huge eagle. I knew its powerful claws could not just gouge my eyes out in a single second but also badly disfigure my face. I opened my eyes once more and saw that he flown past me and landed on the shoulder of the statue of Jesus, which was no longer bleeding.

The eagle looked me deeply in the eyes, his gaze like a laser beam penetrating my brain. It seemed as if we exchanged bodies: I was no longer kneeling before Jesus but on the statue, sitting on Jesus' shoulder. My eyesight intensified to a level I had never experienced before. I could see miles away clearly; I was now seeing through the eagle's eyes with a clear and perfect vision of long range overlaid with a bluish tint. I could see two men walking towards the church, accompanied by the man with the six fingers with the young Vladimir Putin bringing up the rear, about twenty feet behind them.

A few seconds later they were in the door. Putin remained in the rear, as if supervising what they were going to do as the group entered the church. As the two men walked towards where my physical body knelt before the altar, my hands clasped and head down in prayer. I tried to warn myself by yelling, "Murderers! Watch out!" Instead of my human voice, the warning came out as the shrill cry of an eagle, amplified by the vaulted dome of the sanctuary and the echoes which returned from above and the back of the church. Both the men, the six-fingered man, and Putin recoiled in pain. I watched the two men remove two long daggers, holding them clearly intending to stab me in the back.

The six-fingered man and Vladimir stopped, watching what the two men were doing. They also reached inside their jackets for some weapon, waiting as a pair of standbys. The two men stabbed down violently, their daggers going harmlessly through my body and stabbing deep into the wooden rail where my elbows were resting. All the men reacted in fear as it seemed like my body actually wasn't there. At the same time, the eagle took off and flew right at them.

It flew over my image between the daggers and emitted another shrill, irritated shriek. It flew into the men, who were now running away but stopped with its claws on the railing between the two daggers as if it were protecting me. The two men reached into their jackets to put their guns out, but neither of them could finish drawing. There was a whispering sound in the dark, candlelit church which echoed softly, and both of them fell on their knees before the altar, holes in the middle of their foreheads.

The eagle opened its wings as if finishing its mission and flew from the railing over my head. As it opened its wings, I stood up and opened my arms to stretch myself, just as the eagle had before it took off. I looked up at the altar and crossed myself, thanking Jesus for being by my side. As I looked up to give thanks, I saw up the rails on the second story of the church, my good friend the Gentleman of Paris, calmly disassembling a sniper rifle and putting it inside a violin case.

With a big smile, he gave me a casual two-fingered military salute. He pointed upwards and a circling motion, followed by pointing downwards. I knew I was to wrap up what I was doing and meet him when he came down. I wasted not a second and left the church through the same door I had entered by only a few minutes before.

Outside, I saw four men dressed in white overalls in the alley behind the church. Their heads were covered like surgeons, with mouth and nose covered by light mint green masks. They got out of a van which had large signs on the sides in large black and white letters which read, *Empresa Sanitaria de Cremacion y Esterilizaciones*[17]. One of the men gave me the same kind of salute as they passed me. The Gentleman of Paris walked up the alley towards me with the violin case in his left hand. The four men entered the church with laundry pushcarts.

My curiosity awoke when I saw that the Gentleman was not alone. He was accompanied by a Caucasian man of medium build who looked from his features to be either Greek or Italian. He had a thick, muscular neck and a barrel chest, and the most prominent feature of his face being a square chin with a slight cleft in it. His eyes were serious, even pensive, but there was the twinkle in them which marked the sort of man who could find humor even in the darkest situation.

They came over to me, and the man smiled pleasantly, extending his right hand to me as he said, "It's a great pleasure to meet you, Commandantico, and a very great honor. I've looked forward to this for a long time. Call me Agent 24. I know your uncle's mentioned me; I'm from the League." I could tell from his broken Spanish that he had learned it by total immersion and that he was an American by his accent. I could understand him easily in spite of his heavy accent, because it was clear from the Cuban version he used that he had learned his Spanish in Cuba.

I looked at him very seriously without replying. Even though I knew it was rude, I didn't take his hand; I felt this whole meeting was inappropriate. I shook

---

[17] *Sanitation, Cremation, and Sterilization Enterprises.*

my head in discontented surprise. I looked at the Gentleman of Paris. "What's going on here? Who arranged this unexpected introduction?" Agent 24 remained silent in awkward surprise.

The Gentleman of Paris, with confusion in his face, replied, "I think he can explain a lot better than about why this we're having this interview. Maybe it's unexpected, and I'm sorry, and abrupt."

I looked at Agent 24 and said, "I'm sorry, but I wasn't expecting you."

He chuckled ironically. "I wasn't expecting to be here myself."

"I believe it will safer and better for us if we get out of this alley and at least sit down in my vehicle. This is not the most discreet place to discuss any private matter, much less introductions."

The Gentleman said, "Why don't we go to my van? It's not far from your jeep behind the pipe factory. You have a little surprise in your jeep that our friend Agent 24 here left for you as a courtesy."

I was growing more confused by the minute. I didn't really know who this man was, much less how he had arrived where we were, and especially after all that had happened. I was a little dissatisfied, having already specified to my uncle that I did *not* want to be introduced to his contact and he had agreed. What had happened now? Why had my uncle, with no warning, sent this individual, which was a very dangerous thing for me and our whole organization? But in spite of all this, I completely trusted both my uncle and the Gentleman of Paris and knew I shouldn't be rude to him and instead find out what his presence here meant. I asked no more questions and prepared myself mentally for the worst.

The Broken Rainbow: Mysterious Dark Karma

We walked down the alley to the van of the Gentleman of Paris. I used the opportunity to straighten my poison ring, preparing it for action in case it was necessary. We entered the van through the back cargo doors and sat down on the benches against the walls. I sat next to the Gentleman of Paris, while Agent 24 sat across from us.

Once we got comfortable, he leaned towards me a little and put his hand into his right-hand pants pocket, pulling out a pocketknife. We both reacted slightly, the Gentleman reaching inside his long coat for a pistol and I getting ready to jab him with my ring. Agent 24 noticed and said reassuringly, "Wait, don't freak out. I need this pocketknife to get something out of the sole of my shoe."

WE looked at each other and I said to Agent 24, "Go ahead and do what you need to do. No problem."

He raised his left shoe onto his right knee, inserting the tip into the front of his shoe. Instead of nails, it was secured by a series of safety brushes. He undid them all the way to the heel, carefully not to break any of the brushes. He inserted the pocketknife into an interior piece of leather and pried it up as well. From beneath that second layer he removed a small, flat, transparent plastic envelope. He pulled it open from one end and removed three ID cards, each of them with his picture. One at a time, he handed them to me. The first one was a U.S. Navy Intelligence ID with his rank, skills, and level of clearance: Top Secret. After I examined it, I handed it back to him, and he gave me the second one: The International Anti-Communist League. Then he passed the first one to the Gentleman of Paris. The final one he handed me was from the CIA, indicating the highest level of clearance.

He said, "Now you know who I am." He looked directly into my eyes. "I want you to understand that these are *only* supposed to be shown in a case like this, not to anyone else in any other circumstance. Not even my wife knows about this. The only reason I brought them with me on this mission is to verify my identity with you. If I were discovered with these documents, I would never leave Cuba alive. But this mission of mine is more important than my own life. Not only does the life of my President depend on this mission but also the future of my country. The objective his assassination is to destabilize the nation and so collapse our democratic Republic and replace it with a new Marxist-Leninist regime."

I leaned back against the van wall. I understood at that moment that this man represented no danger for me at all, that he was not only a great patriot like my great-grandfather but also without any doubt in my mind a great man, capable of sacrificing everything, including his family, in order to prevent his President's death. There was more to it; he wanted to prevent the suffering and abuse of innocent people and nations who didn't understand the magnitude of evil that this small group of mercenary corrupt politicians were trying to implant this disgusting system represented. He clearly knew it, and would stop at nothing to prevent it, even if it meant his own life.

I smiled, more relaxed. "Welcome, my friend, to our club of Misérables by Victor Hugo."

He smiled ironically and chuckled again as he gave me a casual salute. "Yes. I understand perfectly your feelings. I know my President hasn't really acted honorably with your compatriots. To be completely open with you, I didn't vote for him. I campaigned hard for Nixon." He paused as he returned his IDs back into his shoes, meticulously making sure the seams were undetectable. He finished closing up his shoe and inspected it carefully. As he did, he asked, "Do you think that we should then let him die rather than save his life? It's undeniable he's acted stupidly and made disastrous decisions out of political naivety."

I shook my head firmly. "I never said that, under any circumstance at all have I even insinuated such a barbarity. I can assure you, though, with what little I do know about the plans of Che and his associates within your country like Jack Ruby and other political elements that only God can save him or prevent that assassination. It's really a pity, because I don't like any human being to be slaughtered in that way, especially not by my enemies. Because someone isn't ethical or conducts himself inappropriately is no reason to wish him dead. But there's extremely little if anything that you or I can do to avoid this happening. I tell you this with certainty because there's too much money invested in this operation. Also, your President, like his brother Robert, has cultivated so many enemies that even Che told me that even Vice President Lyndon B. Johnson probably might throw a party after the formal mourning period."

Agent 24 shook his head regretfully. He rested his hands on his knees and stared at the floor of the van in deep thought. Still shaking his head, he said, "It's very sad to say, but I have to agree with you." He leaned back and reached inside his coat, pulling out a leather paper wallet with his right hand. He removed several 8x10 photos and handed them to me one at a time. "Well, I can see there's very little you can do to help me in my primary mission. But maybe I'll be able to help you and myself in my secondary mission." He held up one of the pictures and showed it to me. "Have you seen this picture before?"

I took the picture in my right hand and held it up against the interior light of the van. I was frozen for a moment at what I saw. It was the same picture I had discovered under the mattress of Sonya's bed. Only now, as I looked at it, I saw it was unaltered. This photo had been taken in a garden similar to her mansion's, but not in Cuba. There was a snowfield behind her. The architecture in it looked Russian, it was most certainly a country not possessing tropical weather.

I hadn't recovered from my surprise when Agent 24 added, "Turn it over, read the dedication."

I turned it over and read, "To my brother, Vladimir Putin, from his sister with love, Yoanka." I looked him straight into his eyes. "Where did you guys obtain this picture?"

Agent 24 smiled and caressed his square chin. "Surprise, surprise, from the family album of Putin's mother, Marina Ivanova Putina, *née* Shelomova. This young woman has been impersonating your young love Sonya, and she is nothing less than a highly trained master spy. Her real name, as you can see from her dedication, is Yoanka. She is the illegitimate daughter of Putin's father and a member of the Soviet KGB. The little boy's name is also not what you've been led to believe; his name from his real birth certificate is Nikolai. All these manipulative traps come from the top ranks within the KGB designed very carefully to entrap you and authorized by both Fidel Castro himself and Che Guevara. They're not entirely convinced that you are what you are. But they've been convinced by the KGB that you are the most dangerous spy that they've ever met, precisely because you have their trust. The KGB determined to show their superiority in intelligence by bringing you down. That is what the whole plan is about." He looked at me very directly. "Are you really the Cuban Lightning?"

I smiled and recovered from my surprise at learning about the fake Sonya. I opened both arms and replied, "I wish. I'm only the messenger."

Agent 24 grinned at me. "Don't worry about it. Even if you are, your secret is safe with me. I understand your position perfectly."

"You don't. A secret, from what my uncle and my father both said, is no longer safe once someone else knows it. Thank you very much for your compliment to compare me with the Lightning. But I don't think I'm mature enough yet to even go as high in the sky as the Cuban Lightning can be."

Agent 24 grinned again. "The reason that your uncle Emilio authorized me for this impromptu interview is because he knows you very well, and he knows that unless I showed you irrefutable proof of all of this, you would not give us any information. Even so, I now realize who you are. Your uncle, with all his experience is an old wolf and master spy. He knew that when the Russian ambassador and KGB failed as they have in getting any information out of you through their spy, the next step would be your assassination in order to avoid admitting their defeat to Castro and Che. They were going to make you disappear, go back to Che and Fidel, and report that they did what they had promised. That's the only reason your uncle authorized me to get into contact immediately with the Gentleman of Paris and his team, and with my people try to prevent your attempted assassination. If you still have any doubts in your mind," he added emphatically, caressing once more his square chin, "you can ask Putin for yourself. We got him when he tried to escape from the church with his accomplice with six fingers and have him tied up and gagged as a gift for you in your UAZ." He grinned impishly. "Here's an idea: why don't you take this little vindictive creature to Che and Castro? I assure you that when they see you with him tied and gagged, they will have diarrhea and urinary tract failure at the same time."

"You know what, Agent 24? Thank you very much, not only for that idea but also what you did today. I have no way of repaying you for it and I don't want to promise you anything about your President I can't comply with, because that wouldn't be dignified or possible; unless he changes his itinerary by going to Texas."

He looked at me in grateful affection. "Thank you for your honesty. Now that I know you, I am certain you would do exactly the same for me as I did for you."

"Thank you again. I want to apologize to you for my previous conduct. I think I might take your suggestion about taking Putin to Che and Fidel personally to rip the mask of the Russian ambassador off once and for all." After a brief pause, I asked, "Can I keep at least one of these pictures?"

He smiled again. "It's all for you—you can keep all of them. Just don't say where you got them from. It's a present for all you've done for us without receiving a single dollar in exchange for such great work all these years."

I smiled once more. "I repeat to you again what I said before: I'm only—"

He said with me, "the messenger. Yes, I know. But even the messenger takes a big risk in doing so."

I smiled. "Of course, but never as the Lightning."

He laughed, and the Gentleman of Paris could no longer contain himself and joined in the laughter.

"There's something I want to ask you before we part today," I said.

"Ask whatever you want," Agent 24 replied.

I scratched my head and showed him a picture of Marina. "Why did they assassinate this woman? What did she have to do with all of this?"

He smiled. "Marina was working with us. Clearly, they found out and decided to eliminate her at the same time they cleared up the entire operation. They'd been watching you from the minute you walked into the house, even while you made love to that woman. They were listening as well as watching, and realized they weren't going to get anything from you. They decided to get the kid and remove the double agent from the picture. Likely they didn't intend to harm their agent; she may have gotten caught in a crossfire, but since we weren't there, we can only speculate about that."

I nodded. "I understand perfectly. I've been played very well."

"Unfortunately, my friend, feelings are very delicate and human. It's our weakness, and they used your feelings to get to you. But you proved to them that you wouldn't give anything away. You won't even give *me* anything! I could bring semi truckloads full of IDs, and you would still insist you're only the messenger." We both laughed. "What is your other question?"

"I know your team, along with that of the Gentleman of Paris, intervened to save my life, and I can't thank either of you enough for that, but I have an unanswered question in my mind of something which will sound strange to you. Did you guys bring with you that enormous eagle with sky-blue eyes, or did that eagle come from another place?"

Agent 24 looked at me in complete confusion. "What on Earth are you talking about? An eagle? Which one are you referring to? Like the bird flying in the sky?" I nodded. It was clear he was completely lost. He looked at the Gentleman of Paris. He asked, "Do you know what he's talking about?"

The Gentleman of Paris was even more confused and shook his head. He opened his arms helplessly. "I don't know."

I smiled and said to them, "Don't worry about it, guys. I already have an idea. I have to thank somebody else for being alive today." I got up from the bench. "OK, I think we'd better get out of here and not give time for our enemies to regroup."

We got out of the van. The Gentlemen of Paris closed the back door, and the three of us walked back to my UAZ. As we got there, we saw the gag an ropes which had served to tie up Putin on the pavement. Agent 24 said, "One of the men from the embassy they left behind must have used our discussion in the van to release that little devil Putin and the man with the six fingers."

I smiled rolling up the rope and gag. I shook my head. "Remember, you guys, I wanted to have that conversation in my UAZ." The Gentleman of Paris shook his head apologetically. Wanting to make him feel better, I patted his shoulder. "Don't worry about it. Even though I loved Agent 24's idea of dropping that little devil in front of Che and Castro, we have to flush it down the toilet now. But God knows whatever He's doing, and maybe He let him go because one day I might encounter this kid again and give me a better opportunity to get back at him. God doesn't want me to waste it this time. At the same time, remember, he'll run to the Russian ambassador, which will be a major embarrassment to the ambassador and the KGB before Fidel and Che. Gentleman, that proves that the good and nobility that we embrace is a lot more powerful than the evil and malice that they embrace."

Agent 24 smiled in satisfaction. He patted my right shoulder. "I don't have any doubt that you really are a very loyal and faithful servant of God and His Son Jesus. I cannot say I'm very religious man, but I admire people who have integrity and devotion for anything good in life. I do believe in God, or at least a Master Intelligence, designed and directs events. And I certainly believe in good and evil and am a lover of what is good, just, and honorable."

"Yes, you're right, and I'm a Christian warrior to my death."

We hugged each other, and after I thanked him once more for intervening in my behalf, I said, "God be with you and protect you and your family. If the information I'm giving you now can serve you in anyway, please communicate to your President that according to the information you received from the Cuban Lightning, who has yet to provide you with any wrong information, which is verifiable for his record over the last three years including that the missiles arrived three years ago, if he goes to Dallas, he will not get out of that city alive."

Agent 24 nodded. "I got it. Thank you very much." He turned his back and walked away accompanied by the Gentleman of Paris.

The Broken Rainbow: Mysterious Dark Karma

Chapter 17: The Revelation from the Eagle's Eyes

18 Eagle Spirit

I started my UAZ, thinking for a moment of that beautiful experience inside that old church and the clear vision I had, like an experiment in viewing through the third dimension, looking through those sky-blue eyes of that eagle. I felt a profound tranquility and peace which moved my spirit, even though the devastatingly profound deception I had received from that nasty dark-spirited woman, who with so much exactitude in details had been able to convince me into believing that she was somebody that I had loved and kept in my memory for so many years. I wondered what high level of evil any human being could possess to be able do something like that. I concluded that only those in the service of Satan could possess that high power of persuasion.

At that moment I felt revulsion at the memory of having sex with that despicable and miserable creature. I slammed the wheel of the UAZ, and without even thinking twice, drove to the hospital where I had left that imposter. I hoped in my soul that she was recovered from the anesthetic completely so I could confront her with the pictures I had from Agent 24. I left the parking lot near the flower shop rapidly to rip the mask away from her. She had a lot to explain to me for her despicable conduct.

I drove rapidly towards the hospital with tremendous anxiety in my chest. I knew very well the Machiavellian conduct that these communist leaders usually conducted themselves with after observing them for over four years now. I knew quite well not only their tactics but also their weaknesses.

This was not the first time that the cynical chief of the oppressive intelligence apparatus of the Cuban G-2[18] tried to accuse me of being involved in counter-revolutionary activities in the hope of discrediting me with Fidel, Che, and the other leaders of the revolution. His narcissistic insecurities and weak personality made him consider me extremely

---

[18] The Cuban state secret police, similar in function to the Soviet KGB or Nazi Germany's Gestapo.

dangerous and a threat to his position. Fidel Castro himself had mentioned on several occasions, some in my presence and the other leaders, that if he continued to be able to put behind bars the infamous spy called the Lightning due to his constant negligence, that I was the best option to take his place. I was a lot younger and more intelligent than he was and had completely proved my efficiency and conduct on every assignment I had taken.

I knew that those remarks from the highest leader earned me the most conniving and powerful enemy in the government. From that point on, he never stopped taking every opportunity and occasion he had to try and connect me with the most dangerous enemy the Cuban revolution had, the Cuban Lightning. With no evidence at all, only using assumptions and his own theories, he tried for the past four years to convince Che and the Castros that this spy could only be me, who had such high levels of clearance inside the socialist government bestowed by Castro himself. When I was confronted on several different occasions, I defended myself and explained so logically that I destroyed the case he was trying to make against me.

Instead of parking the UAZ in the hospital parking lot near the doors like I usually did, I chose a space far away from the doors so that I could arrive unobserved. I walked through the lobby and hallways, going directly to the room where the doctor had taken me before, hoping that the imposter pretending to be Sonya was still there.

As I entered the room, I saw to my frustration that the bed was empty, and the imposter was gone. The bed was freshly made, so it had been a while. As I scanned the room, I noticed a small closet whose door was ajar; in the gap I saw something that looked like the heel of a woman's shoe. My heart skipped a beat in excitement as I thought she might be hiding in there. I crept over to the closet door, taking all precautions now that I knew what sort of skills she had. I prepared my ring just in case she attacked me and put my weight on my left leg, holding the rail of the bed with my left hand. I used my right foot to nudge the door open very slowly. I kept my right hand high, ready to strike with the lethal poison should I be attacked.

As the door opened, I saw to my surprise a woman's body, a beautiful young nurse with long, black hair. It was the first girl to greet me when I brought the imposter Sonya to the hospital a few hours earlier. Her body wasn't moving, so I leaned over her to take her pulse. She was dead. There was a very deep mark along her neck, indicating she had been garroted, and there was a little blood on her forehead. She must have been struck in the head before being strangled. I touched the line of fresh blood on her forehead. It was not yet coagulated as I looked at it, rubbing my index finger against my thumb.

I shook my head sorrowfully and crossed myself, wondering what kind of people could kill this innocent nurse just to avoid being identified. I nudged her body back inside and closed the door fully. I stood up and walked to the nearest sink, thoroughly washing the blood off my hands. As I prepared to leave the room, I looked into the outside corridor to make sure everything was clear through a crack in the opened door. A man was walking straight towards the room. He was of medium height, dressed as a hospital surgeon with a mask and cap which covered his face and head. I had no time to run to the closet, so I straightened my body flat against the wall so that I would be behind the door when he opened it. I hoped that I would be concealed fully behind the door.

A few seconds later, the door opened, and the man came inside, but he did something I hadn't planned on. To ensure his privacy, he closed and double locked the door behind him, leaving me fully exposed in the open. I prepared to defend myself. Fortunately for me, the curtains in the room were closed across the window. I didn't move a muscle, glued to the wall. In his rush towards the bed, his focus was on that part of the room and so not on me on the opposite wall. He went straight towards the closet and opened it, discovering the body of the young nurse. He did exactly as I had, kneeling down to check her pulse, crossing himself, and then looked under the bed as if he was searching for someone. He saw no one under the bed. Before he stood up, he saw me as I moved towards him and flinched backwards.

In a panicked motion, he removed his mask with one hand and his cap with the other, all in one move. He said with wide eyes, "It's me, it's me!"

"Doctor Hector Zayas-Bazan? What are you doing here?" I pulled myself back so that I didn't accidentally inject him. I moved back to give him room to stand up. "What are you doing here, Professor?"

He stood on his feet. "Trying to avoid you getting in the same predicament this poor young lady is in now. Your Uncle Emilio and Doctor Vallarte communicated with me. They are extremely worried by your tardiness with their meeting. You were supposed to be there two hours ago."

I nodded. "Yes. Unfortunately, several unexpected incidents happened which obligated me to improvise and adjust my itinerary. One of them is as you see now, the assassination of this poor nurse by the woman impersonating Sonya, the master spy from the Russian embassy acting as a double agent. She's trying, under the orders of the ambassador himself or his entourage, to get close to me and obtain compromising information for them to offer to Che and Fidel that proves I'm a spy in order for them to put me in front of the firing squad. That is according to the latest debrief from our source inside Guantanamo." I raised my arms high. "I better give you the rest of my debriefing once we reach my UAZ. We should leave this place at once, before someone comes in and discovers that woman's body and tries to involve us in this trap."

He shook his head as he started to remove his clothes. I looked at him in surprise. "No, no. You cannot even get close to your Russian vehicle. There are four killers from the Russian embassy waiting for you there, and they don't have good intentions. They at least want to kidnap you in order to take you to Mother Russia and then Siberia." He handed his clothes to me in one hand and some car keys with his other. "Dress in my clothes, go to my car, which is parked in the staff lot for the Surgery Department behind the hospital. We'll see each other when if all goes well in Guanabo, where everyone else will be waiting for you. I'll give you more details about everything later on. Now change quickly and get out of this hospital as soon as you can."

Without saying a word, I took my tuxedo off and handed him my hat, which he then put on. As I was leaving through the front door, I went towards the rear exit of the hospital as he had directed me. I found his car, a white Chevrolet 1958 with a turquoise blue line. To my surprise, her right hand resting on top of the roof, was Chandee. the daughter of Mr. Xiang and the owner of the antique store in Old Havana and corroborator of my Uncle Emilio's team. Her left hand gave me a small military salute. She said, "I'm ready to cut the Devil in half, Comandante."

I replied, "You can keep both halves."

Chandee smiled. We exchanged a cordial hug and jumped into the car. I started the engine and drove off. She said, "Don't leave the hospital immediately. Stop a prudent distance from your vehicle so we can observe the reactions of your enemies when they see that who they stop in the tuxedo isn't really you."

We parked at a secluded angle and watched Dr. Zayas-Bazan leave the hospital and walk towards the UAZ. From this strategic position, we watch as he was stopped by three men who got out of a black GAZ31105 Volga. The driver remained inside the car. The other three followed close behind, their hands on the weapons they had beneath their jackets. They stopped Zayas-Bazan and grew confused. They turned around nearly simultaneously to look for instructions from the driver.

Chandee pulled out a walkie-talkie and said into it, "Now. Don't let them escape. We want them alive for interrogation."

Several men from different cars in the parking lot surrounded the three men, pistols in hand. They raised their hands and dropped their weapons in obedience to the commands shouted at them. The driver, seeing his adversaries had superior numbers, ran away and abandoned the parking lot at full speed, leaving his friends to their own luck.

Chandee saw that everything was under control. "You are the target. Get out of here and go to your meeting with my father and the rest of the group. I'll take care of this here with Dr. Zayas-Bazan." She started to get out of the car.

"No, I'm not going to let you be by yourself here," I said. I got out of the car and approached the group. The three men's eyes were filled with surprise and terror. I recognized them from the embassy. They saw me approaching in a surgeon's gown. I tossed the keys to the Chevrolet to Dr. Zayas-Bazan as he tossed the UAZ keys to me.

Dr. Zayas-Bazan said with a smile, "We'll see each other in a little while in Blue Location 00. If for any reason it takes me a little longer to get there, start the meeting without me. I cannot predict how long we will take."

I nodded. "I will communicate your message to the others and debrief them about what transpired here."

Hoods were thrown over the heads of the three assailants, handcuffs on their wrists, and shackled at their legs. One after another, they were shoved into the trunks of three separate cars. This was a procedure, so that if one car was intercepted, the other cars would arrive with the interrogation subjects.

Chandee said, "I don't think they'll need me. I'll go with you to make sure you arrive safe and sound."

She jumped into the UAZ, and I drove at a moderate speed towards Guanabo Beach. A little while later, we arrived at the beach house of Dr. Vallarte. The two men from Chandee's team who had followed us remained on the porch with two other guards while Chandee and I went inside for the meeting.

As we walked into the beautiful residence, Dr. Vallarte's wife received us affectionately. She brought us a couple of glasses of lemonade, saying to me, "We've been worried about you. You're normally very punctual, to an extreme."

She walked with us into the large trophy room we used for its long table and our meetings. Chandee's father, Mr. Xiang, the Gentleman of Paris—who had already debriefed the group as to what had transpired that day—and my brother-in-law Canen, the husband of my youngest sister Disa, were there along with my uncle Emilio. Canen was also the captain in charge of the missile troops on the Occidental side of the island. He was, of course, dressed in civilian clothes and in complete disguise.

As he watched us enter the room, he grinned broadly. "Brother, we've all been worrying and talking about you."

I said jocularly, "Good or bad?"

He raised his arm high. "For you, there's nothing to say bad about. Everything is good." He grew serious. "Unless whoever is talking about you is a conniving communist. In that case, it will all be bad, since they are famous for inventing tales and disinforming people."

I smiled. "Thank you very much for your compliment." I greeted everyone else and sat down, Chandee next to me at the long conference table. "I hope that the Gentleman of Paris here has explained in detail what transpired today in the past few hours. You should understand the reason for my late arrival for our meeting today." Everyone raised their arms in perfect understanding, waving it off.

Uncle Emilio said, "You don't have to apologize. We are the ones who should apologize to you for not only being unable to uncover that imposter but also for not being able to prepare you to be able to handle the situation. According to the Gentleman of Paris, it nearly cost you your life."

Canen said, "Yes. We all truly should be very, very grateful to Agent 24. His valuable and opportune information caught every one of us by complete surprise."

I said, "My brother Canen, I'm in perfect agreement with you and extremely grateful to Agent 24. I'm also very sorry I could not provide more help to him. I believe he is an intelligent man, understands what has transpired, and that what I told him was 100% honest. I believe that not only do we have a good contact there now, but I think I've also cultivated a friend.

"I want to make a point to be completely honest and fair—there's someone else we have to be very grateful to, and I have to give infinite thanks to, and that is the Supreme Being who has always, as you guys know, been behind my back all these years. Maybe the Supreme Architect of the Universe used His animal kingdom in perfect disguise: the most beautiful bird I've seen in my life, completely white with eyes the color of the blue sky. It transported me at the precise moment of the attack by those two men with very long, sharp daggers into my back. It took my physical body and left behind only my image and spirit kneeling before the altar. The most unbelievable experience so far; you guys know I've had quite a few, but this one is the top. At the precise moment of the attack, those two assailants were completely disconcerted because my physical body disappeared right before their eyes, though my image continued to be there before them. They could not understand; it was beyond their imagination.

"We can talk about this," I finished, "though, on another occasion. We have a lot more important things we need to urgently discuss. By the way, Dr. Zayas-Bazan is completing a mission of extreme importance and asked me to relay to you not to wait for him. Start the meeting as he could be delayed for several hours before completing his objective."

The others nodded in agreement, and Canen said, "There is a most powerful reason why I called this emergency meeting today. According to the latest secret information I received in the staff meeting at the missile troop headquarters is that we're on high alert. The orders come from Fidel Castro himself. We should prepare our troops and the intercontinental missiles to be ready for a counterattack. We have a great possibility that after the death of President Kennedy, which we all know here will happen in a few days, the new President might use nuclear weapons to retaliate, so we should be on high alert and prepare for the worst."

Mr. Xiang stood up and said indignantly as he shook his head in distress, "I have no doubts in my mind that this imbecile Fidel Castro is a disciple of Satan, and his mission is to destroy all of humanity. In any nuclear confrontation, there will be no winners or losers. We'll all be losers. What is this moron thinking? It's one thing to scream insults at the President from the Plaza of the Revolution and threaten the most powerful military nation in the New World, and it's another to send professional assassins to kill their President." He shook his head once more in frustration. Then he added sadly, "Of course, it will be in retaliation. That's logical. We would probably do the same. All our families will be vaporized off the face of the

The Broken Rainbow: Mysterious Dark Karma

Earth unless one of us can put a bullet in the head of this communist Fidel Castro at the same time President Kennedy is assassinated." He said emphatically, "This way we *might* avoid a retaliation from the Americans—eye for an eye, tooth for a tooth."

A profound silence descended on the table as we deeply thought about and digested what Mr. Xiang just suggested. It was very logical. As he pointed out, a nuclear confrontation would result in millions of dead, most of whom would be innocent people, including our families.

Mr. Xiang broke the deathly silence a few seconds later. "If you are all in agreement with my proposal, and maybe it won't be a solution, but at least there will be a great possibility to avoid the total destruction of our beautiful island. The radiation will make Cuba uninhabitable for several generations." He stood up. "Who of us has the sufficient training and facility to get close enough to this communist beast to blow his brains out with a single shot in the head?"

We looked at each other in silences for a few seconds. I thought twice quickly, raised my arm, and said firmly, "I'm the only one, unfortunately, in this group who has been trained but also has direct access to the beast. I don't like the idea at all of taking the life of another human being, even my worst enemy, but I believe that put in the divine balance in order to save thousands of innocent lives if not millions, I believe that I could live with this exception." Everyone looked at me seriously, their eyes open wide with admiration. I never forgot that or ever will.

Uncle Emilio raised his arm high and shook his index finger from one side to another. "Your bravery and disposition and dedication is admirable. But I believe your sacrifice will be unnecessary. Whoever attempts this suicidal mission on the leader has a 99¾% of being killed in the act, even *if* he manages to accomplish it. There are simply too many well-trained people around him, and they will die for him.

"This is not the only point I want to make in disagreeing for you to be the choice. Let me explain the reasons your sacrifice would be hopeless. I am completely assured that there will not be any type of retaliation from the Americans, even if they manage to assassinate President Kennedy. Every plan a human being makes, no matter how perfectly it is done, all has a risk of failure due to human error. Even if we consider it absolutely certain, which of course doesn't exist, because in the end we are human beings, and we're far away from being perfect. It simply doesn't exist. Because of that, everything without exception is subject to human error, for better or for worse.

We remained silent for a few moments. Uncle Emilio leaned back in his chair. "As I've said to you all before, in my analysis and calculated intelligence, there are many logical reasons to believe there will not be any retaliation against our country. The main, most powerful reason is that aggression against Cuba at this moment won't be views as being against the Castro regime; it will be considered as directly against the Soviet Union. We and US intelligence know from our sources that many Russian military regiments are in our armed forces bases. This means that if they drop bombs here will not only kill communist soldiers serving under the Castro brothers. Many, if not thousands, of Russian soldiers will die in the process at those bases. The man who will replace the young President Kennedy will be his Vice President,

Lyndon Johnson." He put his index finger to his temple. "Just think about it—Lyndon Johnson is not a young, inexperienced, and naïve politician like Kennedy. He's an old wolf, and he'll try to do the possible and impossible to prevent a confrontation of this magnitude. Under no circumstances, being the new President, will he want to provoke a thermonuclear war. It would be the end of both civilizations.

"Reason #2," he continued with an ironic smile, "this plan to assassinate President Kennedy is so perfect and meticulous that one hundred years will pass before anyone can prove for certain who actually is behind this criminal conspiracy." He leaned back in his chair and massaged his forehead with the fingers of his left hand. He added with conviction in his voice as he shook his head, "I am completely convinced that, unfortunately, this crime will go unpunished in the eyes of men; of course, not in the eyes of the Supreme Architect, because whoever kills with iron or lead will be killed with iron or lead without remedy.

He looked at us with a great sadness in his eyes. "To avoid making this too long, I'll say to you guys today that there will be no retaliation. Politicians in the immense majority are not that friendly to world wars. These wars affect their own families and the luxury they live in gets disrupted. Suddenly, instead of living the good life, they actually have to roll up their sleeves and get their hands dirty. I mean by this 99% without exception when it comes to politicians."

Everyone around the table smiled and nodded their heads in agreement with my Uncle Emilio's savvy and wise words. We all knew of the mercenary nature of politicians.

The Broken Rainbow: Mysterious Dark Karma

Chapter 18: The Emergency Debriefing

19 Dr. Hector Zayas-Bazan

There was a knock at the door, and Dr. Vallarte said, "Come in—the door isn't locked."

The Broken Rainbow: Mysterious Dark Karma

The door opened and Dr. Zayas-Bazan entered, now dressed in an elegant dark grey suit with pinstripes in a lighter grey. He held a hanger with my tuxedo in his right hand, but he was still wearing my hat. As he walked into the conference room, he hung my tuxedo up, removed my hat and put it on top of the hanger. He said to me with a big smile, "I'm returning your elegant tuxedo. Thanks to God for both of us I'm doing so without any bullet holes."

I smiled. "Thank you, but the most important thing is that my hat doesn't have any holes in it."

He smiled again, more broadly this time. He raised his right hand high and said, "I'll be back in a few seconds. I need to bring something from my car." A few minutes later he reappeared in the door with a small box in his hand. It looked like a hat box, only deeper. He put it next to his seat at the conference table and went to close the door. My attention was caught when he double locked the door. It was clear that he wanted absolute privacy and that not even the guards should know what was about to happen.

With a mischievous smile, he drummed nervously on top of the box with his fingers. He looked me in the eyes and said, "I have a very beautiful and extraordinary surprise for you." His expression grew serious. "And another one not particularly pleasant that I want to show everyone. Which do you want first—the good or the bad one?"

Everyone at the table stayed silent, including my uncle. I replied without hesitation, "I've been told to always take the good news first, because that good, pleasant experience will minimize the impact of the bad, making it easier to bear."

Dr. Zayas-Bazan nodded his head in agreement, pursing his lips as he did. He gave me a small smile. "I never considered that before, but now hearing you express it that way, it makes a lot of sense. In agreement with your decision, I will tell you the good news first. We made the bird, the most trusted man of the Russian ambassador, sing like a canary. We found out that your friend Sonya is not only alive but also in perfect health."

I could not hold myself in. "Really?"

He nodded again. "Really."

I asked again, "Where is she?"

He understood my anxiety. "These political delinquents have both her and her mother in a very run-down hole in the wall place in Old Havana. But we already relocated them to one of our security houses in Cojimar—Location #10. You know."

"Yes, yes! It's a beautiful place right by the beach."

He said "If you want to see her, you must do it tonight. We've already arranged in the very early morning hours to your Uncle Emilio's team member, Captain Marrero, take them out of the country. We know that if they remain here, they won't live for long, especially after what happened today."

"OK, I'll go and see her as soon as we finish with our meeting."

Canen was sitting next to me. He patted me on the shoulder with a smile. "Finally—you've been looking for her for three years, and now you'll be with the real one instead of an imposter. Just remember, God works in mysterious ways. If you hadn't met that imposter, we would never have discovered where she's being held." He smirked joyfully. Always very religious, he added jocularly, "I believe God, before He became God, was a very professional master spy and a master of surprises."

The Broken Rainbow: Mysterious Dark Karma

We smiled at Canen's expression and choice of words. We all knew how devout he was to his Adventist church and was a staunch adherent of Christian principles. Chandee curiously asked Dr. Zayas-Bazan, "Well, we already know what the good news is. Now everyone here is probably anxious to know what the bad news is and the unpleasant surprise."

Dr. Zayas-Bazan's fingers drummed on the box again. His demeanor changed to a serious one and said apologetically, "I want to tell you guys that the decapitation of the most trusted man of the Russian ambassador was unintentional. It was an accident through his own stupidity—or perhaps Divine Justice. This royal imbecile, thinking he could escape from us, asked one of our guys to take him to the bathroom. When they took him, he decided to jump out of one of the windows on the second floor, not knowing that beneath that window on the first floor they were running a flour mill for grain, and he landed inside the grinder. The only thing we were able to recover was the head. The rest went to feed the animals in the pig farm in Santiago de Las Vegas. By the time we finally managed to stop the grinder the whole body was already mixed with the flour already. The head was completely separated." He looked at Chandee. "You might want to leave; it's not a pleasant sight."

She shook her head. "Don't worry about it—I've seen worse."

"As you wish," he shrugged. As he spoke, he opened the box and grabbed the head of the Russian ambassador's assistant by the hair and pulled it out of the box. It was the same man I had seen in the church next to the six-fingered man. Everyone was shocked when he pulled the head out of the box; it looked ghostly with the flour covering the face. He added sadly, "This is not exactly, like I said before, how we planned this. You know we don't like to go to any extreme, but as Brother Canen said before, God works in mysterious ways. I considered it would be just as well, since this son of Satan lost his head, for us to use this opportunity to send a terrifyingly scary message to the Russian ambassador. Maybe we'll manage to intimidate him to the point that he'll fear losing his own head. We can send him a note that the next head in a box will be his if he doesn't stop his intrigues against our citizens and leave Cuba in the next twenty-four hours. It will be up to him whether he chooses to leave or have us make another example of him by taking him to the flour mill."

Uncle Emilio smiled and said, "Colleague, I have to agree with you. Your idea might result in something very productive. All these individuals adore Lady Violence when she strikes everyone else, but when she knocks on their own doors, or in this case the embassy, then they get scared and run away. They abandon that romantic dalliance with her as the adulterous man is confronted by the wife's husband and runs for his life."

Chandee was the first one to laugh. "I can offer to put that head as a present on the ambassador's desk in his embassy; of course, in a more presentable and fancier, attractive wrapping."

Canen interjected, "I think that going to the ambassador's office is extremely dangerous and unnecessary. I think it will work the same and even better to leave it in the back seat where the ambassador is accustomed to sit in his limousine. It will be less dangerous and perhaps more effective. He'll think that the same way we can leave that box in his car we could also leave a bomb. I think psychologically that will have a better effect."

Dr. Vallarte nodded in agreement. "I think I like that idea a lot better, and I agree with Canen that it's an unnecessary risk due to the extremely high security at the embassy, especially situated as it is in the Havana Libre. Whoever does this, whether it's Chandee or any of us, has to be prepared. I know for a fact that diplomatic cars normally have two alarm systems. One is the loud siren and the other one is silent. Both are controlled by monitors inside the car with remote control cameras. The cameras inside the car monitor an intruder's activity so they have enough evidence to legally prosecute."

I smiled. In support of Chandee, I said, "I believe Chandee has been well-trained and is perfectly qualified to do it in either location. She can conduct the operation in a successful manner without any problems."

Chandee looked at me and grinned thankfully. She gave me that two-fingered casual salute once again. "I believe that I've had the luck of being not only trained very well but also by one of the best of us, a master in everything. I know for a fact that I can do this without any problems, and I can assure every one of you that after I finish my work the Russian ambassador will find a way to create whatever excuse after my visit to his car to leave Cuba in less than the twenty-four hours that we give him."

Dr. Zayas-Bazan put the head back and closed the box. He pulled out of his inside jacket pocket a small object the size of a pencil sharpener. He showed it to everyone and said as he looked straight at Chandee, "Look at this thing. This small pump is a lethal weapon that's been used by Russian spies for a long time now to get rid of their enemies without a trace. I know it's only a few of you guys have seen before. They got it from the Nazis."

He opened it on top of the table and showed us how it worked. He added in profound concern, "We found this in the possession of this man." He tapped the box top. "He was a very dangerous spy. It's like a manual pump that is pushed into the face of your enemy. It expels a poison gas which blocks your trachea as an acid penetrates all the way into your lungs. There is no antidote, and it completely shuts down your body within minutes. If any individual gets close to you and has something similar to this in his hand, immediately cover your mouth and nose with a handkerchief because this is a lot worse than being shot at various angles all over your body. From bullets we can save you and many times survive; but with this mortal poison, nobody so far has survived. My tremendous concern is that if this master spy and criminal had in his possession this object, others in the embassy must have them, too.

"I took it and examined the contents meticulously in my lab," Dr. Zayas-Bazan added. "That is why it took me so long to come to the meeting. I'm very sure that all of them, including the ambassador, might have one with them. The security staff certainly possess this weapon, and they absolutely won't hesitate to use it on one of you guys, especially when they see one of you doing something which would jeopardize the ambassador's security. According to my study of the contents of the little pump could also contain luminolnitrophenylpentadienal[19]. It can be applied to doorknobs, floor mats, or cars, and it's been converted now into something more dangerous—it's been aerosolized with hydrochloric acid. Instead of tracking people, spraying that in anyone's face instead results in certain death in a matter of minutes. As a chemist and professor of pharmacology at the university, it took me a while to find the composition of this poison.[20]"

He passed it around to us and added, "Examine this meticulously, each one of you guys. This is like preventative medicine. If you get to know it and see what it looks like, you'll immediately recognize it when you see one in your hands or those of an enemy. That way no one will ever take you by surprise."

My uncle smiled as he took the pump and examined it carefully. Before passing it to me, he said, "I remember this from World War 2. It was used by the Nazis, and yes—no one was ever able to figure out how someone was killed. It could look like this or have a different configuration. With today's technology this could be battery powered—but the basic principle is the same. It blows the toxin into someone's face where it is inhaled. That is why I'm going to suggest to you guys that from now on you carry two handkerchiefs, one in each pocket of your pants. That way you can cover your faces in case an attack takes place. The most important thing then is

---

[19] Also called NPPD, the dust was used by the KGB as a tracking agent. The addition of luminol would make the dust glow under an ultraviolet light.

[20] Dr. Hector Zayas-Bazan was the founder of the International Pharmaceutical Congress.

to run to the closest bathroom as fast as possible and then blow your nose and rinse your mouth beneath the faucet to remove any residuals from the poison that was able to penetrate the fabric.

"Another way to prevent this is to prepare yourselves before you go on any mission that you consider, using your common sense, that you could possibly be attacked by this, is to take bits of cotton and put it inside your nose. That will act as a filter which will trap the majority of the particles of the poison, whatever small amount gets past your handkerchief in an attack. Carry a container in which you can blow the cotton in order to preserve it because having this with you after an attack will give the physicians who will be treating you the knowledge to neutralize what toxin gets inside you. Most people don't survive these attacks, but you will increase the odds of your survival by preserving those pieces of cotton."

The Gentleman of Paris had remained silent. He shook his head with an extremely serious expression, clearly showing his discontent. "I've known for many years the evil of these unscrupulous individuals within the Russian KGB. They trained under the totalitarian regime and dictatorship of Stalin's NKVD. I know they possess the worst lack of conscience, but I never even dreamed or imagined the magnitude of those diabolic, criminal minds; with no doubts in my mind now we see all the evil they possess. But when we think twice what can we expect from the men that created the most bizarre lie and deceit in the entire world?

"Stalin, after the Russians invaded Germany, was the one who created the name for his enemy—'the ultra-right.' Today, continually, the communists use it as a slogan for their enemies ever since World War 2. After they took part of Germany, they came up with that deceitful invention because in reality the ultra-right never existed, nor will it ever exist in the future. Only in the minds of the Marxists who are masters of disguise that all agree and gave that name to the Socialist Democratic Nazis[21]. That way, they wash their hands like Pontius Pilate, trying to dissociate one Leftist movement from another Leftist one, creating the invention of the ultra-right. Very ignorant people have it in front of their faces and still swallow that pill and believe the Socialist Democrat Nazis are extreme right-wing; if you remove the 'nationalist' part from 'Nazi', what's left is nothing more than Marxist-Leninism, formed under the same ideology."

Uncle Emilio grinned broadly and stood up as he applauded the Gentleman of Paris. "Bravo! I have no doubts that you are well read and educated to know the facts and the truth, and never swallow the pills from this sour, Satanic tyranny. This ideology has massacred millions of human beings around the world, and it is extremely important to read and educate our future generations, because that way we know the weakness of our enemies and the sophisticated lies that they create and use to distort history. Without that education, they can get away with false promises, conquering the masses of uneducated people. This is the way they destroy our democratic institutions—with lies, deceit, and inventions."

---

[21] "Nazi" is a shortening of the party's name: National Socialist. They would also refer to themselves as Socialist Democrats.

He smiled ironically as he shook his head. "Why do you think, in every country in the world where the communists take over, they rush to burn our books? Wherever they control a society, they instigate the mobs to burn publicly all the valuable knowledge that we've cultivated for hundreds of years. The answer is very simple—only in ignorance can they manage to manipulate and cheat the less educated with fraud and false promises to convert everyone into slaves."

He sat down. Everyone, especially Dr. Zayas-Bazan, stood up and applauded his savvy words. Uncle Emilio raised both hands to thank us for our praise and said, "I believe that we've done everything we can today, and we can end our meeting on this note. We all have a lot of work pending. Unfortunately, time is something no one has been able to stop."

We smiled at his expression and said goodbye to each other. Following our usual protocol, we left ten minutes apart from each other. I drove my UAZ towards Cojimar and Location #10.

The Broken Rainbow: Mysterious Dark Karma

Chapter 19: The Sadness of Goodbyes

20 The Farewell

As I drove several doubts and unanswered questions ran through my head: to what extreme Sonya had corroborated with the KGB and what she could be telling them to save the lives of herself and her mother were foremost. I could not completely comprehend how that female imposter had so many details about that particular and only sexual encounter I had with Sonya to use on me. They were so personal that I had been utterly convinced that she was who she said she was. How Sonya could share that kind of moment was beyond me. My hands started to sweat as I grew closer to my destination, my heart pumping faster and faster like a locomotive at full speed.

I could see the colonial structure not even half a block away and on the sandy beach was a very beautiful woman dressed all in a white linen sun dress. She had long, red hair that shone under the last rays of the sunset which marked in the distance the end of the day. She walked towards the shore, looking lost in thought.

I slowed down and pulled over between the mangrove and coconut trees, trying to hide the UAZ since I wasn't sure who that person really was. Full of curiosity, and under the assumption that it could be Sonya, I turned off the engine and pulled the binoculars out of the glove compartment. I got out of the UAZ, hid behind a coconut tree, and adjusted the magnification on the binoculars. She was looking away from me, but my surprise grew larger as I saw that she began to remove her clothing slowly until she was completely nude. Then she started to walk towards the water, possibly to refresh her body in the salt water. Even though it was near the end of November when the normal temperature in Cuba was cooler, today it had been hot, a perfect Indian summer day.

Even though the sun was setting, the heat and humidity of the tropics could still be felt on that beautiful beach, especially as there was no breath of wind at that hour of late afternoon. I continued to observe her beautiful naked body, and something caught my attention as I saw the right side of her butt cheek that proved it was indeed Sonya. It was a birth mark which looked like a half moon. I had noticed it during that beautiful, romantic encounter. I made up my mind immediately to meet with her.

Thinking of the old saying that one nail pulls out the other, I put away my binoculars in the glove compartment and started to take my clothes off, folding them up on the passenger's seat of the UAZ until I was nude. I walked in the direction of the beach not even knowing whether I was going to be welcomed or rejected. I had made that rapid decision with optimism supported by that beautiful memory Sonya had left with me, hoping that I was able to leave the same memory with her in her heart and mind.

With a big smile on my face, thinking of the tremendous surprise that she was going to have when she saw me naked. At the same time, it crossed my mind that those who are willing to risk everything in life were the ones who could enjoy the exquisite flavor of the honey of victory.

I determinedly walked towards the water. The sun was nearly below the horizon, but a little twilight was left. It was as if Nature was my accomplice for that beautiful and splendid surprise that I intended to give to the first love of my youth, my Sonya. Not too far away, as I walked into the water, I saw that she had become aware of my presence and stood up instinctively. With her left hand, she attempted to cover her breasts while with her right she shaded her eyes to try and identify me in last reflection of the sun dying in the distance, wondering who the naked man was who was walking towards her.

Sonya indecisively began to walk towards me slowly, this time using both hands to cover her breasts. As she got close to me, she frowned slightly, still trying to identify me. She stopped about a hundred feet away and yelled, "Julio Antonio del Marmol? Is it really you? Please, let me know before I start to run in a different direction."

I smiled. "I believe the only person here who should ask that question is me after all I went through with that diabolic woman who impersonated you so well that she managed to seduce me sexually."

She laughed when I said that, a little more relaxed now. She looked at me. "You've changed—you've grown too fast." She continued to walk towards me slowly, a large, satisfied smile on her face. "I believe with great conviction that that imposter managed to convince you not because of all the details, more like you wished to see me so much that you wanted to believe her. That's because your mind has such a great memory of our last encounter."

I smiled. "Conceited? This is something I didn't know about your personality!"

Sonya laughed again. We were only a few feet apart now. She said, "I believe you have a lot to learn, Cuban Lightning. All intelligent women are conceited."

"Really?" Her casual reference to my codename made me serious again.

She got closer to me and caressed my cheek with the back of her fingers of her left hand. "I would be lying to you if I said to the contrary. You have nothing to regret for yourself. If I were in your shoes, I am absolutely certain I would have made the same mistake. My wishes to see you again, I believe, are even bigger than yours. It's been almost four years."

"Not quite that long—three and a half. It's been almost four years that I couldn't find you. What was that 'Cuban Lightning'? What's that about?"

She smiled and looked at me mischievously. She put both arms around my neck and looked me deeply in the eyes. I felt the warmth of her breasts against my naked chest which gave me goosebumps all over my body. "That is the name of the famous spy who has done so much damage to these communists for years. They told me that they were very sure that it's you." I could not avoid my mood from changing completely, and my face grew very serious. She smiled. "Don't be serious." She shook me teasingly. "You don't have anything to worry about. I'll back you up. For my part, I managed to convince all the Russians and even the Cubans there the reason I hadn't ever seen you again was because you are a completely brainwashed, indoctrinated communist by Che Guevara and the Castro brothers, and that wasn't compatible with the feelings of all my family."

"Thank you. No wonder they tried Plan B."

"What?"

"Never mind, don't worry about it. Proceed. What else?"

"Well, they promised me two options. The first one, if I was willing to cooperate with them, they would not only reduce the prison sentences of my father and brother, but they would also allow them later to be freed and they would facilitate that we could leave the country as political exiles to the country of our choice."

I smiled with a hint of sarcasm as I shook my head. "Yes, the same way Fidel and the others promised to the Cuban people years ago that they would have cow's milk in their kitchens from his Utopian dream *las niñas bonitas*[22] for free from a special faucet in every home."

"I know, I know." She also spoke with a tone of irony. She added, "Only a few useful fools still believe in all these false promises. I only followed their game and pretended so that I might manage to get an elephant out of a flea. The most important thing here is that you are OK. Unfortunately for us, we found out that all the crap they promised us was nothing more than a tale, because my father and brother were already to be released under the International Red Cross. We'll leave the country in a few hours, to Costa Rica, where my father and brother will eventually reunite with us. Thank you for your help and thanks to God for your Uncle Emilio and his good friends; my family has no way of ever repaying all you guys for what you have done for us."

I smiled. I took her face in my hands, saying, "You owe us nothing. Whatever we've done for you we've been doing for different people over the past four years: those who have been persecuted by this disgusting communist totalitarian regime."

We looked at each other. I kissed her lips tenderly and her eyes moistened with gratitude and love. She responded to my kiss with a passionate one, and slowly our naked bodies grew aroused in excitement as we caressed each other until a larger wave than normal practically dragged us to the verge of the surf. It was like someone wanted to break the mood up. We continued to make love and repeated the beautiful experience from years before. We exhausted ourselves from the intense exercise and passed out on the sand beneath those

---

[22] Dairy cows

beautiful coconut trees. A very strong breeze and some drizzle woke us up. We smiled at each other and stood up. She picked up her clothes and we ran towards the UAZ, where I grabbed my clothes and dressed. As we sat, the rain started to come down harder. I tried to dry her face with my handkerchief. As I did, we started to kiss again until we heard a hand tapping on the frame of the passenger side door.

When we separated, I saw the face of a little red-headed boy of about four years of age. He waved his little hand to say hello to us. He yelled in a glad voice, "Mommy! Mommy! The captain is here already. He'll take us on board the ship to that place you've been talking about where I can eat all the ice cream with any flavor without having to stand in line for hours."

I smiled as I listened to that. I was still caught by surprise—I had thought this part of the tale was a lie invented by the imposter. It would still be a pleasant surprise. I looked at Sonya with a smile on my face and pointed questioningly at the little boy.

She looked me in my eyes and nodded with a small smile. She said, "Yes, he is your son, Julius Christian. That is the only truthful thing that diabolic imposter probably told you that had any reality."

We both got out of the UAZ and picked the boy up beneath his arms and lifted him over my shoulders. I danced with him, happy to know that part was true. At that moment, Sonya's mother Lola, Captain Marrero, and two sailors came out. Seeing my joy, Captain Marrero, even though he knew the urgency to leave quickly and the danger each additional minute meant, allowed me a few minutes to joke and run around with the boy. He fully understood my happiness. Mr. Xiang had, it turned out, already fully debriefed them as to the details.

I noticed his stress and impatience as he paced back and forth, but he gave me some time which I used to the max to run under the palm trees along the beach with that young boy on my shoulders, making myself the horse and him the rider, the boy squealing joyfully. I had no doubts that he enjoyed it as much as I did. Everyone looking on understood what the little Julius Christian, too young, could not understand. At that moment was our introduction after such a long time, and perhaps a sad and permanent goodbye between us. Julius Christian, in his innocent mind, when I returned him to the arms of his mother, asked, "I want him to be my Papi."

Sonya and I looked at each other intensely as if she were consulting with me and inquiring for my permission. I smiled slightly in acceptance, shrugged, and nodded. She held Julius Christian out to me and said in a loving, maternal voice as she grabbed his chin, "Yes, yes, love. He is your real Papi." She kissed him tenderly on the cheek.

He said in genuine, spontaneous happiness, "Really, Mommy? Really?"

Two tears in her eyes showed how touched she was by his display of joy. "Yes, my son. He is your Papi."

The boy joyfully squirmed out of his mother's arms, grabbed my right leg, and gave me a hug. "Are you coming to Costa Rica with us, Papi, and come with me to that place where we can eat all the flavors of ice cream and never have to stand in line again?"

I could not control my emotions and tears filled my eyes. I made an extreme effort to contain them but failed. I quickly wiped my eyes on the back of my shirt sleeve in the darkness. I picked him up and spun him around like a helicopter to try and induce him to forget. He laughed in that innocent, childlike manner for a few seconds. Then I let him down onto the sand and leaned down to him. "I will try to follow you very soon, but now you have to leave here quickly. Some very bad men want to hurt your Mommy, and you don't want that, do you? I need you to be with her to protect her, OK?"

"OK, Papi." He looked at me, unconvinced and not very happy. He nodded in affirmation. "But you'll come to us soon?"

"I will try to enjoy you later."

Julius Christian, still unconvinced, grabbed his mother's hand and replied, "OK, but don't take too long, OK?"

Sonya gave me a big hug and a kiss on my lips. They started to walk away, followed by Captain Marrero and his two men down the beach, where other men waited by the rowboat. I stayed by the UAZ. When they were about a hundred feet away, Julius Christian let go of his mother's hand, turned, and ran towards me, ignoring his mother's call to stop. He ran to my side, and my heart twisted within my chest. I knelt down by him and opened my arms to give him a big hug.

My joy didn't last long because from over his shoulders I saw the light of a car coming along the road rapidly. I rushed to let go of my son and showing him the car lights, I said in his ear, "Go with your Mommy and Captain Marrero quickly, because I think the bad men that I told you about are coming to hurt your Mommy."

Julius Christian looked at me and sniffed back some tears which had filled his eyes. He looked a little scared, but obediently ran to rejoin Sonya, who had been walking back to retrieve him. She waved her goodbye to me as she noticed the approaching car. She knew that road only led to the house they had been staying at.

They started to run in the sand, thinking the same thing I had, that they could be Russians or perhaps Cuban G-2. The men with Captain Marrero were already pushing the boat into the water and helped Sonya and the boy to board. Once all the men were aboard, they began to row towards the ship that was anchored a short distance offshore.

My instincts kicked in at once. My mind acted in a way to be able to distract whoever was coming in our direction along that road. Those uninvited guests could be fatal to the success of their exit. I got inside the UAZ and started the engine, switching the large lights on. I had parked towards the ocean; I now backed up and turned around so that my lights shone directly towards the car to blind them to the ship at sea and give them time to reach their destination.

A few minutes later, the car which had apparently been heading towards the residence slowed down and pulled over next to where I had parked the UAZ beneath the mangroves. When the car finally stopped, I was prepared for the worst. I had pulled my pistol out of the glove compartment and readied for use to defend not only myself but also the retreat of Captain Marrero and his precious cargo. I gave a last look at the rowboat through my binoculars and saw they had arrived at the fishing boat and had been raised onto her deck.

I breathed with a sense of relief, thinking that in a very short time they would leave Cuban waters and enter international waters, where they would finally be out of danger from any attempts by that totalitarian tyranny.

The Broken Rainbow: Mysterious Dark Karma

I bent over to replace the binoculars in the glove compartment and when I straightened up when I looked at the car, I could see only shadows inside. It was a black Volga, which was used by the high-ranked officials in the communist government. I could swear I saw an individual inside, but when I looked again, he was gone. This got me worried. I kept the lights of the UAZ on, but the mangroves blocked a clear view.

The mangroves, coconut trees, and bushes offered a perfect camouflage for anyone who didn't want to be seen on that dark, rainy night near the end of November. I opened the driver's door, not wanting to take any chances. I slid, pistol in hand, very carefully, and crawled on my elbows and knees among the trunks of fallen coconut trees, trying to hide among that debris, only twenty feet from the UAZ, where I could have a good view and remained silent, waiting to see the shadow of the driver or other men from the Volga.

The Volga's headlights switched off. Long minutes passed which felt to me like hours. I heard in the distance the diesel engines of large fishing boat of Captain Marrero. That gave me a sense of tranquility as I listened to that sound disappear into the distance until it was heard no more. My patience started to reach its limits. I looked at my wristwatch and saw that twenty minutes had passed. I began to consider the notion that this individual had stopped on that road looking for privacy or a peaceful place out of the usual traffic where he might need to relieve himself.

I had already decided to abandon my hiding place when something stopped me at once. From the bushes in that darkness sporadically lit by lightning from the approaching storm, the silhouette of a tall man in civilian clothes loomed out, but I could not make out his facial features. He held something white in his hand; when he crossed in front of the UAZ, it looked like a roll of toilet paper. I also saw that he held a pistol in his right hand.

As he approached the UAZ, he tried to look inside it. Seeing no one inside, he opened the door, leaned over inside, and turned the engine and lights off. With almost half his body inside the UAZ, I came up behind him slowly. I waited behind him until he straightened up and put the muzzle of my pistol in the back of his neck. I said in a determined voice, "Drop your pistol and step back very slowly if you don't want to splash your brains all over my windshield."

The man froze. Without moving a muscle in his body, as he felt the cold metal of my pistol against the back of his head, he asked, "Julio Antonio, is that you? It's Canen, your brother-in-law. Be careful, that weapon could discharge, and then you would leave your sister a widow and my daughter fatherless."

I recognized his voice at once and removed my pistol. I asked in surprise, "What are you doing here?" I was a little upset with him at that moment. I stepped back to give him space to recover from his moment of fear.

He replied, "Fidel and Che sent me to take you to them. They want to bring you tomorrow morning with them to Pinar del Rio where they're going to inaugurate one of their Agrarian Reform Farms. They're calling this Sandino after the famous guerilla who fought for the farmers in Nicaragua. They grew several forms of produce here, and at the moment they were focusing on tomatoes. I told them you had another attempt on your life, and they, both being hypocrites, pretended they had no idea what was going on with the Russians or anything that happened. They're probably dying of curiosity to know how you survived from your own lips. I don't believe they have any special interest in your attending that inauguration—they've never invited you to any event unless it was a military one."

I smiled and pointed at the roll of toilet paper in his hand. "Have you been having stomach problems, and you had an urgent need for a number two?"

"You must be kidding! I had some Russian canned beef and have had such diarrhea that I've been running to the toilet for two days now."

I smiled ironically. "I believe Che and Fidel will need a few of those rolls without eating any of that Russian beef when Chandee finishes with the Russian ambassador. If there's anything I can assure you of, because I'm the one who trained her, is that the ambassador is going to have a nightmare tonight if he manages to survive this *chinita cubanita*. She will not limit herself to whatever we told her to do. I know for a fact that she will find an excuse to improvise. I don't think we'll ever see at least this ambassador in Cuba again."

Canen looked worried and shook his head. "I hope to God that she follows what I instructed her to do and doesn't go overboard. Extremes never bring anything good, and the government has the power. It could take retaliation and personal vengeance against all the members of the opposition." He looked at me sadly. "You know very well how bloodthirsty these people are. Especially when they're trying to intimidate innocent and defenseless people."

"Brother, I know. But remember, we are at war. Those who are afraid and maintain silence from the abuses of these bullies don't even know that through their inaction they support and glorify the very abuses that they themselves receive. They then create more victims."

Canen shook his head again. "Why can we not live in peace and harmony like God commanded us to in this beautiful world He gave us to enjoy as brothers and sisters?"

"Unfortunately, for all of us, human beings have no worst enemies than his own species. Only piranhas devour each other like we do—and we're supposed to be rational beings! I don't want to know if we would do to each other if we were irrational beings!"

He patted me on the shoulder. "Remember—the bad people are a small minority. It's just that the minority of people are noisy, which is why they get more attention than those like you and I who live our lives saving innocent and defenseless people without making false promises or bragging about the free milk faucets in their houses."

I smiled. "You're right, Brother Canen. You're right."

He returned my smile, satisfied by my agreement. "Well, I think the most prudent and secure thing now is to get out of here, before the G-2 or elements from the Russian embassy come to visit us. Besides, we have to get up early tomorrow morning to go to that ghostly milking and Agrarian Farm and other Utopian dreams of our Commander-in-Chief."

"Where did you get that Volga?"

"Oh, Fidel gave it to me today."

"No wonder I didn't recognize that vehicle. You caught me by surprise; I was expecting the enemy."

As we left that place, I crossed myself and prayed to God and Jesus Christ, that Sonya, her mother Lola, and our son safely reach their destination in Costa Rica without any major troubles.

The Broken Rainbow: Mysterious Dark Karma

I found out later from Chandee's lips that she had tried to follow the plan as Canen and the others had recommended and avoid unnecessary risks. However, due to recent events and setbacks at the embassy that the ambassador had been having, and based on the report Putin had given, their security had been multiplied, and they had brought in reinforcements from the G-2, undoubtedly sent with pleasure as their chief, Piñeiro, rushed to serve his masters.

When she came into the parking lot where the embassy was supposed to keep their official vehicles beneath the Hilton, she encountered nearly ten men patrolling around the parking lot where only one or two cars were parked. A barricade had been erected, separating the secure parking place from the rest of the lot.

When she saw that, she discarded the initial plan and prepared her own plan. She discovered the name of the personal attendant and cook for the ambassador, a woman of Asian origin, middle height like Chandee was, and middle-aged. Her name was Lijing. She was the most trusted person to the ambassador; he only ate the food she prepared for him. She intercepted that woman on her way to work and managed to drug her, interrogated her about the standard procedures to serve his meal, stole her clothing, and made herself up to look older, with the prescription glasses the woman normally used. She managed to pass through the guards on security and left the original Lijing tied up, drugged, and gagged in the trunk of her father's car in the street.

She managed to get into the kitchen, prepared to serve the already-made meal, and pretended to do things in the kitchen. As she prepared the stainless-steel containers to cover the trays, one of the bodyguards entered the kitchen. With abrupt and disrespectful manners, he yelled, "Lijing—did you fall asleep or something? You're already fifteen minutes late and the ambassador is asking for his dinner."

She bowed and avoided eye contact. "It's done."

"Well, what are you waiting for?"

She took the various trays and with steady hands followed the bodyguard to the private office of the ambassador. She looked at the guard over the rims of her glasses as he walked into the office. The man escorted her inside and then remained outside in the reception area. The ambassador was on the phone with someone. He placed his hand over the receiver and grunted, "You're late."

She bowed. "Sorry. Sorry."

As she deposited on the tray on a side table like Lijing usually did, she took the utensils and brought out of the tray the various stainless steel covered trays and organized them on the table in order. He put his hand on the receiver again and said, "Finally, you brought my dinner. I thought you wanted to kill me through hunger."

Chandee kept her back to the ambassador and continued to slowly lay out the dinner, taking care to show as little of her face to him. Distracted by his conversation on the phone, the ambassador didn't notice. He put his hand on the phone again and said, "I hope that what you prepared for me today was worth the wait. Why are you so late today?"

Chandee bowed and nodded and smiled slightly without saying a word. She unwrapped the napkins and laid them out on the table as Lijing had described. She walked towards the door wordlessly, like usual. The ambassador stood up as he hung up the phone. "Wait,

Lijing. I'm curious about the meal you prepared that took you more time than usual."

Chandee tried to control herself and not allow panic to prevent her from improvising. Before she could do anything, she nonchalantly double-locked the door. She turned around and put her hand beneath her apron on her silenced pistol[23]. She kept her head half down in submission, she looked at him over the rim of her glasses. He started to check the food, one container at a time, making approving noises each time and smiling in satisfaction.

It didn't last very long. He uncovered the container for the main dish at the end of the line and screamed in a voice blended with surprise, fear, and anger, "What the hell? What is this?" His eyes bulged out of their sockets.

Chandee stepped back a few steps and put her back against the wall next to the door. She pulled the pistol out and prepared to fire, pointing it at the ambassador, who still couldn't believe what he saw. His eyes remained glued to that container. He put both hands on top of the table. "Bitch! What is this all about?"

Now in the midst of his panicked surprise he took a better look at her. "You're not Lijing—you're an imposter!" He raised his voice and yelled, "Imposter! Guards! Guards!"

There was a battering at the door, but the door was too thick. He thought she felt insecure since she hadn't fired, and seeing as his guards couldn't help

---

[23] Because of the awkwardness of the additional length a noise suppressor creates operatives at this time had pistols issued which had the suppression apparatus built into the barrel of the weapon.

him, he picked up the lids of the containers to throw them at her. It didn't take the ambassador very long to realize that this woman was very well trained as she expertly dodged each thrown lid like an expert martial artist. In the end, when he had run out of things to throw at her, he picked up the head of his assistant from its position on the main dish platter.

Chandee yelled, "NO!" She put her head down by her knees and rolled like an armadillo all the way to shelter under his solid copper desk, pistol still in hand.

The ambassador, when he saw what she did, he looked at the head. At that moment, the head exploded, taking the ambassador's head off as well. The entire place shook so bad that half of the decorative ceiling fell down, hanging by the wires. The massive door she had locked blew outwards, killing the four guards outside. The fire alarm began to ring, and the sprinklers switched on. Debris, dust, water, and smoke from the exposed wiring provided the perfect confusion and concealment for her escape from the hotel.

As she walked through the lobby towards the front door, she passed by several police and firemen in full firefighting gear. As she was about to go through the door into the valet parking, a young policeman stopped her, claiming that he was worried about her because of the way her clothing was so ripped and dusty. He was clearly suspicious because of it and thought she was either there or in close proximity to the blast. Chandee told him repeatedly that she was OK, but he still called a paramedic and compelled her to sit down to be examined by the first responder.

To avoid creating a fuss, she took a seat on the stool the valet parking attendants would use when things were slow. The policeman didn't leave, observing as the paramedic took her vitals and checked her for injuries.

Once the paramedic was done, he gave her a mask. He said, "Your lungs must be full of dust, so breath into this respirator."

Chandee later told me that the young policeman started to wonder about her with such an intensity that she grew concerned. She blamed herself of not taking the precaution of changing clothes and cleaning herself up in one of the restrooms of the hotel. She noticed that he was writing down the answers she gave him, and her concerns grew.

He asked her, "Are you staying in the hotel, or just working here?"

Luckily, before Chandee could answer the question, the young policeman was called by one of his superiors, interrupting the interrogation. At the same time, the paramedic took her pulse and checked her blood pressure. The paramedic said when she removed the respirator, "Don't take that away. That will help you clear the dust out of your lungs."

Chandee's worry about the policeman increased as she kept her eye on him while he spoke with two different officers who appeared to be his superiors. She saw him pointing at her and understood that he was not worried about her health as he claimed previously. Like a good communist he was indoctrinated by that psychological, Machiavellian system to promote his career to his personal benefit no matter what the cost was to anyone else. He continued to try and convince the older men that Chandee was one of primary suspects.

Chandee understood at once that this imbecile in his greed for power and thirst for promotion could blow her cover. One of the fire trucks entering the driveway of the valet parking, completely blocking the line of sight between her and the other policemen at the door. One of the firemen, as he entered laid his helmet down on the concierge desk. She used the opportunity to put into motion her Operation Harry Houdini, distracting the paramedic by asking for water. She removed the mask and picked up the fireman's helmet, putting it on. In less than a few seconds, when the paramedic returned with a paper cup of water, all he found was the respirator mask on the stool.

The policeman walked over with his supervisors, having convinced them that if she wasn't involved, she at least knew something about it. The policeman looked at the paramedic, about a hundred feet away, who gestured in complete confusion. They wondered where that older Asian woman could possibly have gone, evaporating completely before their eyes.

At that moment, the fire truck began to leave. It maneuvered towards the exit to 23rd Avenue, slowing down to allow traffic to drive around them, with Chandee hanging on the rear steps on the side of the truck opposite to the hotel door and allowing her to leave the parking lot without being seen. As the traffic stopped to allow the truck in, she jumped off. She was then able to lose herself in the crowd in the darkness, heading towards where she had left her car with her prisoner.

The Broken Rainbow: Mysterious Dark Karma

Chapter 20: The Assassins in Motion

21 Farm in San Dino

The next morning, Canen and I left the capital in the caravan behind Fidel and Che to the inauguration of the Agrarian Plan in Pinar del Rio. When we arrived at the location a few hours later, we had a group of people waiting outside the facility applauding us as we drove, yelling "Vive Fidel!" Everyone in Cuba knew the people screaming were members of the communist party and used by the government at every gathering to give the impression to anyone watching in person or on TV that they had the support of the majority of the Cuban people.

But with a little common sense, one would see the ones yelling were well-dressed and looked well-fed, while the peasants had poor clothes and long faces and applauded half-heartedly without feeling. By now the peasants were suffering more that even before under Batista's dictatorship; they had lived their lives in a democratic, free Cuba, and those freedoms were evaporating each day. Under the new Marxist-Leninist government and its declared Supreme Leader, Fidel Castro, Cuban society underwent a fundamental transformation from a democratic country into a communist one. The government didn't care about the suffering of the majority of the people, the ones who had lost the incentive and hope of getting rid of those bandits, especially after the failed invasion at the Bay of Pigs.

This sense of deception was seen clearly in the faces of the people. I noticed it and together with Canen we observed a small deputation of these people approach us to ask to speak with Fidel about these reforms which they didn't want. The apparent leader said, "I represent the Worker-Peasant's Alliance[24]."

My curiosity kicked in to find out who the man was who had the courage and audacity to express his discontent with the Agrarian Reform, supposedly created to help the peasants who in the past had been abused by the landlords, who demanded from them higher rent of the land than the income they were able to produce on it.

---

[24] A group which had existed for several years before the revolution. They were more like a syndicate, but the government respected them.

They had created this association to protect the peasants from the landlords. That group of brave men represented the silent majority. A compromise was all they were asking for. The group was well-organized and represented most of the people there who feared to express themselves lest they be retaliated against.

According to that man, the Agrarian Reform went against the personal freedoms of the farmers because they were forced to sell all of their produce to the government at the price it established and could not sell even a portion of their crop to private entities. This government enterprise's name was ACOPIO[25]. If the farmers refused to sell to the government, they would be accused of speculation. The government, which provided them with seeds, pesticides, and other agricultural equipment so that they would be able to successfully achieve their work. If anyone was caught selling contraband to the speculators, they would be arrested for embezzlement and high treason as thieves against the people and sentenced for up to thirty years in prison or worse, executed by firing squad, depending on the value and quantity that was stolen. Of course, they always used "the people's interest" to make the government case, which was typical demagogy.

The leader was a tall man, nearly 6'6" with reddish hair and an Italian nose. He came up to me as I was speaking with his group. I was fascinated with them. He very discretely put his arm around my

---

[25] The State Procurement and Distribution Agency of the Cuban government.

shoulder and whispered into my ear, "Julio Antonio—can we talk in private?"

I recognized him at that moment. It was my uncle on Mima's side, her brother Juanito. He was the youngest and favorite brother of Mima's. I smiled and replied, "Tell me where."

We shook hands. "Nice to see you again," he said with a smile. "I'm the rebel and the leader of this group."

My cousin Tatico, tall like his father but a little hunchbacked was next to him. He asked, "What's up, cousin? How are your Commandos doing? You better watch out with these guys. Today you're a Commander and in the pink elite of the revolution and tomorrow you end up in the firing squad."

I smiled. "I know what you mean. I assure you, before I end up before the firing squad, I'll be a real pain in the rear to all these guys."

He laughed in his funny way. I followed them both, accompanied by Canen. They took us to the mess hall where the workers would come to eat. We sat down at one of the tables and my uncle called one of the ladies over. "Bring us some *pinareña la jupiña montes*[26]."

Canen and I were very grateful for this. In the rush to leave the capital, neither of us had any breakfast. Juanito asked if we wanted anything to eat, and I said, "Canen and I are starving."

He turned to the lady who brought the sodas. "Prepare for us a chorizo and spinach omelet." When she brough it out, we devoured it. He asked me, "What is your opinion? I would like to talk to Fidel in private in order to be completely open with him and tell him this arbitrary law has already cost the life of the son of one of my friends

---

[26] Local pineapple soda

in the Alliance. In the twenty years of experience as President of my association, I can assure you that you cannot squeeze them any further before they will rebel and strike. We'll have a serious problem then. I've been in this syndicate for as long as I can remember, and I've never seen anything like that before in my life."

I asked, "Why? How did this happen?"

"They caught his son selling some of the grain as contraband and they gave him a warning. He continued to do it. Don't take me wrong—I don't see anything wrong with selling your crop to anyone you want. The government pays pennies. The end of the whole thing was they took him before a popular tribune and accused him of being a speculator and an embezzler of the people and executed him by firing squad twenty-four hours later. Do you think Fidel would be willing to listen to me? All we want is the option to those who don't sympathize with this law the independence to sell the product to whomever they want as a democratic and mutual respect for anyone on the part of the revolutionary government."

I had several pieces in my mouth at that moment. I kept silent as I chewed until I was able to swallow what I had. With a sad expression, I looked at him and said, "Yes, he'll listen to you and whatever you want to tell him. But I also want to warn you that what you did today you put your life in danger. Whatever conversation you have with Fidel, in the end the only thing you will earn is having him as the worst enemy you ever dreamed of having in all your life." I paused and stopped eating. I put the fingers of my right hand to my forehead and rubbed it. "Remember, what

Fidel did to his best friend, Commander Huber Matos."

Uncle Juanito shook his head in resignation. With sadness in his face and deception in his voice he said, "Yes, they sentenced him to twenty years."

I nodded and looked at him in frustration. I put the last piece of omelet on my plate into my mouth. Canen had already finished and said, "I am in agreement with your nephew 100%. I don't believe that you will gain anything to tell Fidel what he already knows. You will put yourself and your family in great jeopardy with the government and probably Fidel will add you to his paranoid blacklist of his enemies."

Uncle Juanito replied, "Well, I'm the president and leader of the Worker-Peasant Alliance. Even if I make Fidel my worst enemy, which I will try to avoid doing with every method of diplomacy at my disposal, I have the responsibility as the leader to tell him the truth, which is that every one of us disagrees with the Agrarian Reform."

Canen replied with a sad face, "In this case my friend Juanito, good luck and God protect you. You are crossing the ugly red line with Satan on the hallway to Hell." I nodded in agreement.

Juanito replied, "Well, I promised my followers last night that I would let Castro as well as all the other leaders of the revolution know their feelings at this inauguration. I need to comply with my promise."

At that moment, Che Guevara walked into the mess hall with his escort. He walked over to where we were sitting. With a sarcastic smile, he said in mock surprise, "Commandantico, Canen. What are you doing, sitting here with the opposition?"

I replied, "Unless you have another way to convince the opposition to bring them to our side other than discussion and persuasion, please let me know what other suggestion you have."

He pulled his pistol out in a grandiosely intimidating manner, raised it high above his head, and said, "I have a most persuasive way to bring them to our side: six feet under the dirt."

Uncle Juanito didn't like that at all nor appreciate the joke. He raised his eyebrows in concerned puzzlement. "If that was a joke, it's not in good taste," he said.

I knew Che actually meant that but would excuse it as a joke; I had seen him do this before. Juanito stood up, towering over Che. "What, you can't take a joke?" Che said as he put his pistol back.

"Only cowardly men try to intimidate others and pass it off as a joke," Juanito said.

Che smiled hypocritically. "Come on, for God's sake. I don't need to intimidate anyone. I just kill them."

Canen and I exchanged glances. Canen said to Che, "With all my respect, Commander, I believe that your method or alternative is the last one we should deploy when we have no others left."

Che laughed. "That is precisely the problem that many people have. If they leave for later things of importance that they could resolve now when they have the opportunity, they end up never having another chance to conclude it."

I replied with a small smile, "I'm in perfect agreement with you, Commander. We have a perfect example of your theory in the men in the Russian embassy and the ambassador himself. The ambassador lost his head last night."

Che stood up before our table, petrified and confused. His face registered different emotions. Each time a different emotion he jerked and contorted his features and eyes. First surprise, then terror, and finally disgust. Completely taken by surprise, it took him a few seconds to reply. "How the hell do you know this?"

I put my hand inside my uniform coat and pulled out a folded copy of the newspaper *Granma*. I showed him the headline: *Ambassador decapitated. Many killed in an explosion that appears to be a gas leak.* I added, "It's for certain that one thing these Russians know is how to get ahead." Che thought about that for a few seconds, massaging his forehead with his fingers. He remained silent in confusion. I added, "It appears the ambassador didn't use your methods and the dirty laundry at his house caused him to lose his head."

A little more recovered from his intellectual embarrassment that made him lose for a moment his egotistic attitude, he gestured with his right hand to Juanito. "Come with me. Fidel wants to talk to you."

I extended the newspaper to Che. "Did you want to take this to Fidel?" He snatched it from me. "I grabbed it early this morning before we left the hotel."

Tatico stood up with the intention to accompany his father. Che said, "No—Fidel told me very clearly that he wanted to speak with Juanito in private. I'm sorry, but those are my orders."

"That's OK," Tatico said as he returned to his seat. Juanito followed Che closely as they left the mess. Tatico turned to me with a worried expression on his face. "I hope my father doesn't end up the same way that Constantino's son did, in front of the firing squad."

"No, it won't be like that," I replied. Your father is a public figure, especially in the labor syndicate sector. This would be a provocation to the syndicates and the work force across the nation and not just in agriculture. I can tell you one thing, because I know these communists very well, inside out: if they take any retaliation against your father, they won't do it obviously like that. This kind of stuff they handle in different ways. For example, an accident, or poisoning from industrial chemicals, or even a car accident, or anything else that will seem to not involve them, but never the firing squad. That's used not only to punish somebody but also for intimidation to the rest of the population, to send messages. That is the principal objective of psychological coercion."

Forty-five minutes later, Che returned with Juanito, who was grinning from ear to ear is if he had won the jackpot in the lottery. It appeared that Fidel, with his charm and deception, offered Juanito a Kool-Aid, and Juanito didn't just take a glass; he drank the whole jar. We remained silent as Juanito sat down by us, but Che remained standing by our table, something which caught my attention, wondering why he was here. As if he was reading my mind, he said to me, "Commandantico, Fidel wants to talk to you before we return to the capital."

I stood up at once. "OK, let's go."

Juanito said with a grin, "When you come back, I'll tell you everything. It went better than I expected. Imagine it! Fidel didn't know that I was your uncle, your mother's brother. When I told him that, he became absolutely fascinated because he has a great admiration and gratitude, not just for you but your father Leonardo and his sacrifices which made the revolution possible as well as bringing you to him and nurturing you into the military revolutionary leadership."

I smiled as I walked towards the door with Che and turned slightly. "Don't go away. I'll be back shortly, and I'm dying to hear what you're so happy about. We'll continue our conversation when I get back."

Canen smiled and raised his right hand high. "Well, it all depends on whatever topic Fidel wants to discuss with you. If it's a complicated one, I believe that I see myself sleeping tonight on this farm. Nothing is short or simple for Fidel. Thank God we're in the best location in the entire farm—close to the food! We won't have to worry about being hungry."

I smiled and left the mess towards the farm's main office. As we walked through the building and into the enormous, sophisticated offices, I was taken by surprise. Even the ministers in the capital didn't have the luxurious furniture that I saw there. I thought to myself that if there was anything these communists were good for it was to aggrandize the bureaucracy, since they practically lived in their offices, even when they had nothing to do but cutting their toenails. I had seen some of them in the sleeping in their offices to pretend how much they were sacrificing to their jobs, even creating frictions within their families.

I could not contain myself and a big smile spread on my face as I walked into the office Castro was using. I gave Fidel a crisp military salute. He waved me to be at ease as he returned my salute. "Sit down, please." He looked at me with his tiny, rat-like eyes. "The one who smiles for himself is the one who's thinking of the mischievous things he did."

I replied, "My smile as I entered this beautiful office had no relation at all with memories. On the contrary, it's related to what I was watching right now as I entered these extraordinarily well-decorated offices. I don't know who designed them, but it's very unusual in an isolated farm so far away from civilization to find such refined offices. This could be the envy in the city from any architect, attorney, or high executive in one of our ministries. I see this instead in an agricultural farm program!"

He smiled. "Well, even though the director of this plant has a great office, too, a little smaller in size, this is not his office but that of the Comrade General Secretary of the Communist Party."

I smiled. "Ooh-la-la! Leave the poor to the world!"

He could not hold it in and burst out laughing. "You always make me laugh."

I answered, "Well, we have to take care of our people. Vive la difference."

He smiled again and his laugh was genuine. "I don't know how you manage it, but whenever I see you without exception you make me laugh."

"Well, Commander, that gives me a great satisfaction. That is our purpose in life—to put smiles on people's face and everyone in our road, never tears in the eyes of anyone."

He nodded. "Well, unfortunately that is a lot more difficult, in fact the most difficult thing in life, because someone unfortunately always has to cry." His demeanor had changed, as if he was thinking of the number of tears he had brought to the eyes of the Cuban people, the island that was the Pearl of the Caribbean before his crazy experiments. He grew serious as he leaned back in his comfortable executive chair behind that beautiful solid copper desk with a transparent glass top. "All that happened last night in the Russian embassy has come to be a very intriguing mystery, especially about the woman who tried to cheat you by assuming the identity of one of your friends from your youth." He looked me directly in the eyes. "Who do you think could be behind all of this? Do you have any idea?"

I looked at him silently. I thought how much of a master of hypocrisy this man was. At the same time, I looked over at Che, who sat to my left, and nodded. He had remained silent the entire time, smoking one of his big Havana cigars. After a few seconds, I said, "Eye for an eye and tooth for a tooth. I know you're not very religious, but that's called Divine Justice, which no one can avoid or ever stop. Everyone involved in trying to hurt an innocent always winds up paying for not only what they tried to do to me but also what they did to that defenseless, innocent girl and her son, who had never even for a second involved in politics or hurt anyone."

Fidel looked at me but could not hold my gaze. He dropped his gaze and looked down. I knew that both he and Che had certain knowledge of all that had transpired, gone along with it, and allowed the operation with the ambassador and KGB to proceed. Maybe he wanted to convince himself of my loyalty or had some doubts about it. "Who do you think," he repeated anxiously, "*really* prepared and is behind this attempt on your life?"

I leaned back in my armchair and took a deep breath. I said with a lot of resentment in my voice, "Who do you think, here in Cuba, possesses the power and the tools to mobilize so many people and try to put down a young man like me? You guys know that the only who could perpetrate this kind of operation against any one of us. You know the answer better than me, Commander. Please. I don't even want to pronounce that name."

Che said, "Of course, it has to be Piñeiro." Che just fell into the trap I had carefully prepared for both of them.

Fidel said, "Of course! The only one who has been trying anything against you is Commander Piñeiro."

Che took his beret off and put it over the left knee he had crossed over his right leg. "Is that the name you've been looking for and didn't want to tell us?"

I smiled sarcastically and bit my lip as I shook my head. "Not only Piñeiro. There's a lot more involved than just him. It's a lot deeper."

"What do you mean?" Fidel asked.

"Well, we can say the Russian ambassador was involved. And many of his men. I saw a couple of them in the church when they tried to put me down. As I said before, Divine Justice is implacable, especially when you attempt to put down innocent people." Both hypocrites exchanged looks for a few seconds, now knowing for certain that I had something to do the night before in the embassy. But they had failed in everything they had been doing and the beauty of it was they still could not accuse me of anything. Once more, in their search for the Lightning and intention to really find out the identity of that mysterious spy, they had instead encountered the smoke of the phantom that in the dark night mixed with the mist and the fog that disappears, leaving behind no trace, no fingerprints—just the undeniable signs of the Divine Justice.

Che and Fidel lied to each other and faked surprise. I knew Che's was feigned because if he wasn't the incarnation of Satan, he was one of his most devoted followers; a great difference from Fidel

Castro who had been educated by the Jesuits. In Castro's case, as we say in Cuba, the dress doesn't make the monk. But we at least thought that something good had to come from the goodwill of those Jesuits who had been educating him, and so the people in Cuba assumed that he might be a good leader. Unfortunately, those assumptions had been evaporated by three years of the hypocritical, egotistical mercenary personality which Castro showed was a little mixed with the necessary ingredients to produce a very conniving dictator and assassin.

This degenerate, unscrupulous man, as he had demonstrated during his three years in power, had brought with him the mysterious dark karma for all the Cuban people, planting not only mourning for the hundreds of thousands of firing squad victims but also shedding more innocent blood than the entire time the previous dictator in power had. The long list of murders committed by Fulgencio Batista now was a very short one in comparison to what Castro had done in three years.

Fidel, his expression displeased by my answer, stood up. He might have been trying to prevent a possible confrontation with me based on my answer and so got control of himself. He said in a more friendly tone and demeanor, holding out his right hand, "Well, the most important thing is that you're alive and in good health. I promise you I will take care of this and talk to Commander Piñeiro as soon as I get back to Havana." He held his thumb and forefinger a small space apart and added with a hypocritical nod, "If I discover that he had even the most minimal responsibility in all this turgid mess, I will remove him from his position as the Chief of the G-2 and I swear I'll put you in his place to give him once and for all as a very good lesson he'll never forget in his life."

It was clear he was pretending to be incredibly upset with Piñeiro, but I was unconvinced. I knew for a fact that all the anger and distress he was pretending to display to me was nothing more than a hypocritical simulation to try and prove to me that neither he nor Che had anything to do with that attempt on my life.

He raised his voice, nearly yelling, "If I find the proof that Piñeiro is involved with the Russian ambassador and his men after I have told him clearly to not bother you and leave you to work in peace, that would be it! My glass will be overflowing, I can guarantee you that."

"No, Comandante, please," I replied. "Thank you very much, but I don't want to be a spy or involved with them, much less than to be the chief of all of them. I take no pleasure in all the lies and intrigues that Piñeiro enjoys so much. I believe with great conviction that your election of putting him as the commander of the G-2 could not be better. It's very suited to his personality and character. He is the perfect Machiavelli, a conniving person suited for that position."

Che stood up and held his right hand out to shake my hand. "I agree with you 100%. I never like intrigues, and I like Comandante Piñeiro even less, because he is a very insecure man, filled with an inferiority complex."

I smiled. "Thank you for your support. Now, if you don't have anything else for me, I'd like to go back. I have a lot to do. I want to see if I can convince these people in the syndicate my uncle leads to come aboard with us, become more involved in the revolution, and support the Agrarian Reforms."

"Bravo!" Fidel said. "Thank you, Commandantico."

"You're welcome, my Commander." I gave him a crisp salute and turned to return to the mess hall where I had left Canen and Juanito.

The Broken Rainbow: Mysterious Dark Karma

Chapter 21: The Conspiracy of Power

I entered the mess and sat down next to my friends. I put my elbows on the table and rested my chin on the back of my hands. I nodded sadly. I said to Juanito, "Go ahead—tell me what Fidel promised you and I will tell you if he intends to comply with them or not."

He looked at me in wide-eyed astonishment. He glanced over his shoulders fearfully to see if anyone would overhear us and put his index finger to his lips in a cautionary manner. "Lower you voice. I don't know if you guys in the capital have as many informants as we have here, but everyone is trying to hear what you say to get themselves in a better position with the government. Things as insignificant as what you just said have had many people here serving ten, fifteen, twenty years in jail for being counterrevolutionaries."

I smiled and lowered my voice to make him more relaxed. It was clear that he had a really bad experience from something he had said previously which had been overheard. "You're right—we cannot give any excuse to our enemies which justifies them to persecute us and abuse us."

My uncle put his finger to his lips again. I smiled. It was clear that the G-2 and other security agencies in the government had been more severe here to suffocate the disappointment of the population. The most basic necessities had been rationed and everyone was suffering. Each day it got worse as the government consolidated its totalitarian power, trying to control every private property, factories, banks, confiscating everything under the demagogic slogan that everything was in the best interest of the people and the proletariat.

My uncle said, "I'm very happy because it appears that Fidel and Che, under the pressure of our union have conceded to make an exception for us in their plan. They're going to allow us to sell our product to whoever pays more for it."

I smiled. "That is the biggest, most grotesque lie I can guarantee you. Fidel and Che have told me repeatedly that there will be no exceptions for anyone. The Marxist-Leninist communist plan will apply equally to everyone."

He pursed his lips, the deception showing plainly in his face. "Really?"

"My uncle, I'm sorry, but tell your people in the syndicate to not expect anything at all and instead expect a retaliation. If Fidel tells you one thing, he'll do another. I wouldn't be surprised if they squeeze you and put more pressure on you to intimidate you. Be prepared and be careful; these people are worse than gangsters. They'll tell you what you want to hear but will never deliver anything."

I said goodbye to them, and Canen and I departed to the capital of Pinar del Rio, Canen going separately to his house while I went to mine because my mother had requested that I stay with them for a few days. She complained that she never saw me anymore due to the busy itinerary the government demanded of me and that I was completely forgetting my family. That hurt my feelings, so I agreed to sleep that night in my old childhood room at the house on 116 Avenue Cabada.

My parents had kept my room intact, the pictures on the wall from my musical group Los Gatos Negros and all the things I had done in my early teen years, just as I had left it before. She had promised to make me tropical fruit tartlets for breakfast, like she had always done before. I could not resist that promise and my mouth watered at the thought of the next day. Unfortunately, I never got to eat those fruit tartlets, because the next day, early in the morning I woke up to screaming, crying, and lamentation from my brothers and sisters.

According to my cousin Tatico, who had called early that morning, after we left the farm yesterday afternoon my uncle, accompanied by some of his workers, went to inspect the irrigation system of a tomato farm. That farm was sprayed by one of the fumigation planes without any warning instead of the next week, like planned. It had dropped the entire load of the deadly pesticide Parathion. The pilot had perfect visibility and must have seen the group of men with someone wearing Juanito's hat walking in the tomato field between the rows of plants. Eighteen men from that group were killed by it almost instantly, poisoned by that insecticide. Only a few of the entire group managed to survive, and that only because they were far to the rear. What was curious was that they had five different farms and the only one the pilot fumigated was the one run by the union who had protested the Reform.

Juanito had survived and transported to the regional hospital in a coma. According to my family, he was in intensive care. As I arrived at the hospital with my family, as a member of the hierarchy of the government, I used my influence to allow me to go see him.

When I finally was allowed into the ICU communal ward, it broke my heart. His face was swollen like a balloon, and I didn't even recognize him. Canen, as soon as he heard what had happened, he drove to the hospital in full uniform as a Captain in the Army. He came up to me and said, "I have no doubts that this is a macabre maneuver of Che and Fidel's to silence the opposition." He shook his head disgustedly.

We left the room as there was nothing we could do. When we entered the reception room, my mother, the brothers and sisters of my uncle, his wife Maria, my grandparents on my father's side were all extremely concerned, some of them crying.

Mima asked Canen, "How is he doing? Is he better?"

Canen was silent for a few seconds and shook his head slowly. "He's in critical condition. But at least he's breathing better, according to what the nurses told me."

I looked at him and raised an eyebrow. I hadn't seen him talking to any nurses. It was true there were several nurses, but they were all very busy trying to insert catheters and hang IV bottles. They were too busy to talk to anyone; but I understood that he had just said that to put the family more at ease.

I said goodbye to my family, got in my UAV, and drove to the Sandino Agrarian Project. I wanted to assure myself that whatever had been said to the families was actually an accident or another criminal act from those cannibals of society, the leaders of the communist regime on the direct orders of Che and Fidel.

A little while later, I arrived at the farm and saw Tatico driving a tractor with a trailer filled with boxes of tomatoes, taking it to a warehouse where several trucks waited to be loaded. A group of workers were unloading the wagons as they arrived and put the produce into the trucks bound for the large warehouses in the city. Tatico stopped the tractor when he saw me, gave some instructions to one of the workers, and left his driving gloves on the dashboard of the tractor as the assistant continued his work.

Tatico approached my UAZ, shaking his head in distress at what happened to his father. He said, "You must have a crystal ball hidden somewhere. Exactly what you told us is exactly what happened yesterday after you left."

I grimaced in revulsion, touching my stomach as I did. "I wish in my guts I wasn't so right. Unfortunately, I've spent so much time around these disgusting birds that all I can see are their droppings. I know exactly what kind of birds they are."

He gave me a half-smile in revulsion. "I know how you feel. What's more painful is that my father believed the lying promise that those degenerate cannibals of our society don't care about anything at all."

"Where is the pilot?" I asked.

He pointed to the office building. "Right there, with the Secretary of the Communist Party and several leaders from the Reform plan. They might be preparing the PR to sweeten the Kool-Aid of lies that they always make to cover this mass murder up and make it look like an accident." Tears appeared in his eyes. "In the conference room in the building for the large group meetings. It's written on the board on the wall that the fumigation would happen on Friday, November 22nd."

"Can you take me to that building?"

"Of course. It's a good idea before these sadistic criminals try to hide the truth. Let's go right now."

We walked optimistically towards the building close to the mess hall. When we entered the room, not only had what he described to me disappeared, but the entire board was covered in red paint. It looked like blood was dripping down the wall. It read *Death to the communist system and its leaders.*

I smiled and said to my cousin, "Typical tactics of the Marxists. Let's get out of here immediately. We're close to being accused to be counterrevolutionaries. They have to produce some victims to be able to justify their crimes, and those victims will be whoever is in this room when they come in."

Tatico looked at me with terrified eyes. "Let's get out of here!"

Before we could leave the room, something like a premonition raised the hairs on the back of my neck, prompting me to open the blinds on one of the windows to see what was going on outside. There was a group of five men walking in our direction. Tatico was walking towards the door, getting ready to leave in his hurry.

I said, "Stop, Cousin! There's a group of people coming this way."

He came back and peered through the blinds, identifying some of the men in the group. One of them was the director of the Farm dressed in a militia uniform. I recognized the man in charge of the Agrarian Reform program. One of them pointed at the room where we currently were located. It looked like they and the three men were looking for someone, as if they knew we were there. One of the other three was the heavy-set General Secretary of the Communist Party for Pinar del Rio; another man who had a massive Pancho Villa mustache was the head of the G-2 in the province. Tatico identified the third one, a man with red hair, as the pilot of the airplane.

Tatico grabbed my right arm in panic. "I'm sorry about bringing you here. I now realize that this is a well-prepared trap to accuse me of being a counter-revolutionary and put me in front of the firing squad. I'm in command of the union now that my father is in the hospital. Of course, the communists want to put their own men inside the union, and they don't want me because they know that I think and feel the same as my father."

As I heard him say that I understood at once that we were both in serious trouble. I ran and double-locked the double doors and secured the hurricane bar across both doors. I turned to Tatico. "Is there any other exit from this room?"

He shook his head. "But I know where we can hide. Don't worry. I know my way around. They won't be able to find us."

"Good! Let's go!"

"Follow me." We rushed until we got to the end of the building and went inside one of the bathrooms.

He pushed a narrow window open. "We could get out this way, but we're only going to pretend that. Let me climb on your shoulders." He pushed the narrow window open.

He went over to a utility closet and pulled an aluminum extension ladder out of it. Extending it to its maximum height, he put it against the wall and pushed one of the panels of the false ceiling over the utility closet to one side. He climbed up to the double ceiling and gestured for me to follow.

Once we were inside the double ceiling, he turned to me and said, "Hold me by my legs." He lay down on his belly as I secured his feet. He pulled up the ladder, collapsing it as he did, and hauled it up with us, replacing the panel afterwards.

He put his index finger to his lips to caution me to silence. We could hear the banging on the door as the men started to break it down. This was definitely meant to be a mousetrap.

A few minutes later, we heard the sound of a grinder cutting away the hinges on the door. Then there was a large boom as the door fell inwards heavily onto the floor.

One of the voices of the men said loudly, "Bandits! Terrorists! Destroyers of the people's property! Better come out—we all have weapons, and we don't want to kill anyone! This is your only warning. Five minutes, and we're coming in!"

A few minutes later we heard them rush inside the building. The same man said, "Bandits!" I realized by his use of the plural that someone must have seen us entering the building and was on alert to tell them if anyone entered, especially Tatico.

One of them entered the bathrooms beneath us. Another voice said, "I think they escaped through this window." I peered down at them through one of the holes in the decorative ceiling and could see every movement. The man was sticking his body half-way through the window, searching around. He said, "I think we missed them."

Another man said, "We took too long."

The Broken Rainbow: Mysterious Dark Karma

The Secretary and the G-2 chief remained in the bathroom to use the urinals as the others left. They opened their flies to do their business. The man with the large mustache caressed his facial hair with his right hand as he urinated. He said to the Secretary, "In confidence, *compañero*."

"Of course."

"I want to make it clear that Che told me that under no circumstance could the Commandantico be hurt. This would be a great fiasco to the image of the revolution that we aren't even capable of protecting our leaders. Also, it would show to our opposition, the counterrevolutionaries, that we are weak and can get hurt. They could even plan more personal attempts against us. That won't be good for any of us."

The Secretary said, "I understand perfectly." He nodded. "Che's plan is only limited to eliminate Juanito's son, so that we can put one of the members of the communist party in his position, someone who won't bring to us any more headaches with this stupid union."

"Of course, that is the objective: eliminating the opposition and the enemies of our Marxist-Leninist doctrine."

Tatico looked at me in panic when he heard that. He put his right hand to his forehead as if he listened to the voice of Satan himself expressing his morbid feelings. He shook his head and clenched his jaw in frustration, biting his lip as he did. He pointed to his ear with his index finger and pointed down to where the men were talking, making sure that I heard what he had.

His assassination was clearly well-planned. I limited myself to shaking my head in frustration as well. The man with the large mustache only confirmed what I had already been thinking. I breathed deeply and slowly, trying to remove that frustration from my chest.

The G-2 chief said, "Well, the only thing I feel sorry for is that you will lose one of your best pilots. Che has promised to Jaime, your pilot, a better job in the capital for the great work he did yesterday in our behalf."

I shook my head. There was no longer a single doubt. From the lips of the head of the G-2 to his associate in crime we heard the details of Che and Fidel's plans to not only assassinate my uncle Juanito but also his successor, Tatico in order to completely destroy their opposition.

Both men finished urinating, washed their hands before the long mirror under two of the many faucets. They dried their hands with paper towels and left the bathroom. We remained in the same positions, squatting on our haunches, in silence without moving a muscle. After we heard that conversation, we both knew that even if they received orders from Che not to harm me, if they discovered us there, in order to save their own skins, they would not stop at killing both of us. There was a chance that they might leave someone there to see if we appeared, so we remained there for over forty-five minutes after no longer hearing any voices.

It took tremendous patience to remain in that position for so long. Tatico said, "Let's very carefully remove the grill over the heat extraction vent. We can lower the ladder through there. At that point, we can go immediately into the tomato fields."

He began to remove the extractor fans and then the grill. We managed to lower the ladder down and escape the mousetrap, hiding the ladder in the bushes growing

The Broken Rainbow: Mysterious Dark Karma

next to the building. We went out into the fields, making a large circle in order to return to where we had left our vehicles. Making sure that no one was around, we agreed that, if for any reason we got stopped, we would say that we were in the tomato fields the entire time because Tatico wanted to show me how splendidly the tomato crop was coming in. The government had classified the produce as first-class A-1 for exportation to other countries.

Tatico said, "Let's not get out yet. Give me a little time."

"What are you going to do?"

"Don't worry—I have a plan. Sit here in the field until I come back and then we'll go to our vehicles. Fifteen or twenty minutes will allow us to justify that we were far from where the vandalism took place."

I sat down for around half an hour on a rock and eating some of the ripe tomatoes. Finally, he showed up with a big smile on his face. I said, "Who laughs by himself is remembering the mischievous things he's done."

We got out and walked towards our vehicles. When I reached my UAZ, I pulled my binoculars out of the glove box and scanned our surroundings. I had heard the engine of a plane on the landing field and saw the chief of the G-2 getting into the aircraft. The Secretary got in afterwards, followed by the chief of the Agrarian Reform Plan. I handed the binoculars to my cousin, who smiled after watching them for a while. We watched the plane take off, shielding our eyes against the sun as we did.

Suddenly, the plane exploded in midair with its diabolic load. Tatico held out his right hand to me, I shook my head, and then his hand. He said, "Divine

Justice. Tooth for tooth, eye for eye." He squeezed my hand so hard that it hurt as he clenched his jaw with a sad expression mixed with profound peace in his face. He released my hand and we both crossed ourselves. He opened his arms, and we exchanged an embrace. Wordlessly, we walked to our respective vehicles and drove off in different directions.

As I drove, I looked at the black clouds covering the space like the approaching storm, followed by the thunder and lightning in different directions that could be the welcome to the entry of those demons in their return to Hell.

The Broken Rainbow: Mysterious Dark Karma

Chapter 22: Meeting the Triple Agent

22 Alicia Alonso

I returned to the city of Pinar del Rio. As I entered, I stopped by the hospital where my uncle Juanito was in intensive care. To my great pleasure and surprise, the many members of the family rushed to give me the news that my uncle had come out of his coma and was awake. Mima said that even the doctor, Sergio Cuervo, called it a real miracle. He was another member of our family, a great surgeon famous for his skill at skin grafts. The youngest brother on my father's side, Francisco, was married to Dr. Cuervo's sister, Holga Cuervo.

I breathed a sigh of relief as that news made me very happy, since I was very close to my family. I realized now also that the doctor in charge of his treatment was a member of the family, and that made me feel lot better. He was no mercenary in the government's service. As I left the hospital, I had a sense of relief knowing that he was in good hands. Before I left, I promised Mima that I would be back in a few days to check on my uncle and take her up on her promise for those fruit tartlets. I got into my UAZ and drove back to the capital, where I found several messages from Uncle Emilio waiting for me at the front desk.

He wanted to invite me that night to the ballet in the Gran Teatro de la Habana. The prima ballerina and choreographer, Alicia Alonzo, was dancing that night in her portrayal of Giselle in the ballet version of *Carmen*. I called my uncle at once. He was unhappy to hear what happened to Juanito, but he was more at ease when I related his current condition.

He said, "Thank God. Was this an accident, or was it another thing as you and I know?"

"It was another thing. I'll debrief you when I see you in person."

"I'll come by around 8 pm. The performance doesn't start until 9."

I knew that he didn't invite me to this just to enjoy ballet. I hung up and said to myself, "What has he got cooking in his brain now?" Every time he had a social invitation like this, as he had said to me repeatedly, his contacts and relations he wanted me to meet were like a sandwich which contained a little bit of everything.

In our double lives as spies, that complexity is extremely essential because we were never completely sure where we would find the most precious information from the most unexpected individual. This information sometimes could destroy the life of someone or the political structure of some country and could land by a fluke in our hands.

As I got in the elevator and went up to my suite, I realized that the floor for the embassy was out of order. It looked like Chandee went over the line just a little bit, miscalculating the damage she would cause. The entire floor was left in ruins.

I arrived at my floor and entered my suite. As I did, I noticed that my tuxedo had been cleaned by the concierge. It was wrapped with a plastic cover with the initials of the hotel: HL. I smiled at the irony—from the Hilton to the Havana Libre.

I showered, though I usually preferred to soak in a bath for a while. I was saving time, and a shower was quicker. As I knew he would, my uncle was very punctual and arrived in the lobby at 8 pm precisely. We exchanged an embrace and walked out to his newly acquired 1960 black Chevrolet Impala with white stripes.

We drove out of the hotel towards the theater. He said, "Don't be surprised, because I know that I broke the protocol a little bit, but I think it will be worth the risk. I'm going to introduce you tonight to someone of tremendous importance because she asked and begged me to meet you. I had some doubts at first, because until today no one ever knew who the Lightning really is. But after I took it into very deep consideration and consulted with Drs. Vallarte and Sayas-Bazan, and we decided that, if you feel comfortable working in corroboration with her, you could do a lot more damage to these communists than working by yourself like you have done until now for the last three years." I grimaced uncertainly. "Why are you making that face? What is wrong?"

"I don't like to change our M.O. or improvise unless it's absolutely necessary. My question for you is what happened so drastically that made you change your methods and techniques so abruptly? You told me from the beginning of my initiation into this business that bringing new people in could be sometimes not only dangerous but many times fatal."

My uncle smiled and raised his right index finger high. "Ah ha! It gives me tremendous pleasure that you remember and bring to my face my contradictions, because this means that you really get it, and you actually are on the ball with your training. I'm really pleased that you question any order that you don't find as making any sense, which is exactly what we've been teaching you and that I am repeating to you right now. In this case, we're making an exception, which every rule has when the circumstances require it. But even though I'm going to give you the logical reason for this exception, you should never stop doing this. Always demand a logical explanation, no matter how high in the intelligence this individual is in terms of position. You deserve an answer to convince you and he has an obligation to satisfy you with logical reasons. If he doesn't do it, you should stop if you have a shadow of a doubt. In some cases, it could be a well-planned trap by our enemies and could cost you your most precious treasure: your life."

The Broken Rainbow: Mysterious Dark Karma

I nodded. "I don't know if you remember, but those exact words you said to me a few years ago when you introduced me to the Gentleman of Paris in Dr. Vallarte's home in Guanabo."

He smiled in satisfaction. "Of course, I remember. Even though I have a few years more than you in life, my memory is still in perfect order. Everyone in our family lacks the gene which causes forgetfulness. We recall the slightest details of everything."

We arrived at the theater. As we got out of the car, he squeezed my right shoulder as he saw Alicia Alonzo signing autographs in the lobby as a promotion. She was giving away some of the tickets for summer season of the next year. He added, "I'll give you more details later." Seeing us, Alicia left her fans behind and the prima ballerina came in our direction with an ear-to-ear smile on her face, both arms open to hug my uncle.

She said in genuine joy—or at least well-pretended, since she was a spy, "You don't know what satisfaction you're giving me, knowing how many responsibilities you have, taking the time to come and see me and our ballet performance."

Emilio kissed her on both cheeks, which she reciprocated. He replied, "How could I deny coming and see you in this beautiful, original production, especially when you displayed such class in your invitation by including wrapped that box of Belgian bon-bons, the best in the world?"

She smiled again. "For our great friends, without exception, we always gift the most exquisite presents with all the love in our heart."

He grinned with pleasure. "Thank you very much, not just for the ballet but also for those multiflavored liqueurs in the bon-bons. It's been a while since I could find such a delicacy in Cuba, but you're always so diligent and have known me for so many years to understand my palate, remembering me in your trips around the world with these beautiful surprises." He moved to one side slightly. "This is my favorite nephew, and the man of the day for his song 'My Sonya' all over the country."

She said to my uncle, "I really like very much that you've brought with you the Prince of Modern Music." She extended her hand, and I took it and kissed it with a slight bow over it. She smiled in satisfaction. "Oh, ho! We have a real gentleman here!"

My uncle smiled proudly. "In our family tradition, chivalry, respect, and admiration for all you beautiful women motivates our lives."

Alicia, moved by my gesture, pulled me into her, and gave me a hug and kiss on my cheek. She said to me, "Oh, you smell so good! I like your cologne very much! Who is providing it to you? I know it's not from Cuba." She was burning with curiosity. Like other products, cologne had disappeared under the communist regime as being unnecessary.

I smiled. "Friends. Good friends. I always say a friend is more powerful than a sugar cane mill."

"Come on. Who is that friend? He must have good taste, because this is French cologne. If it's not too indiscreet."

"It's not at all. The man who brings this to me is the French Ambassador to Cuba. He's very generous and fond of me."

She stepped in and sniffed by my neck. "What is the name of it? I have to buy it for my husband."

"Monsieur Givanchi."

"Oh, Givanchi!" She stepped back and looked at me mischievously. "By fluke or coincidence, that is one of the French colognes which contains masculine hormones to seduce all of us older women through our sense of smell?"

I shook my head dubiously. "I don't know. All I can assure you is that, knowing the French culture which I've studied extensively in books I've read, I wouldn't be surprised if what you just said is true. If there's something the French have pride in and mastered, it is in sex books and culinary recipe books. I can tell you this from personal experience, even though I'm very young. My mother studied high cuisine in the Cordon Bleu in Paris, and she is the one who brought me those books because she wants me to be an educated man."

She looked at me mischievously and smiled seductively with half-closed eyes. "Your mother has brought you cookbooks?"

I smiled and shook my head with my own mischievous look. "No, she not only brought cookbooks, but she brought me both kinds in order to make me a master. She said that the man has to have two things in life to conquer the heart and love of a woman. One of them is a stomach; the other is being a good lover."

She opened her eyes wide in astonishment. "Ah, ha! I see you've been well prepared and educated to do well in life. Almost everything that we do in our lives takes us to the same place through these two things. You have a wonderful mother! The principles of happiness and satisfaction, without being vulgar, are great sex and delicious meals."

My uncle was listening and observing our conversation in silence. He spoke up then with satisfaction in his voice. "Well, I have no doubts in my mind that you two, who have never seen each other before, possess a tremendous affinity in your personalities and characters. I've enjoyed your conversation tremendously. It's been so pleasant to watch you dialogue. For me, I can stand here for hours watching you guys and listening to what you say."

She looked at him gratefully, though a little embarrassed. She blushed a little. "Thank you very much for your words." She looked at me tenderly and smiled. "It's been a great pleasure to meet you in person."

I replied, "The pleasure is mutual. I've had a great time with this short conversation."

The bell of the theater rang, announcing that the performance would begin shortly. Alicia said, "I have to go. It would disappoint people if the prima ballerina didn't show up. Thank you for everything; I'll talk to you gentlemen later."

My uncle breathed deeply as she walked away and shook his head. He put his arm around my shoulders. "I don't know how you manage it or what kind of magic you possess, my nephew, but I can tell you for sure, without any doubt, that you have a magic gift, probably divine. I don't know anyone since the time you arrived in this world, with quite your gift. And the things you did even while you were still and infant turned the heads of everyone in the family, fascinating everyone. I envy your father.

"I'm going to tell you something you might not even know' stop me if you already do. One big dinner on Christmas Day, when we all were together in your house in Guane, when you were only three years old, my brother

The Broken Rainbow: Mysterious Dark Karma

Leonardo was about to serve the suckling pig, since everyone in the family we expected was present. Your favorite uncle, Juanito, had already said he couldn't be with us because his wife was sick. As your Papi picked up that big knife in his hand to cut up the pig, you stood up on your chair and looked over the whole table. Because you were so little, not even learned how to put sentences together, you yelled, 'No, no Papi—one moment. Uncle Juanito isn't here yet!' Before Mima could convince you that he wouldn't be coming, the doorbell rang. She went to answer the door, and you jumped down and followed her, exclaiming, 'I told you, I told you!' You got ahead of her and waited, since you couldn't reach the knob. She opened the door, and to everyone's surprise, she saw Juanito, his wife Coco, and his little boy Tatico. Coco was feeling much better that Christmas morning, so they decided to surprise all of us by bringing their son with them. Everyone was completely mystified how you knew that they were coming and at the door. There was no logic to it, even for me, as a man of science, and everyone simply concluded that you must be a psychic.

"That was one of the first things you did; as you grew up, you did things which showed your extraordinary capability to do things no ordinary person could do. Every single thing you did made your father the Mason rack his brains for a reason why and how he had a son who could do these things. I explained to him that you evidently had an extraordinary psychic, telepathic, or simply divine gift that allowed you to do things we could neither understand nor comprehend. Many of those things you have done right before my eyes, things I never saw any other human being be able to get close to understanding."

We had by now entered the theater. As we sat down, he asked me, "Why are you so quiet?"

I replied, "I've been thinking about what you just told me many times. This is one more that I don't even know—I don't remember anything from that age." I leaned over to whisper in his ear, "But to be honest with you, if its any consolation, I don't understand the things I do or why I'm able to do them with my mind either. I don't know how I can separate my body from my spirit and float around like I'm going to other dimensions while my body is still in one place. I find out sometimes days, months, or years ahead of whatever I see happens, and I confess honestly that these things have confused me a lot. They also terrify me."

He shook his head and took me by the chin to look me in the eyes. He whispered, "Don't allow yourself to ever be intimidated. Whatever divine or psychic gift you have, use it properly, as you've done, to stop the injustice. The Satanic forces will use this to try to confuse and terrify you of yourself in order to weaken you. They know the power you possess within and that it is capable of destroying their work. Your mind and spirit you should keep controlled so that this gift is used for good all through your life."

The lights dimmed to black as the ballet began. I looked at my uncle with a smile of satisfaction and gratitude. I said, "Thank you very much for always being like a second father and giving me psychological courage when I most need it."

We exchanged smiles in the darkness, and he nodded. The orchestra began to play the overture and the ballet began. Spotlights lit the stage as the dancers entered.

The Broken Rainbow: Mysterious Dark Karma

A couple of hours later, the ballet had concluded. As we walked through the hallways, my uncle said, "Alicia is a very trustworthy person. She's worked with me for many years, since her teens. She helped us in our fight to stop the Nazis from taking over on our continent and the Caribbean. But remember our rule: from the very beginning first you can trust, but before we move forward and compromise ourselves, we have the duty to verify whatever anyone proposes to us. If necessary or if you have any doubts, you consult with whoever can assure you that you are on the right track. OK?"

I replied, "You have nothing to worry about. I'm not accustomed to improvising unless the circumstances require it." He nodded and gave me an affectionate pat on my shoulder. I added, "If you don't mind, I'm going to stop in the restroom. I need to discharge my weapon."

He smiled. "Be careful—don't kill somebody. I'll wait for you outside. I don't want to be close to your weapon when you're discharging it."

I smiled. "Very well." We got separated by the crowd as I walked towards the restrooms.

To my surprise, there was a line for the urinals. As I waited in that line, a very young mulatto with straight hair and European features came over to me. He asked, "Are you Julio Antonio del Marmol?"

"Yes. Who wants to know, and what can I do for you?"

He was still dressed in his costume from the ballet, identifying him as a member of the company. He handed me a folded-up slip of paper. "This note has been sent to you by the prima ballerina. She told me to wait for your answer before I bring you to her."

I didn't understand what this was about. I opened it and read it. *I need to speak to you about something of extreme importance, if you can meet tonight. Let me know immediately through Fernando. Please send on the back of the note to me the number of your suite. I know you are staying in the Havana Libre. Write the time and your suite number on the back and I will meet you when you say. Thank you, your friend Alicia Ernestina de la Caridad del Cobre Martinez del Hoyo.*

I took my pen out of my inside tuxedo pocket and wrote a note on the back. I folded the paper to conceal what I had written and handed it to the young ballet dancer who waited next to me. I said to him, "Thank you very much, Fernando. Please tell the prima ballerina because the paper is too small, I cannot express everything I want there. It will be a pleasure to meet with her as well as an honor."

"OK," Fernando replied with a small smile, "I will do that." He gave me a little bow. "Nice to meet the author of that beautiful ballad 'My Sonya.' Everyone here in the capital is talking about it, and I'm sure the rest of the island is as well. Your song has received a lot of love, after so many years of being unable to listen to that modern music here in Cuba. It's really extremely refreshing. We have the pleasure to hear it in our own language in a voice with such romantic tones and modern, manly, romantic beautiful melody. I believe you are also the composer." His mannerisms were just a little too effeminate for my comfort.

"Yes. Thank you very much, Fernando." He was coming out of the closet, and people in the bathroom began to leave as his exaggerated feminine manner disturbed them. I rushed to say goodbye and hurried to a urinal. The bathroom was now empty, and I didn't want his infatuation with my voice and music to cause him to offer me any assistance in my physiological needs.

After I finished with the urinal, I saw the bathroom was now completely empty. I thought it might have been a rush from people wanting to leave the theater to go home; but it could also have been Fernando's flaming mannerisms which had scared every man there who possessed any testosterone. It was, after all, 1963, and any sign of homosexuality in Cuba could result in one facing years in prison the government called a "re-education camp" which the Castro brothers had established as part of their Marxist government. All they needed to validate any accusation was a single witness, who many times fabricated the story. Anyone who found themselves around an openly homosexual man, even a heterosexual, could be described by the government as "the scum of society."

Chapter 23: The Triple Agent's Betrayal

23 The Havana Libre, formerly the Havana Hilton

I left the theater and rejoined my uncle, who dropped me off at the hotel. I went to the bar where I asked for a heated Grand Marnier, which was to me was the best medicine to have sweet dreams and was accustomed to having this before bed. I finished my Grand Marnier and ordered a bottle of chilled champagne with a tray of appetizers of prosciutto with ham and cheese rolls, cranberry Brie cheese puffs, grilled cheese, shrimp and lobster tails with cocktail and tartar sauce on the side, and some pastries to be delivered to my suite. I walked away from the bar, took the elevator, and went to my suite where a few minutes later the bell rang, announcing a waitress with my order.

After the waitress set up the cart with the goodies, I gave her a generous tip, even though that was prohibited in Cuba by now as such gratuities were considered degrading to the service. She hesitated, and I finally convinced her to take it as something which would be between the two of us. She said with a big smile of happiness, "Thank you, sir."

After she left, I opened all the stainless-steel covers, savoring the delicious presentation and odors, and my brain sent a signal to my mouth which made me salivate in anticipation. I didn't feel it was proper to eat before my guest arrived, but I decided that a little taste wouldn't hurt.

I put a small bit of everything on a plate from the cart. I was ready to sit down at the dining table when I heard the doorbell. Assuming it was Alicia, I shook my head slightly in discontent. I hadn't eaten all day, so I was hungry. I took the plate to kitchen, covered it, and put it in the refrigerator; then I walked towards.

I looked through the peephole and saw the smiling face of Alicia waving at me. I opened the door and said, "Good evening, for the second time."

"Good evening," she replied, extending a very beautiful yellow rose. "This is a symbol of lasting friendship and true loyalty."

I took it in my left hand and held it to my nose. "Ooh, this rose has an exquisite aroma of French perfume." I looked at her playfully. "Did you spray this rose with estrogen?"

She laughed, remembering our earlier conversation about my cologne. Her eyes twinkled mischievously as she shook her head. "No, I don't do that sort of thing; I'm a good girl. I wonder how many girls your age would give an eye to be right here in my place and have the opportunity to seduce you."

"Age has never been an impediment for great and wonderful love. Like a flower which exists with many fragrances and colors, it is up to a person's choice for what he or she wants."

Alicia stepped forward to enter the suite. I moved back to allow her in. To my surprise, instead of entering the suite, she put both arms around my neck. She looked into my eyes for a few seconds and then leaned in to give me a tender kiss on the lips. I was surprised; then she parted and stepped back. "I'm sorry for my impulsiveness, but since I saw you in the lobby with your uncle, I have had a tremendous desire to know how those fluffy lips taste. I wanted to find out if I imagined it right."

I smiled. We were both still in the doorway, close to each other and one of her arms still over my shoulder. We were also in full view of any passersby. I asked, "I hope I haven't disappointed."

She smiled and shook her head. "No. On the contrary, the only problem is I want more and have awakened my appetite for continuing even longer. I feel as I got a taste of a delicious delicacy."

I took her by her small, delicate waste and pulled her towards me as I closed the door with my foot. I reached over her shoulder and double-locked the door. I put both my hands on her face and kissed her passionately. Her mysterious and sexual game had managed to turn off my appetite for food and start the flame of a great sexual passion which she injected into my blood now.

As we kissed each other, we walked together towards the bedroom in search of the comfortable bed. She allowed me to lead the way while we took off our clothes, leaving a trail of spontaneous, uncontrollable passion behind us over the carpet.

We reached the bed; by now she only had her translucent bra on, revealing her small breasts, firm and beautiful for her age. They looked more like those of an eighteen-year-old girl with nipples like rose petals. She laid back onto the bed, opened her legs for me to climb on top of her. I kissed her breasts and removed her bra as I kissed her abdomen. We gave each other our bodies and souls in between hyperventilation and sexual moans.

I heard her voice say in extreme pleasure, "Julio Antonio, who taught you to make love so masterfully?" She could not hear my answer because my mouth was busy producing that great pleasure for her. She said again as she released a loud groan, "If you learned this from those French books your mom brought you from France, *vive la France!*"

I smiled and continued my work without interruption until she finally reached a fantastic climax, which she revealed to me later. Amid all that moaning, she grabbed my hair and nearly tore it off my skull, screaming, "Hallelujah! *Vive la France!*"

Afterwards we shared a showered during which she grew excited once more as she began to kiss me from the waist down. We both reclined against the thick glass of the round shower and made love yet again, this time more calmly and romantically. When we finished, I turned off the faucet of the shower and she took my face in both her hands and gave me a tender kiss on my lips, tears rolling down her face this time.

She asked, "Why did you take so long to come into my life? I've been so unhappy."

I gave her another tender kiss. "Just remember, it is never too late to discover your true happiness. Since it's right here with us, let's hold on tight and don't let it go."

She smiled and nodded. She kissed me once more as we left the shower and replied, "You're right. We should hold on to something as beautiful as this for as long as we can. I've never felt this way with anyone, including my husband of so many years."

"Have you already had dinner?"

"No. In the rush to come and see you, I left my dinner for later."

I smiled. "Unbelievable—I did exactly the same thing. I already put a plate for myself together, and if you doubt me, check the refrigerator. I have a little surprise for you in what I ordered. I hope you like it."

We wrapped ourselves in bathrobes and went into the dining room where the food carts awaited. I took the bottle of champagne and a bottle of fresh orange juice from the refrigerator and began to prepare mimosas.

As we sat down, Alicia said, "This is not a dinner. This is a first-class buffet!"

I smiled. "It's a great pleasure for me that you like what I ordered. In the future, I won't have to worry about it at all because we have the same tastes and our palates are perfectly coordinated like a musical harmony, as in our sexual tastes. That's difficult to find in life."

She nodded in agreement. "You're right."

We finished eating and sat down in the living room, taking our glasses of pineapple cordial with us. I put my latest album with "My Sonya" on the record player. The pineapple cordial was a gift from the producer of the radio station in Pinar del Rio, Cadena Occidental de Radio, where my music was playing every Sunday for the entire province. The DJ of this program was Andres Losano, who was grateful to me because whenever I made any new record, I brought him the masters so he could play it before any other radio station. I remembered that he was the first one to play my music, and considered it a duty to let the people of the province of my birth hear my music before anyone else on the island.

Alicia looked me deeply in the eyes. "You are a very talented young man. I'm very proud of you. Don't ever give up your dreams and continue with your music. You're a great composer and a good singer."

"Thank you. You are a great ballerina, and I hope I get close to being as known as you are all over the world."

She put her hand out to me, I took it and kissed it. "Thank you." She grabbed my hand before I could release hers. "Can I trust you completely?"

"Of course. If there's anything I describe myself as is being loyal to my friends and family.:

She grinned. "Well, I hope I qualify to be on that list." She grew serious then. "I'm not referring to our work because your uncle and everyone surrounding you have a great respect for you and admire your integrity and dedication for our cause to return freedom to our beautiful Cuba. This is a personal matter. Whatever I'm going to ask you for, I don't want anyone to have knowledge of it, not even your Uncle Emilio." Her expression of disgust. "I know what I'm asking is very difficult for you because he is your closest relation."

I raised the index finger of my right hand. "My relation to my uncle is irrelevant; also, it's completely unbreakable. But as always it all depends on what you're going to ask me for or what you're going to entrust me with. If it's not in conflict with anything regarding my uncle, I don't see any reason to communicate to him anything that happens between you and I here tonight. For example, and to be more explicit, you and I have had a great sexual experience, something that is absolutely private between you and I—unless, for whatever reason, you wish to communicate it to anyone, including my uncle. I cannot control that. I have nothing to hide, but I also have no need to publish in the newspaper what I do in my private life." I spoke with great conviction. "For me, there are certain things in life which belong to two people only in complete confidence. I don't see any necessity for anyone else to know about this, especially in your position as a married woman as well as a public figure."

She smiled. "You don't have to worry about that at all. I know you are very young, but you are a gentleman. This is part of your personality, which is what attracts me." She stroked her chin with her fingers with a small smile.

"My husband and I have a private understanding and intimate rules. Each of us, with discretion, can manage our lives and relations with others in the way we consider best for ourselves to produce happiness. We have no social restrictions which only pave the way to divorce and break up the nuclear family."

I nodded. "You're right, especially now under this communist system where so many people are confused by the propaganda and misinformation of the Marxist-Leninist ideology."

She nodded this time. "What I want to entrust you with, even though it's related with our daily clandestine fight, is more personal. Should this by any chance come into the public eye, not only will it blow my cover that I've maintained for so many years, but it might cost me my life as well as those of my family's. I cannot ever afford exposing my double life for any reason." She smirked ruefully. "Whatever you hear now, if at any moment you consider it to be in conflict with what you want to know, please raise one of your arms high and I will stop speaking immediately."

"OK," I replied. "No problem."

"Very well. I love the way you communicate—very clean and very clear. Well, the matter is one of my confidants among the dancers in the ballet is in jail with the G-2. His name is Nicholas Perez. They've accused him of illegal contraband and international espionage." She shook her head. "Of course, the charges are false without foundation and exaggerated out of proportion. They want to intimidate Nicholas, and I'm convinced that Commander Piñeiro and his G-2 are trying to involve me in all this crap. They know that Nicholas is my assistant and confidant. If they manage to turn him against me through that intimidation of executing him in the firing squad, then Piñeiro will get his brownie points for merits and honors that you know the revolution gives to anyone who produces such a high-level prey. Fidel and the rest of the bunch of hypocrites are always looking to devour somebody involved in the revolutionary process like I've been for so many years."

I raised my hand and asked, "Where have they detained him and what type of contraband did they find in his possession?"

She breathed a deep sigh of relief since it appeared I didn't want to be involved at first. She said with a small smile, "They arrested him in Jose Martí Airport. The contraband was twelve ampoules of Botox. It was just $10 per unit, but they found it in a false bottom of his suitcase. This they interpreted as him smuggling illicit drugs into this country. Of course, the fact that he hid it multiplied the charges."

I could not hold it in and laughed with a shocked expression. "Where did these G-2 'scientists' invent that this cosmetic is an illicit drug? At the same time, you, I, and everyone in this country knows that this government is the major client of the Colombian cartel and biggest importer and exporter of cocaine around the world."

Alicia smiled and nodded. "Remember, the flavor lingering from the communists is that you do to the letter what they tell you to do, but you should never do what they do because that could cost you your head, very similar to the Roman Empire. The worst of the whole thing is that I cannot admit that these injections are for me. According to my attorneys, this would make the situation worse and tremendously complicate their efforts in getting him out, not including getting myself into trouble for nothing. According to the new communist laws, drugs like the cocaine you just mentioned are brought from Colombia to be sold to all the tourists in the hotels by the G-2 agents in order to make more dollars for these bandits. And then the tourists sell it at double the price to our youth or give it to them in exchange for sex. But if you bring any medication, including aspirin, in your bags upon your return to Cuba, they consider those illicit drugs and hand out sentences of ten years in jail."

I shook my head. "Where do they have your friend Nicolas Perez?"

She looked at me sadly. "In Villa Marista."

"Unfortunately, this is part of the beauty of the socialist regime. What can I do for you? You, as a woman, maybe, have more influence and power through your fame as a prima ballerina and director of the National Ballet of Cuba through Fidel and his brother, more even than I or anyone in this country."

She shook her head and clucked her tongue. "That's what it looks like, but not everything is as it appears."

I said in surprise, "Really?"

"Yes," she said guiltily. "Maybe it's all my fault." She took a little sip of the cordial. "The last time Fidel came to visit us during our rehearsals in the theater, he brought once more his demands of how and who should be playing which role and how the scenery should be in a very coercive attitude. One of the things he told me was that I had to consider the expenses and sacrifice the Cuban people make to maintain that national ballet in proper function. He had the audacity to tell me that the expenses in the choreography had been too high lately.

She took her fingers of her left hand to her forehead and massaged it. "Unfortunately, he caught me on the wrong day. He's done this many times, and I blew my fuse this time. I told him to remember of the hundreds of thousands of dollars we produced for the people of Cuba during our tours around the world with my dancers. If I didn't remember wrong, my dancers were very underpaid compared to the standards of the rest of the world in terms of salaries. This was not taking into consideration that they were being paid in Cuba pesos, which you know as well as I do don't pay for their food and clothing. They couldn't even afford to buy the right colored threads to sew their tutus, which are outdated, from 1950, that we are using in our country."

I again could not hold it in and laughed. It was not a matter for laughing to her, but her face was absolutely red and the veins in her neck were standing out and throbbing. I loudly said, "Ho, ho, ho! Now I can explain perfectly where your problems are coming from." I shook my right hand high and shook my head. "I know Fidel Castro like the palm of my hand. I can assure you that your friend and confidant Nicholas is in jail on all these outrageously fabricated charges on Castro's order. Commander Piñeiro is Castro's loyal dog and doesn't move a single finger without consulting Fidel first. All this is nothing more than the product of that Machiavellian, conniving cannibal of society, Fidel Castro. It cannot come from anyone else. He's sending you a message of intimidation and terror to bring you to your knees. How dare you confront him like that? Remember, he's a king, and this is his dominion. I can bet you anything you want that after your argument with him, Fidel never came back to your theater."

She nodded in affirmation. "There it goes!" I exclaimed. "This egotistical, maniacal schizophrenic who adores himself like a perfect narcissist won't tolerate critics or ideas which go against his opinions. Whoever dares to do so with courage and reasons, like you did, has to be humiliated unnecessarily and punished to an extreme."

She looked at me, her face enraged. Tears of anger stood in her eyes. She rushed to wipe them away with the back of her hand and shook her head. "How is it possible, Julio Antonio, for us all to be so wrong about this man?" She vigorously shook her head now, adding, "Out of the crucified Christ in the pictures they sold us at the beginning of the revolution in 1959 to the poisonous Satan without scruples to now in the '60s that now we have to live with."

I bent over and refilled her glass. "Remember, Satan never shows his true face, just like the communists. They come like thieves in the night with false promises of happiness and prosperity and deceive everyone by dressing like sheep. Then, after they rip your freedoms away and take power, that is when they show the horns.

"But I don't think you have much to worry about, to be honest with you," I added to try to reassure her a little. "Eventually this rage Fidel has against you right now will go away and he probably will order Piñeiro to release your friend Nicholas. I believe now at this moment when things haven't been going well for them, the last thing they'll want is for you in your frustration to leave the country and go into exile permanently. You could imagine what that would represent to the Cuban exiles in Miami and the rest of the world. It would become a tremendous slap to his ego. I cannot share with you what I know, but I don't think he's ready to take another punch right now."

Alicia half smiled and shook her head. "Unfortunately, I'm not telling you my biggest worry which hasn't let me sleep since the moment Nicholas was arrested." She took a deep breath to muster the strength for what she had to say next. She caressed her forehead again with her left hand. "Nicholas has in his possession, in his body, something extremely valuable, not just for all of us in intelligence but for me personally. That is why I need to get him out of Villa Marista as soon as possible, even if we have to kill a few people and put him in a boat to go into exile. If the G-2 discover what I'm talking about, not only will it put him in front of the firing squad but also a large number of our allies."

I asked, "Do you have a plan in mind to get your friend out of Villa Marista? From what I saw on my very few visits to that macabre place, they have an extremely high security system, practically impenetrable. They made it equal to the Gestapo headquarters in Berlin under Hitler's Nazi control of Germany that in order to protect them against retaliation by the general population; it is very similar to what the G-2 has created in our capital of Havana."

She smiled and took a small sip of the cordial glass. "No, I don't have a plan at all in mind. According to my information I obtained from the Gentleman of Paris, what you did with the uncle of one of your best friends, Yaneba, is absolutely amazing. You saved him from the firing squad only a few hours before his execution[27]. This story gave me tremendous hope in addition to the many other

---

[27] The full account of which is in *Montauk: The Lightning Chance* and *The Lightning and Montauk: Reality vs. Fiction*.

The Broken Rainbow: Mysterious Dark Karma

things I've heard about you and motivated me to speak to your Uncle Emilio at once to introduce me formally to you. I hope in my heart that you will be the right person to help us in resolving this huge problem."

I looked at her very seriously deep into her eyes, trying to reach her mind as I swirled the liqueur in my glass I held in my right hand. "This obviously is the principal reason that you came to see me so urgently tonight."

She looked straight into my eyes with a steady gaze. "Yes. To be honest with you, this happened before I got to know you in person and established such an interesting dialogue in the lobby of the Gran Teatro tonight."

I nodded. "Our encounter and conversation made you change your initial plans?"

Alicia hadn't broken my gaze, gauging my reactions. "No. It made me change my mental image of you; it also made me change a lot after I spoke with you—something started in my daily work in espionage now has changed into something a lot more personal and pleasant. Maybe my internal desire to get closer to you and know you better and a great challenge to be able to work with you."

"If you keep flattering me my head is going to burst like a water balloon."

She smiled. "No, I'm just being fair and honest with you. Of course, that's if you accept me into your circle. I believe that whatever I can say about you is little; I also believe that we can learn from each other. At the same time, we can create an indestructible force and be unstoppable by our enemies."

I looked at her straight in the eyes again, just as she had a few seconds before. It looked like we were drilling into each other's brains to see what was really going on there. "This is extremely strange," I said. "What I feel now I never experienced before. And like you, probably, I'm accustomed to following my instincts. So far, I have a good reading about you. I hope I'm not cheating myself, but I'm willing to take a chance and unite our forces, not just because you've been highly recommended by my uncle. I will put all my expertise to resolve your problem and try to save your friend Nicholas' life, and for that I'm going to give you your first mission."

"Whatever you need."

"Very well. The most important thing between us is to be in perfect coordination in whatever we do, without egotism, to try to achieve our goals. The only to do that, I've developed a plan which might be effective. But first, we need the schematics of the original building of Villa Marista from the bottom ground of its construction. I know you have a very good and great personal relation with the bishop here in the capital. I know that this building was originally built as a school run by the Marist Brothers. To execute a rescue of your friend Nicholas from that horrible place we need the schematics."

"I see that your mind works fast and gives good credit to your secret code in intelligence: the Lightning."

I looked into her face with a surprised, innocent expression. "I don't know what you're talking about or referring to. But I'm going to tell you something I learned from my old friend, the great writer Ernest Hemingway. Never admit to anyone anything that could be detrimental to your business or your personal life. In the first place, you don't have any idea whether or not that person pursues it in order to find out something that could be derogatory and detrimental to you. The second thing and worst is that you never know who is listening to your conversation behind the walls. Why incriminate yourself over something that is no one's business?"

Alicia nodded. "I'm sorry. Very savvy advice from your friend Hemingway. Very stupid and unnecessary remarks on my part."

I smiled. "Don't worry about it. You have nothing to apologize for. Your comments, I know, were innocent and spontaneous. At least, I want to believe so."

She looked at me in surprise. "Thank you for your maturity, class, and great understanding. Yes, it is as you just said—why would I say it in any other way. I didn't know you are a good friend of Ernest Hemingway. I knew that there was a great friendship between him and Fidel, Che, and the other leaders of the revolution."

I smirked sarcastically. "I can assure you that with friends like that, you don't need enemies. I believe that I don't even need to say that, since you already have experimented with that."

She nodded again in agreement. She made a sour face. "Yes, you're right—very close and very hurtful. Do you know if it's true what the newspapers say about your friend Hemingway committing suicide? Or is the other version from his wife that it was just an accident when he was cleaning his hunting rifle the truth?"

I shook my head and clicked my tongue. "I can assure you that neither of those versions are true. The first version is promulgated in the North American press through the paid propaganda from the G-2 as a coverup of a horrendous crime that was committed in retaliation for Hemingway's supposed betrayal of their cause. The second one created by his wife, probably full of love and devastated at losing the man she spent half of her life with and trying to publicly cover the image of the man she loved."

Alicia looked at me, her eyes bulging in terror. "What? Are you sure of what you're saying?"

"I don't say anything. What did I say?" I shook my head and looked into her eyes. "You repeat once more an incriminatory question."

She raised her right hand high over her head and shook her head as she bit her lower lip. "I'm sorry. I'm sorry. I didn't' intend to repeat the same mistake twice."

I smiled. "Don't worry about it. This time, I'm not going to incriminate myself. I'm going to repeat Che Guevara's words. If I said this to his face he couldn't deny it, so I'm not incriminating myself. He told me that what happened to Mr. Ernest Hemingway will happen to everyone who follows along his path by betraying the Marxist-Leninist cause, because the arm of revenge by them is a really long one which is not limited by countries or frontiers. Wherever these traitors go, they'll pay for their betrayal with their lives."

She couldn't control herself and clapped her hand to her mouth in utter shock. She might have been thinking that she could have the same ending as Hemingway at that moment if she were discovered and exposed as a traitor to the communist revolution. I observed her mentally disturbed state and said with confidence, "I don't think you have anything to worry about. Maintain your calm. All what Che was saying was only propaganda, and you should never allow fear or terror to dominate you. This is precisely what they're looking for."

The Broken Rainbow: Mysterious Dark Karma

I saw her hand which held the cordial glass was still trembling as she put the glass down. I got up and walked over to her to put my right hand on her shoulder. "Calm down. You give yourself away very easily. Learn to control yourself. If you were in front of one of these people, you would blow your cover completely. I don't know how you've survived in this business for so long—or are you just pretending? In that case, you're a master."

She looked at me slightly offended. "Why did you say that? Why do I have to pretend to you?"

I said with conviction, "Remember, we have to trust everyone but verify. Sometimes a simple conversation can give you the reading of what that person really has hidden in his or her mind. I will tell you something: I never promise anything to anyone, because the only promise you never break is the one you don't make. I don't like to say something and to not be able to deliver it, even though sometimes it's not up to us but to the circumstances. I can assure you that if you put into my hands the plans of the construction of that building, I will do my best to get your confidant and friend out of that place. You can go to sleep in peace."

With a look in her eyes and face of gratitude, she grabbed my hand after she put her glass on the little table beside her chair. She stood up and put both her arms over my shoulders and gave me a big kiss of thankfulness on my lips that turned into a passionate one.

After we separated, she said, "I'm going to retrieve my clothing from your room. Thank you for everything, but I believe if we're going to do all of this

I need to move fast. The faster I bring it to you, the faster you can put your plan into motion."

She left the living room to go into the bedroom. When she returned a few minutes later she was completely dressed, with her handbag slung over her shoulder. We kissed each other again and I walked her to the door.

She said, "I'll be in touch with you as soon as I get the plans you need."

"I'll be waiting for your call." I stayed in the door, watching her thin but beautiful feminine figure disappear towards the elevators in the hallway.

The Broken Rainbow: Mysterious Dark Karma

Chapter 24: Dangerous and Sophisticated Ballerina

24 My Room in the Former Hilton

Before I closed the door, I looked at both sides of the corridor. I had been feeling uneasy in my guts, as if something wasn't right after she left and during our conversation in the living room. I closed it and double locked the door.

I felt the old danger sensation as my neck hairs raised. It was like someone was watching me while I spoke with Alicia saying goodbye at the door. Applying logic, I discredited the feeling. I looked around the hallway several times and assured myself that the other doors of the other suites were closed. I decided it must have been a false alarm, which had never happened before. But there was a first time for everything.

At that moment, the telephone rang. I went to the bar to answer it at that phone. "Hello?"

An unfamiliar voice, possibly disguised so it wouldn't be recognized, said, "Open your eyes, because many eyes and ears have been observing you."

"Hello, who is this? Who are you?"

But the sound of the cut line was heard as he hung up. I tried to reconnect, but I received now a busy signal. After receiving that strange message, I looked at the walls in puzzlement. I saw a glint of reflection inside the grill for the air conditioning. I looked inside and saw nothing, so I dragged one of the bar stools over. I stepped up and saw that small reflection again as I moved from one side to the other.

I pulled a toothpick out of my pocket and inserted it between the grill and fished out a very thin wire. I pulled on it, and it kept coming until I found one end which had a small microphone and another a tiny camera lens. I yanked it out and broke the connection before closely examining it. I realized it was both camera and microphone attached to all those cables. I wondered at once that if someone had been able to put this in the living room, where else could it have been done?

I swept the entire suite and found sixteen devices, hidden at different angles in the false ceiling and realized that they were not there before. It must have been installed that same day because there was dust on the carpet beneath most of the locations from where they had been drilling. I had never felt until this day that someone had been watching me.

From that day on, I never doubted once that psychic signal in my brain again. It had protected me in time from that imminent danger. I dressed and prepared to immediately communicate this to my uncle. I put every device into a plastic bag and shoved the bag into one of my pockets. I dressed elegantly and put a raincoat on. The phone rang again just as I was about to leave the suite. I hesitated about answering but decided to do so in case it was a repetition of that anonymous caller.

I picked up the receiver by the bar. "Hello? Listen, if you don't identify yourself, I don't want to hear anything more. Hello?"

Alicia's voice said, "Julio Antonio, it's me, Alicia. Is everything OK?" I could hear the concern in her voice.

"I'm sorry, yes, everything is OK. Something of not much importance. What can I do for you? Have you got everything done?"

"Meet me at the Fox and the Crow in one hour. At this moment, I'm driving with the bishop to retrieve the package you need in the place where they archive all the documents. He assures me that we will find what we're looking for there."

I smiled. "Very well. A strange coincidence, this particular night club is the location of my final meeting to say goodbye to Ernest Hemingway."

"Do you want to change the location?"

"No, no—I'm just making an unimportant remark to you as I was speaking to myself. I want to share it with you. I have a great memory of that last meeting with the old wolf of the sea."

"Very well. It's about 11:30 pm. Let's synchronize our watches. I'll see you in the club at 12:30 am."

"Very well." We said goodbye and after I hung up the phone I left my suite, took one of the elevators down to the lobby, and went through the lobby to the telephone cabinets near the restrooms. I entered one of the glass cabinets and called my uncle in Miramar, checking my watch impatiently.

Even though I had called him late in the night several times, I didn't like calling after hours. He repeatedly had told me that, in an emergency, it was never too late or too early. Emergencies in the business of espionage like food and the stomach—when the stomach calls with hunger, it has no clock. It rang for a while until my uncle finally picked up.

"It's Julio Antonio. I'm sorry to call so late, but I have a very acute abdominal pain and the area is kind of swollen. I'm a little worried." This was of course a code to identify an extreme emergency.

He immediately woke up like the experienced master spy he was and replied, "Come over immediately. I need to examine you. Don't take any kind of fluid, even water."

"OK, I'll leave immediately. I'll see you in a little while."

I drove from the hotel to Miramar. I parked my UAZ upon arrival and walked across the sand on the beach towards the umbrellas where we usually sat to discuss our business. He was already there, waiting for me, wrapped in a thick, long black winter coat with a black and white scarf. Two steaming cups of coco sat on the table on that very cold night of November 20th, two days before the assassination of John F. Kennedy. The winds from the north blew spray from the gigantic waves over the umbrellas we sat under. The moon was waxing crescent in the cloudy sky, like a fatal premonition that something morbid and extraordinary was about to occur. Something that would shake the entire world and change the course of history, something that was utterly unavoidable.

We exchanged greetings and I sat down under the beautiful white canvas umbrella. I pulled the plastic bag with my discoveries out of my pocket and handed it to my uncle. "I have to break the wishes of Alicia in showing this. She didn't want me to share with anyone, including you, anything she just told me a few hours ago. But my priority and loyalty are to you. Even though I don't have to share details of my personal and sexual relationships, which I consider private, with you or anyone else as a gentleman first and a discrete man secondly. But through the circumstances which just occurred, the signals I received from Alicia, which were very strange, and the success which has occurred in following up her meeting, I believe that I need to put into your knowledge without the luxury of details all that occurred and how uncomfortable I feel now with what transpired in the past few hours after you dropped me at the hotel after the ballet.

"I believe I have several questions to ask you about Alicia Alonso. The only reason I met with her is because you guaranteed me that she was absolutely trustworthy. If I have to be honest with you, my uncle, I'm completely surprised. Until today, no matter the numerous animosities which exist between Commander Piñeiro, his dogs, and his multiple attempts to discredit me with Fidel, Che, Raul, and the others, this is the first time that he completely crossed the red line and ordered his men to put cameras, bugs, and recorders in my personal suite. Especially tonight when I met with Alicia—the same night that Alicia tried to convince me that she needed my help urgently with something that looks like of such great value that she considered it life or death for her and all her family. That sounds extremely dramatic and put a heavy pressure on my shoulders."

My uncle stopped me with an expression of consternation. "Whoa! What is going on here?"

I smiled. "That is exactly what I want to know."

He leaned forward uncomfortably, very tensely. He pointed at me. "You want to tell me that she asked you for help and also asked you to not share it with me?"

I nodded. "That's right. Exactly how you heard it."

He put his left-hand fingers and massaged his forehead, his signal of profound worry. He grimaced. "Well, my nephew, until today I never asked you to share anything of your relationships and private life, much less sexual encounters with anyone, but now the circumstances just changed dramatically. I have to demand from you, forget about your gentlemanly manners and remove your principals, ethics, and everything, and tell me in every single detail what transpired between you and Alicia. I don't want to alarm you, but I believe, if I'm not wrong, that you could be in extreme danger.

He reached across the table, grabbed my arm firmly, and shook it as if trying to wake me up. "Knowing you as I do, this will be very difficult and embarrassing for you, but in the game we're playing, if it involves the life of somebody, especially someone I love with all my heart like you, we need to forget our more delicate feelings. This could be a very high price for someone to pay. We have to put our heads together and figure out our next move in this perhaps final, fatal game of chess that Alicia has initiated with you."

I nodded. For a good half hour, I told my uncle, omitting not even the slightest detail, beginning with our encounter in the restroom in the theater lobby with Fernando and the interesting note she sent me demanding that I write my answer to her on the back of the note. My uncle said that indicated she wanted the note back so that I would have no proof of what she had sent me. When he brought that to my attention, he explained to me that it could have another purpose—it could be a very elaborate trap to put me before the firing squad for high treason against the revolutionary Marxist-Leninist government.

He concluded, "You will be executed in the name of the people for the people, according to their propaganda." We finished exchanging ideas and his debriefing me of what my next step was to be. He said, "I want you to remember something extremely important. Never forget, I never, never will reveal to anyone your secret code. What you just told me they will want to verify from your own lips to admit to it, including the closest collaborators we have, because they must assume you are that identity. But I have never told them who you are; I sign my own reports to the US Navy Base with that code. The Lightning could be any of us or none of us. That is what has kept you alive all these years.

He added with emphasis, "Only you and I know that secret, and no one else should ever know it. We will continue to keep it that way. Now go to your meeting with Alicia with extreme caution, follow my instructions to the letter, until I can clarify what kind of game Alicia is playing. Everything looks like and indicates that she, unfortunately, has sold her soul to the Devil and crossed the line by converting herself into a very dangerous double agent. That is, if she hasn't always been a double agent that we never detected. If so, you in one single night, Nephew Lightning, have blown her cover. I don't' want to assume anything or rush to any unfounded conclusion until we can convince ourselves. We will prepare for her a remedy from her own medicine cabinet. This will be something she will never expect, and when she drinks it, she'll get diarrhea symptoms that will last for many years.

He smiled in satisfaction as he stood up. He came and put one of his hands on my shoulder. "Thank you for your loyalty and confidence in me. I want you to remember something: you are in fact my nephew, but you are also the son I never had and always wished to have. My daughter is a great gift from God, and I appreciate her very much, you are the best and most gratifying pride that any father could wish to have.

He walked a few steps towards the ocean, opened his fly, and began to urinate. A few seconds later, he returned to the table and said with a mischievous smile, "My little friend is not very fond of the winter and these low November temperatures. It's hard work to get him out of his shell. It was like trying to get the head of the turtle out of its shell when it's in panic."

We both laughed at his comparison. We exchanged a few more remarks for a little while as he reinforced the details of the plan he wanted me to follow to test Alicia's real intentions. I looked at my wristwatch and saw that the time for our meeting was close, so I gave my uncle a big hug and thanked him for his savvy advice, said goodbye, and left the Nautico towards the Fox and the Crow and the meeting with my new enigma, Alicia Alonso.

As I drew close to the club, I realized I didn't have one of my pens to record pictures and videos and checked my watch to see if I had time to swing by the hotel to pick up one of them from the box I had in the safe. I wanted to have proof of any conversation we had from now on. As I stopped in the valet where I usually parked, the chief valet saw me, waving to me in greeting from the valet desk. When I saw him walking towards me, I was surprised, since I never gave them the keys.

When he got close, my surprise grew greater when he whispered to me, "I have something extremely important to tell you. Let's walk away to a distance where no one can read our lips."

As we walked, he repeated the same words the mysterious telephone caller had said. "Open your eyes. Many eyes and ears are observing you."

I looked at him in my greatest surprise, now recognizing his voice. Without saying a single word I walked with him to the other side of the parking lot by the left corner of the building next to a thick column. Jimmy, the tall Brazilian man with a thick Western mustache, a man I had known for a long time, said with concern in his voice, "I'm the one who made that call to try and warn you because I saw the men from the G-2 arrive here earlier this evening after you left. I followed them with their typical large bags of surveillance equipment. This is not the first time they've done this, and I know what those bags contain. It surprised me when I followed them and saw them enter your suite. I know, and everyone here knows that you're working with the leaders of this government."

I asked, "What is your motivation to take the risk of calling me and warning me about this?" I put my hand in my pocket to give him a generous tip.

He stopped me with a big smile. "I work with the Wildflower Group—our leader is the Gentleman of Paris. You don't have to give me any money. We're protecting you here. But if you want to give a tip to anyone, give it to my boys over there. Please be careful, and don't mention this to anyone. I know that you are a great man with a good heart, and without any doubt a great patriot. Everyone here in Cuba that knows who you really are look at you in admiration and respect. But remember, again, this conversation never took place."

I smiled. "What conversation?"

We said goodbye and I pulled out two $100, put them in his front pocket, and walked away before he could stop me. I whispered in his ear, "This is just a decoy, in case somebody sees us talking for so long to not compromise either of us."

I went up to my suite, grabbed one of the pens, and walked back to the elevators. A while later, I left with my pen ready to record and use it for whatever I need in case it was necessary. I returned to the lobby, took my UAZ and drove towards the meeting with Alicia in the Fox and the Crow.

The Broken Rainbow: Mysterious Dark Karma

Chapter 25: Dead Crow, Smart Fox

25 The Fox and the Crow

When I got near the club, I decided to park in the street a half block away, just in case I encountered any kind of hostility in that place. After all, I hadn't selected it; Alicia had. Besides, I wanted to be sure of having my exit covered in case of emergency and they wouldn't know what kind of vehicle I was driving.

I locked the UAZ, walked along the street on the sidewalk, and arrived at the entrance to the nightclub. As I walked in the main door, I saw Alicia through the dancing crowd sitting at a table against the wall, nearly in the corner, strategically situated in a shadowy area. She recognized me at once, which told me she was not only alert and expecting me but also proved to have great skills. She gestured for me to come over with her right hand.

I slowly, casually, walked over to her, not because of the crowd but to use it as an excuse to scan the entire perimeter. Between the forms and faces at the different tables drinking and apparently having a good time I continued to explore my surroundings, table by table, completely alert. I looked at each face I passed, looking for a signal in each man or woman that they weren't genuinely were enjoying the music or were merely pretending. There's a big difference between those there to have a good time versus those who were actually working, waiting for a signal to act on some orders.

Because of my special training, it was very easy to determine the difference. In only a few seconds I could make eye contact directly with the subjects and read their facial reactions. It could be life or death to detect such danger, like predator waiting for its prey. For me, it was enough either to prepare a very good counterattack or an opportune, intelligent retreat if it became necessary and the circumstances required it. As I walked to her table, I saw she was there with Fernando.

I leaned over and whispered in her ear firmly and urgently, "Please stand up and follow me to the women's bathroom. Something extremely important just happened, and I need to speak with you in private immediately."

Alicia nodded and stood up as I stepped away. She turned to Fernando and said, "I'll be back in a little while."

Fernando waved at me with a small smile, and I walked to the bathroom, followed by Alicia through the crowd. The congestion made our progress slow, but we finally arrived there. Before we entered the bathroom, I spotted one of the men seated at a table on the other side of the dance floor, surrounded by several other men. That was the first signal which attracted my attention to him. As I walked towards that table, the man I made eye contact with glanced at another table across the way, as if consulting with them what to do. I glanced in that direction and noticed that table had three men.

Neither group seemed interested in the music, much less the people dancing. They were concentrating more on our movements. We apparently took them by surprise, as they weren't expecting me to take Alicia immediately somewhere, and they had no idea if we were going to the bathroom or leaving, as the bathrooms were near the exit to the club.

I took advantage of their confusion and smiled a little as I turned one of the corners into a side passage off the dance floor by the bathrooms and club exit. We went down the side passage so that they would be in doubt as to whether we left or entered one of the bathrooms. As we turned, I took Alicia by the arm as soon as we were out of sight of the men, forcing her to come into the ladies' room with me.

As soon as we inside, I opened one of the stalls and brought her inside with me. I closed and locked the door, and then shoved her against it firmly with both hands around her throat. She said, "What are you doing? Have you gone crazy?" She was genuinely scared and surprised; but if she was a highly trained double spy, it could be feigned. "What happened for you to treat me this way?"

I released one hand from around her neck and motioned for silence. We heard the door of the bathroom open and close, but no one walked inside. I took her by the neck again shoved her down onto the toilet. I whispered in her ear, "Who are these men who have been following you and watching your back here in the club?"

As I expected, Alicia looked surprised. "I don't know who you're talking about or who you're referring to."

I furrowed my brows in anger. I made a fist with one hand and pulled back as if to punch her while I squeezed her neck with my free hand. I had no intention of striking her; I was simply intimidating her as a test which she failed to pass. As I expected again, she blew her cover and reacted violently to the offered threat.

As she raised her right hand and tried to scratch my face and eyes with her long fingernails, even as she kneed me in the groin with her right knee. The attack launched with her nails towards my face and eyes I easily blocked with the sleeve of my tuxedo. As for her groin strike, little did she know that I was expecting that attack and was prepared for it. I wore a special support over my testicles provided to me by intelligence. Not only did it protect me, but this support was designed to which produced deep and painful wound over the knee of the attacker. The device was something much like corkboard with three very sharp spring-loaded nails behind it. Any violent impact would trigger the springs, which would then retract back and reset in case of further attacks.

Alicia screamed in pain, something I tried to control by putting one of my hands over her mouth. She looked at me in shock and looked down at the profuse bleeding from her knee. She looked at the crotch of my pants as she wondered what I had beneath them.

I whispered in her ear, "If you try to hurt me again, the only one who will be injured is you, and next time it will be severe, as you can see now." I wound some toilet paper around my fingers and handed it to her to clean her bleeding knee. "Remain silent if you want to leave this place alive with me tonight."

She looked at me hesitantly but took the toilet paper and began to clean the blood that now dripped onto the floor and then into the toilet after she sat down. She noticed the slight holes in the pants of my tuxedo left by the stainless-steel nails.

Once she cleaned her still-bleeding knee, she dropped the toilet paper into the toilet bowl and I flushed it. I looked at her resentfully with an angered face. I pushed her back down on the toilet and leaned towards her, putting my face close to hers. "I know you've been lying to me from the very minute we met in person. All I did was follow your lead to see what you were all about and to see how long you could maintain your hypocrisy. I know you're playing a very conniving role in a communist theatrical trap.

She looked at me remorsefully. She denied not a word I had spoken and lowered her head in shame. I took her face in my left hand and forced her to look up at me. "You don't know me at all. You don't even have an idea that I come from a line of noble warriors. My blood has been shed for generations. I never,

never hit a woman. It doesn't make any difference how bad and degenerate and conniving that woman can be. If you knew this before, you would also have known when I raised my fist to you that I would never have intended to hit you. I was only trying to scare you.

"I never want to hurt anyone, but you on the contrary have been conniving and deceiving me, and all you've told me is nothing more than lies, probably with the intention of destroying me. You might not believe it, but even now, I'm trying to help you and find out why you've descended so low to create all these stories about your friend Nicholas. I wonder if there's any part of you which exists inside that head still: the Alicia who fought to stop the atrocities of the Nazis with my uncle, the Alicia who risked her life as a patriot from 1933-1938 when you began your work as part of the intelligence community. Where is that Alicia Ernestina de la Caridad del Cobre Martinez del Hoyo? Where is the honor and nobility of that woman? Or is she dead already?"

Two tears rolled down her cheeks. We heard the door open and the voice of man call out, "Alicia, are you hear?"

Moving so quickly I had no chance to stop her, she gestured for me to climb on top of her and perch on the back of the toilet. She pulled down her underwear around her ankles. She called out, "Yes, I'm here. What's the matter? What happened? Can't I even go to the bathroom in peace?"

"I'm sorry," the man apologized hurriedly. "I just wanted to check on you. Any problems?"

"No. The only problem I have is a little constipation, but I've had it for so many years that I no longer consider it a problem. Just a small inconvenience."

"OK." Then we heard the door close.

The voice of another woman said, "What are you doing in the women's bathroom?"

The Broken Rainbow: Mysterious Dark Karma

Chapter 26: The Deadly Toy Gun and the Liberated French

26 Nightclub Restroom

Alicia helped me step down from her shoulders. She looked me in the eye. Her eyes were filled with remorse and her face grimaced as she tried to control her tears. "They forced me," she said. "They left me no other alternative, I swear. You just made me remember the old me and who I really am. I could not continue feeling as miserable as I have all day long. They promised me all my problems would vanish if I sold you out and got enough evidence against you. Not everything I've said to you are lies. I have a huge problem, but I didn't want to get into that now. I'll find another way to resolve it without compromising my principles and dignity like I have like Commander Piñeiro told me to do. As a double spy, I ask you to please find it in the bottom of your heart to forgive me, and not reveal it to anyone, especially your uncle. I would be very ashamed.

She pulled a small plastic container with several mini cassettes out of her bra. She pulled the magnetic strips out of each cassette, one at a time, and flushed them down the toilet. When she was finished, she smiled and said, "That was all the evidence of the several hours earlier while you and I were talking. You have nothing to worry about because they'll never get their hands on it. All I need to thank you for now are two things: first for the greatest orgasm of my life, and the second is for opening your beautiful integrity and sharing with me your great personality which opened the drawers of my conscience.

She put both her arms around my neck. "I only ask you that you never let, as you grow older, the years to change you. OK?"

I replied, "I will try. I feel very happy with myself. This allows me to sleep peacefully whenever I put my head on my pillow and transport myself to the beautiful world of dreams. All I ask of God is to allow me to continue being like that until I depart from this beautiful world you and I have been living in, only you and I can never stop fighting or allow anyone to make it ugly for everyone else."

"Yes, you're right." Tears were in her eyes as she looked at me. "Will you allow me one last kiss goodbye?"

"Yes, of course, but not right here in the toilet. Let's get out of here and let me clean your knee."

"You're right again. Let's get out of here, but don't worry too much about my knee. I'll take care of that wound when I get home. By the way, what did you put down there?" She reached towards my groin, touching it very gently. "Something you didn't show me before? It caused me so much damage that I can barely walk with that leg now." She left the stall, dragging her right leg.

"When you go into battle, as I figured I would be today, you take all the weapons available. It's a lot better to have it and not need it than to need it and not have it."

We walked over to the sinks, I took one of my handkerchiefs and wetted it under a faucet. I bent over and pulled the hem of her black and red night gown up, asking her to hold it. I saw that she was still bleeding badly. The puncture wounds were very deep, and the blood had not begun to coagulate. As I wiped away the blood with one of my handkerchiefs, a lady walked into the bathroom from behind Alicia.

She looked very European. She bore a wide brimmed had, and all she could see was Alicia with her dress lifted up, me kneeling before her, and what appeared to be my face between Alicia's legs. She smiled and said mischievously in broken Spanish with an accent that marked her as being French, "Oh, my goodness! I thought I would only see this in Europe, but you Cubans are very liberated sexually to have such an exhibition in the bathroom. Don't take me wrong, I'm not offended. It gives me great joy!"

She opened her purse and left some paper currency on the sink. "I demand the same treatment she is receiving now. How much is it? I'm going to be going to the toilet because I've been sweating too much dancing and need to wash myself. I won't take very long; I will be waiting in line patiently."

She walked into one of the stalls. The sound of her hurried washing as she cleansed herself. The stall she had chosen was the same one we had just used. Then we heard her scream. "My God! I didn't know there were any virgins left in Cuba! Or maybe they all got together in a big crowd tonight."

She had not finished speaking when the same man who had spoken before entered the bathroom. He saw me in front of Alicia on my knees and asked in surprised, "What the hell are you doing there?"

I poked my head around Alicia's waist, my hand with the bloody handkerchief and held it out to him. The man, taken by surprise, gasped, "What is going on? What are you doing, man?"

"What is it to you?" I answered. "Is she your wife?"

That struck the man speechless, both my confrontational attitude and casual approach. He recovered himself and said, seeing my left hand filled with blood, in indignation, "Stop! Stop! Whatever you're doing! Or do you want me to put a hole in your head?" He reached inside his coat to search for his pistol.

Rapidly, I reached down by my own knee and pulled out a plastic water pistol. It was a light blue, transparent, the liquid within evident. He pulled his pistol, saw what I had, and he lowered his gun as he laughed uproariously. I pointed the pistol at him.

"What—are you going to kill me with that water pistol?"

Without answering, I stood up and squirted him three times. The liquid soaked his face and sprayed into his eyes. This time he screamed in agony. "What the hell did you just spray in my eyes, you son of a bitch?"

I yelled, "Muriatic acid!"

The man in panic dropped his pistol, which skittered across the floor. He blindly groped towards the sinks, still screaming in pain. Alicia looked at me in terror. She asked with her eyes bulging out of their sockets, "Truly? Is that what you squirted in his face?"

I leaned in and murmured in her ear with a small smile as I held the barrel of the pistol to her nose, "It's only 95 proof alcohol."

She shook her head and smiled. "You are a real enigma, full of surprises. Let's get out of here quickly, before he finds out the truth."

As we left the bathrooms, she pulled out of her purse something folded up several times and handed it to me. "These are the plans from the engineers for Villa Marista. I have no use for them. If you find them useful, give them to your friends."

I put them inside my coat. "I don't think I'll have a use now, but you never know."

I walked towards the door as if we were leaving the club, but before we reached the exit I heard beneath the noise of the loud music and people conversing so loudly the man from the bathroom yelling orders, this time with several others trying to intercept us. I said to Alicia, "Go to your table, and I'll get there in another direction."

We separated at once and I saw the man with his eyes red as tomatoes from the alcohol. I saw me and pointed me out to the rest of the group. I looked around and headed toward the dance floor.

The Broken Rainbow: Mysterious Dark Karma

As I got into the crowd, I looked at them and then bent over. I was very glad at that moment that I was not a tall man and disappeared before the eyes of my assailants. I tried to go around them through the crowd without being seen. Like a submarine, I would periodically poke my head up, look around for my pursuers, and duck down again.

I grabbed my 95-proof alcohol[28] pistol and looked for another one. I tapped him on the shoulder, squirted him right in the eyes, and ducked down again. He screamed like the others had. I went for another searcher before repeating my performance. Each time, I got rid of two, because one of their accomplices had to guide the blinded man to get his eyes washed.

Eventually, I no longer saw any of them and decided on an intelligent retreat and headed back to the side passage to go to the exit. As I reached the telephone cabinets, however, the last one I hadn't seen stepped in front of me and shoved a pistol in my face. "You are under arrest for complicity with Alicia Alonso to plan the aid and abetting the escape of a prisoner from our facilities in Villa Marista."

I clapped both hands on his pistol and suddenly twisted it in one, swift motion to disarm him before his surprised, disbelieving face. He was well-trained, and reacted properly by stepping forward, grabbing my neck with his hand and then cocking back his knee to strike me in the groin. As he tried with his right hand still on my neck to retrieve his pistol, he screamed in excruciating agony as the stainless-steel nails penetrated deeply into his knee.

---

[28] Also called surgical alcohol or isopropyl alchohol

I used the opportunity to use my toy to splash his face. The alcohol could produce irritation and possible damage to the surface of the eye if it was not rapidly washed away. Even then, it could even go so far as irritating the retina and impede vision for quite a while afterwards, possibly even causing permanent blindness if not promptly washed away.

I left him behind screaming in frustration, as he had no one to help him. However, the loud music and all the voice yelling in pleasure in the club, no one noticed. As I walked out the door, I dropped his pistol in the trash can. I left the Fox and the Crow. That ordeal served me as a good experience during the early years of my career as a spy in that particular night club, located at 23rd Street between N and O Streets. It was very close to the Havana Libre and where the most common music played was jazz. It was considered at that time one of the best night clubs in Havana as well as the point of meeting for our espionage team who caused so much damage and headaches to the Castro brothers regime by the Lightning.

November 22nd, 1963

When I woke up that morning, I noticed a strange darkness in the sky, overcast like a violent storm was approaching the island on the horizon. I felt as if a very dark karma was about to envelop the nations around the world in a mysterious form, one that it appeared no one could stop like a thief in the night, protected by that darkness. As I drove, what appeared like rocks came pounding from the sky—this was something we had never seen before, hail the size of golf balls. The windshield of the UAZ I was driving in was shattered by the hail, and suddenly strong hurricane force winds forced me to stop driving and pull over to the side of the road. As the hailstones dented the hood and ripped the soft top of the UAZ, a torrential rain swept down on me, completely blocking my vision to only a few feet ahead of me.

Suddenly, the water stopped as if a faucet had been shut off. It was replaced by a thin. misty drizzle which covered the entire city. Vision was still obscured to only a few feet ahead, only now obscured by fog rather than sheets of rain. Just as suddenly, I saw a broken rainbow in the sky, lightening the darkness only a trifle. It was as if that dark karma had opened the doors to Hell. Something was marking the beginning of some new, horrible and dark times ahead.

I continued driving to pick my brother-in-law Canen to go to one of our military gatherings, I had the radio of my car tuned to Radio Reloj, which gave frequent news updates, and heard then the sad, horrible news of the assassination of President John F. Kennedy. I grimaced and changed the station, searching for another one to convince myself that it was just a communist Utopian dream, but it was on every channel on the station. I remembered Che Guevara's words, "Revenge is the punishment for the enemies of our socialist Marxist-Leninist who dares to betray us or do anything against us. Our arm is very long and has no limitation, country, or frontiers."

I knew then from this evidence this was true; that young President with little political experience had just suffered the same luck as my good friend, that wolf of the sea, Ernest Hemingway. On that cold Friday of November 22nd, 1963, these criminal politicians had another mark of victory in the list of assassinations with impunity. As Che had also said, a hundred years would pass before anyone would be able to decipher who was pulling the strings behind this murder.

Of course, Che never took into consideration that the little boy, the Little Commander, was an enemy he had created through his arrogance, cold-bloodedness, and lack of scruples; indeed, his worst enemy. Instead of conquering the young man's mind and brainwashing him to become another fanatic, frustrated Marxist, he was changed into Che's worse enemy and the most wanted spy in the entire island of Cuba beneath his own nose.

Years later that Little Commander would come to expose with his pen to the entire world the atrocities and crimes committed by all of them as a direct witness to those horrible oppressive totalitarian system. As a historical witness he has been in on each of these horrible plans and listened from the lips of every single leader in that fatal revolution the promises of good and greatness to people turn into deliveries of blood and death.

Chapter 27: The Dark Karma Repeats

27 Pico Turquino

Pinar del Rio, Cuba
1964

Miguel Angel, now nineteen, was growing into a very handsome young man. Sporting his favorite black beret, he laid flowers on the grave of his father. He stood up and looked at the engraved headstone which read *Ramon Famosa, 1915-1944.*

From nearby, Sarah called out, "Are you ready, Miguel Angel?"

He looked up from the grave for a moment before turning to Sarah, who stood behind him silently, still beautiful at the age of 41 in spite of the scar which started at her ear and went down her neck from the razor attack three years ago. He said, "Yes, Mother." As they walked towards the exit, he added, "I want to become a teacher for the poor and needy."

"You are quite young to become a teacher, Miguel," she replied. "But you are nineteen, already a man."

"It doesn't matter, Mother. Anyone who can climb El Pico Turquino[29] five times can be a teacher."

"Why would you want to do such a thing?"

"I'm proud of the revolution in my country! Castro is bringing change for all of us!"

"Sometimes I wonder if we weren't better off before," Sarah mused.

Miguel Angel stopped walking and stared at her in consternation. "Don't say that Mother! Castro promised that all the poor will have everything they need."

"We already have everything we need, Miguel Angel. Your uncles have worked hard for that."

"I want to go visit Englebert in Bayamo, again."

"You're not fooling me," Sarah said. "Bayamo is near El Pico Turquino."

"I want to try, Mother!"

Sarah saw a bench and sat down on it. She gestured to Miguel Angel to do the same. "Sit here, my son." He sat next to her, and she continued, "You can do anything you dream of. I know it. Your father was a strong man.

---

[29] At an elevation of 6,476 feet, the highest mountain peak in Cuba.

He fought for freedom. Do you remember what I told you about our life in Germany?" He nodded. "Freedom is worth fighting for. So are justice, and love, and many other things. You have to choose what is important."

"I understand," he replied, slightly confused. "I think."

"Always remember our story. Remember Uncle David and Grandfather Jacob. Your Uncle Englebert remembers. Ask him to tell you again."

"I know, Mama. I remember."

A friend of the family, a beautiful lady named Adela, walked up to them. Sarah said, "Adela, are you ready to go?"

"Yes," Adela replied. "I'm done visiting my grandparents."

"Did they die recently?" Miguel Angel asked.

"No," Adela answered. "It was years ago."

"Oh," he said, a little abashed. "I see."

Sarah said, "Miguel Angel, I think it will be fine if you visit your Uncle Englelbert soon."

"Tomorrow?" he asked eagerly.

"Next week. First you must do your chores and help your Uncle Solomon at the shop."

"I will!" He sprung up and ran toward the exit.

Sarah and Adela smiled as they watched him run off. Adela asked, "He never knew his father?"

"No. Ramon died before he was born."

"Oh, how sad! I'm very sorry."

Sarah patted Adela on the arm. "Thank you for being a friend, Adela." Adela smiled warmly at her friend.

A week later, Miguel Angel knocked on the door of Englebert's house. Englebert was by now in his thirties and had done well for himself. His living room was comfortable, containing practical wooden furniture. For decoration on the walls, he had hung a picture of Old Jerusalem, a scroll in Hebrew, and a cross. He had been sitting in a comfortable chair as he polished a new shoe, but at the sound of the knocking he put the shoe down as he got up to answer the door. "Ah, my strong nephew! I got your mother's letter."

"Uncle!" Miguel Angel exclaimed as he hugged his uncle.

"Sit down! Rest! Tell me about your trip."

"Oh, it was fine, Uncle."

"So, you want to be a Five Pics teacher?"

"Yes! I will climb El Pico Turquino five times and then Fidel will let me teach others less fortunate."

"Fidel himself, eh, Miguel Angel?" Englebert asked in gentle amusement.

"Well, you know what I mean, Uncle." Miguel Angel stood up to look at the wall hangings.

"Yes," Englebert replied, "I believe I do. You are determined to do this?"

"Yes, sir."

"Well, then I will pray for your safety. You can do a favor for your uncle and visit until tomorrow, of course?"

"Of course, Uncle Englebert!"

"Good, good. Let me show you the improvements in my shoe shop!" Englebert got up and put his arm around Miguel Angel as they left for the adjoining shop.

The next day, Miguel Angel was one of about fifty boys gathered around a man with a military bearing as their team leader. They held their camping gear as they listened to this man, Instructor Perez. "Here is the Sierra Maestra, the mountain range where Castro fought his revolution, *our* revolution. Do you understand?"

The boys answered in a chorus, "Yes, *Compañero* Perez."

"During the next few months, you will show your devotion to the revolution and the cause. We will climb this mountain five times, and all the while you will learn the greatness of socialism and the power of the people. Do you understand?"

"Yes, *Compañero* Perez."

"Not all of you will make it. Some of you are not devoted enough, even now. Some of you are too weak. Some of you may even be cowards. This test will prove if you have what it takes to teach others about the greatness of our new leader. Do you understand?"

"Yes, *Compañero* Perez."

"Good. Then we start our training today as we ascend the great El Pico Turquino!" He turned and headed up the mountain, followed by the only other adult, a climbing expert assistant who carried lots of climbing gear. The recruits followed the two adults.

Back at Englebert's home, Miguel Angel's uncle sat in his chair in the living room as he prayed. "Great Lord in Heaven, protect young Miguel Angel by the power of your Son, Yeshua." Englebert looked up at the cross.

Meanwhile, Perez led the group up a steep hike up the mountainside, the lush green valley below them. He lectured them in a powerful voice. "From these mountains and these very trails our great leader led the fight for freedom from the oppression of the dictator. He fought to free those who are poor from the oppression of the rich and powerful. He took away the power from those who looked down on the poor and gave it to the people."

Miguel Angel had a gleam in his eye as he looked up towards the mountain peak.

A year later, Englebert was working on some shoes when Miguel Angel burst in, thinner, more mature, and jubilant. "Uncle! I made it!"

Englebert put down his work and looked critically at his nephew. "Barely, if you ask me." He got up and hugged Miguel Angel, who pulled out a certificate to show Englebert.

"Look!"

Englebert examined it and said, "It's a great achievement, Miguel Angel. What will you do now?"

"They assigned me a small village to teach in, near El Rio Frio!"

"And what will you teach?"

"Everything, Uncle! Some of these children have never had any education. I will teach them many things."

"Very good, then, Miguel Angel." Both of them exchanged looks of happiness.

A few days later, a Soviet military jeep carrying Instructor Perez and Miguel Angel pulled up to the outside edge of El Rio Frio and stopped. As he got out, Perez said, "This is your new home, Miguel Angel."

"I'm glad," Miguel Angel replied.

"Go, talk to *Compañero* Lopez in that first house and he will take care of you. He's the political commissioner in charge of this region."

"Thank you, *Compañero* Perez!"

"Thank *you*, young Miguel Angel." Perez got back into the jeep and drove off.

Miguel Angel walked toward the small house Perez had indicated. In the distance, he scarcely noticed a pretty teenaged girl with long, dark hair who looked at him shyly before walking away.

A while later, Miguel Angel found himself among his pupils, a group of poorly dressed peasant children between the ages of eight and twelve, in a dingy room with meager furniture and a crooked desk which served as the schoolhouse. Miguel Angel stood in front of the group, holding a book in his hand. His pupils listened to him, and the group included an energetic nine-year-old named Raul and a twelve-year-old boy nearly as big as Miguel Angel named Carlos.

Miguel Angel said, "Today we are going to write a letter."

Raul protested, "But I can't write, Miguel Angel!"

"It's fine, Raul. I'll help you."

"Oh, OK."

"The letter is going to be to our new leader, Comandante Fidel. He is making sure that everyone in this great country can read, and he will show your letters to everyone so they can see!"

Miguel Angel handed out paper and pencils to the class and then went over to Raul, who held his pencil, uncertain what to do.

Miguel Angel asked, "What would you like to say to our leader?"

Raul replied, "I want to say thank you for sending me a teacher."

Miguel Angel took the pencil from Raul and said, "Good. Let me write that for you." While the other students tried to write their letters, he finished and asked, "Can you write your name?"

"Yes."

"Then write it there," he said, pointing at the bottom of what he had written.

Raul took the pencil and wrote his name: *Ral*.

As school let out for the day, the students filed out, thanking Miguel Angel. Carlos came over to him and said, "Thank you, Miguel Angel."

"Of course, Carlos."

"Next week, would you like to come to my house to celebrate Christmas?"

Miguel Angel paused. "Christmas? Well, I—"

Carlos interrupted eagerly, "Please? My family would like to thank you."

"I can come. It will be a good time to talk to them about our new life as *compañeros*."

"Thank you, teacher!" As Carlos ran out of the room, Miguel Angel stood there, lost in thought.

The following week, Carlos and his family were in a frenzy of preparation. He, his father Esteban, mother Yalina, eight-year-old Elena, and his older, teenaged sister Flora, were all preparing Christmas dinner. Poor decorations adorned the small house: paper garlands, popcorn strings, and tinsel stars. For the dinner they had managed to scrape together a meal of roast pork, yuca con mojo, and black beans on rice for nochebuena[30].

Yalina asked, "When is your teacher coming, Carlos?"

"He should be here soon," Carlos replied.

Elena said, "Mama, I see there is a present for me under the tree!"

"Yes, Elena," Yalina responded. "But you have to wait until tomorrow to open it."

"That's fine, Mama. I'm glad I have a present!"

Flora came up and put her arm around Elena. The presents under the tree were small and few. "I helped make your gift, Elena."

Elena smiled up at her sister as Esteban asked, "Did you wrap the present for our guest, Elena?"

"Yes, here it is!" She showed Esteban what was clearly a paper-wrapped book.

"Wonderful, Elena! Did you do this all by yourself?" Esteban asked.

"I did!" Elena said proudly.

There was a knock at the door. Esteban said, "Here he is now. Put that under the tree, Elena."

Elena hurried to put the gift under the tree as Carlos answered the door. "Welcome, teacher!" he said.

Yalina came up to welcome Miguel Angel as well. "Come in, come in! Welcome!" She kissed his cheeks in greeting.

"Thank you," Miguel Angel replied. Elena ran up and stood looking up at him. "Um...hello."

"Look under the tree!" Elena said excitedly.

Carlos pointed at Elena. "This is my sister, Elena."

---

[30] Christmas Eve.

"Hello, Elena."

Carlos then gestured to Flora. "This is my older sister, Flora."

A shock of recognition went through Miguel Angel as he recognized the girl he had scarcely noticed when he arrived in the village. She took his hand bashfully as they shared a moment, looking at each other. Esteban came over and broke the spell.

"Esteban," he said, holding out his hand. "Pleased to meet you."

Miguel Angel shook his hand and Carlos said, "Now, what is under the tree?"

"You'll see!" Elena said excitedly. "Presents!"

Miguel Angel looked at the tree and saw at once the book with the label *Teacher Miguel Angel* beneath the tree. "For me?" he asked in surprise.

"Yes, teacher," Carlos said. "For you."

Miguel Angel took the book. "Should I open it now?"

"Of course," Yalina said.

"Open it! Open it!" Elena said, practically jumping in excitement.

Miguel Angel opened it to discover it was a copy of the Holy Bible. "I, uh—thank you. I didn't tell you before, but I'm Jewish."

The family looked embarrassed, and Carlos started to say, "Teacher, I—"

"No, no," Miguel Angel hastily interrupted, "It's fine. It's good we believe in God, yes? Better to trust in God than in man."

Yalina said, "You're right, Carlos—your teacher is wise for his age."

"Will you keep it, then?" Carlos asked.

"Yes," Miguel Angel affirmed, "I will. Thank you."

"You must keep it hidden, Miguel Angel," Esteban cautioned. "The communists don't like this book."

"What? Is that true?" Miguel Angel asked in surprise.

"Yes, young teacher," Esteban said. "You should not tell anyone about our Christmas here, either. Castro doesn't like it."

Yalina came out of the kitchen. "The pork is done! Everyone, sit, sit!"

Miguel Angel pauses for a moment, then relaxed to enjoy the dinner. Yalina hurried to get the roast pig out of the oven and then placed it on the table. She began to serve.

Miguel Angel looked uncomfortable once again. "I'm sorry, I can't—"

Yalina interjected, "Oh, no! That's right, you don't eat pork, do you? Well, that's fine, you just get an extra helping of everything else!"

She loaded up his plate with the beans, rice, and sweet potatoes and he smiled.

Later that night, Miguel Angel was in his small bedroom as he searched through a small box. He finally found his yarmulke and put it on. He stood by his small bed in the sparsely furnished room and recited, "Hear, O Israel: the Lord our God, the Lord is One. Blessed is the Name of His glorious kingdom for all eternity.

He paused for a moment in meditation. Then he prayed, "Great Lord, thank you for reminding me of Your goodness tonight. Help me to remember You in all I do."

Dr. Julio Antonio del Marmol

Chapter 28: Hard Awakening of Reality

28 Communism Doesn't Allow Religious Thought

The next week, Miguel Angel was addressing Raul as he taught in his classroom. "So, two times fifty would be one hundred. Correct, Raul!"

"Thank you, Teacher!" Raul exclaimed.

Miguel Angel closed the math book. "I want to teach you about another important subject. I'm talking about God."

"I know about God!" Raul said. "He is Jesus!"

"Well, Raul," Miguel Angel said, "Some people think he is, yes. But what is important is that we know that God is there for us."

"What do you mean, teacher?" Carlos asked.

"Look around at each other. Look at your eyes, your hands. Isn't it wonderful how we are made? We are made like God. He gave us the power to choose good or evil."

"I want to be good," Carlos said, "like you, Teacher."

Miguel Angel smiled. "I try to be good, Carlos. I hope I am. I'm glad Castro has given us this chance to be together."

"Why would someone choose evil?" Raul asked. "I think good is better."

"You're smart, Raul," Miguel Angel told him. "I don't know why some choose evil. There was a man I know of who tried to kill everyone who was different from himself. He took away freedom from those people, and then took their lives."

"You mean Hitler," Carlos said.

"Yes," Miguel Angel agreed, "everyone should know about Hitler. Everyone should remember what he did. He promised many things to the German people, but he was evil, and so Germany was ruined by him. He used his power as leader for evil. He killed anyone who disagreed with him. He was an enemy of God."

"Castro is good," Raul declared.

"Yes, he is," Miguel Angel replied. "He gave us freedom from the evil dictator. Someone who gives freedom and fights evil is good. We should all try to be good, and brave, and fight evil." He stood there for a moment in thought, and the class waited. "You may go home now," he said finally. "The lesson is over for today."

The students got up to leave and said their farewells to their teacher. As the last of the students left, Miguel Angel walked outside to see them off. Flora was waiting for him.

"I—I brought you some food," she said shyly. "My mom made it for you."

Miguel took the bag. "Oh. Thank you, Flora." He examined the contents of the bag and looked back up at her. "Would you like to take a walk with me?"

"Yes," she replied. He offered her his hand, and she took it. They walked out of the village together.

That night, after Miguel Angel had said his prayers quietly to himself, he climbed into bed. And that's when the dreams began. He found himself struggling up the side of El Pico Turquino once more. It was evening, and the path was treacherous with rocks and weeds.

He heard Instructor Perez's voice calling to him out of the shadows, but he could not see him. "You're falling behind, Miguel! Look around you. Where did you go?"

Miguel Angel looked around as he tried to find his instructor. He tripped on some brush, fell to his knees, and cried out in frustration, "Where are you?"

But the voice of the instructor was gone. He thrashed around in the darkness on his knees, and then a bright light opened in the sky above him. A Heavenly voice spoke to him, saying, "Miguel Angel, do you know who you are named for?"

"What? Who are you?" He shielded his eyes but tried to look into the light.

"You are named for the Archangel, he is My servant, as you are as well. You will witness the end of a Dark Angel of the enemy."

"I don't understand. What enemy?"

"He is the enemy of everyone. He is near to you, he and his servants. Do not fear, I will protect you."

The light began to fade, and Miguel Angel cried out, "Lord, don't go!" He woke from his dream with a start. "Was it real?" he mused aloud. He paused for a moment before falling back to sleep.

The next day, Miguel Angel was standing outside as he greeted his students as they arrived. Raul walked up happily. "Good morning, Raul," he said.

"Hello, teacher!"

As Raul strode inside happily, a military jeep with several soldiers pulled up, followed by two more with additional guards inside. Miguel Angel stared in astonishment as Instructor Perez got out with his guest, Ernesto "Che" Guevara. Guevara was immediately flanked by his guards, and the children watched in amazement as Perez walked up to Miguel Angel.

"Good morning, Miguel Angel," he said. They shook hands as Guevara casually walked towards them. "And this is—"

"Comandante Guevara!" Miguel Angel finished breathlessly as he eagerly shook Che's hand.

Perez continued, "We are doing an inspection tour of the schools in this area. Have your students ready and we will come in."

A short while later, Perez and Miguel Angel stood in the back, and like the children who sat in front of Guevara, listened as he spoke. "Together, we are Cubans, a nation. You must no longer think of yourself as an individual—that is selfish. You are part of a greater destiny. Together, we can do more good than alone. We no longer need to fear the rich with their power; we have taken their gold and used it to feed the poor...."

Later, the students said goodbye to Che as Perez and Miguel Angel watched. As the last student finally wandered home, Miguel Angel turned to Perez. "Is there anything else I can do for you, Instructor?"

Perez gestured to Che, who turned. "Come with me, Miguel Angel." Together they walked outside and strode along a walking trail outside the village. Che said, "I've heard good things about you, Miguel Angel. Instructor Perez says that you were one of his best students."

"Thank you, *compañero*," Miguel Angel replied.

"I've also heard things that concern me. I have heard that you are telling the students about God."

"God? Yes, I tell them about good and evil."

"Miguel Angel, we do not need God. We have gone beyond the need for him, we are powerful together as Cubans. We are what is good, fighting against the evil in the world, the capitalists and others who hate freedom."

"God is good and wants us to be free."

Che stopped and turned angrily. "Miguel Angel! You are not listening! There is no God, and we have no need of him! Religion deceives the people and keeps them from joining together in community. It is poison in their minds. Do you understand?"

"I—"

"You will not speak of God to the students any longer," Che barreled over any objection. "You will continue to be a good instructor, or you will no longer teach."

"Yes, *compañero*," was all Miguel Angel could say.

After Guevara and Perez left, Miguel Angel sought out his Uncle Englebert. He told him what had happened, and they spoke together solemnly. Englebert said, "I know, Miguel Angel, I know. You must do what is right. What you know God wants you to do."

"I'm afraid," Miguel Angel confessed.

"Miguel Angel, this family has faced fear and we have conquered. Remember where you come from."

Feeling reassured, Miguel Angel nodded. "I will. Uncle, I had a vision, in a dream."

"Really? What was it?"

"I saw a light. It said that I will see a Dark Angel fall, that I shouldn't be afraid."

"Then do not be afraid, my nephew. God is with you."

That night, Miguel Angel sat talking with Flora in the schoolroom. She said, "I don't want to live in a place where God is not allowed."

"I don't either, Flora," he agreed.

"I would feel so alone without Him."

"I would feel so alone without *you*, Flora," he admitted.

She turned to him passionately and he kissed her. She returned his kiss and after a moment they stopped and looked at each other. Gently, he unbuttoned her blouse.

A few weeks later, Miguel Angel stood confidently in front of his class as he taught. "Think about it. What is the use of being good if evil stays in the world? What good is it if we all die in the end? It has no meaning. But when you know God, it *does* have meaning. In the end, God promises to make everything right. The oppressed will be free, evil will be punished, and everyone will get what they deserve. That is why we should be good. But we should also do good because we love other people and want them to be happy."

He dismissed his students. As they left, he saw Instructor Perez waiting. Once the last student left, he walked up to Miguel Angel. "You know why I'm here."

"Yes," Miguel Angel simply said.

"Che wanted to put you in prison. I convinced him that military training would clear your mind of lies." When Miguel Angel did not answer, Perez said, "Come with me, then." Miguel Angel took one last look at his students in the distance and then went along with Perez.

Outside the small home of Carlos, Flora and Elena played happily, not knowing what had happened to Miguel Angel.

Chapter 29: The "Beauty" of Socialism

29 Firing Squad

I had by now walked away from my Juvenile Commandos, who had been transformed into the International Communists Union. As my brother-in-law Canen had warned, since I was no longer actively working with the revolutionary government, I got swept into the *Servicio Militar Obligatorio*[31] and sent to work in a walled military camp which resembled to me more a prison than any training facility. It was

---

[31] Obligatory Military Service; generally simply referred to as SMO.

there that I got reunited with my old friends Hernesto (better known as Kinqui) and Miguel Angel.

We had all been assigned the distasteful and arduous task of digging. With my usual sense of mischievous humor, I jokingly threw some dirt on Miguel Angel. "Hey, Miguel, you got something on you."

He frowned. "Thanks. So do you!"

I looked down at my uniform. "What? I don't see any...." And that is when Miguel Angel tossed some dirt on me. Hernesto laughed at both of us, and then we joined in.

All of us failed to notice Sergeant Lopez walk over to us, staring hard. "That's it. An extra day of digging for all of you," he said.

We groaned as he walked away. Hernesto said, "At least tomorrow is movie night."

"Always the optimist," I said.

Miguel Angel pointed out, "With those movies, you have to be. Translating Russian communist films into bad Spanish? It hurts my ears."

"At least we aren't in prison," I observed. "We are only here because we need to be 'educated' in our 'youth.'"

Miguel looked around to make sure no one was listening. "I'm being educated, all right. I'm learning how Castro and the others are full of lies."

Hernesto hissed, "Keep it down, Miguel! That will take you straight to prison!"

"Sometimes I feel like this is already prison." We went back to our digging.

A few days later, Miguel Angel was eagerly waiting in the visiting room. There was a table and a few crooked chairs, and a Cuban flag as well as a communist flag hung on the wall. He fidgeted in his seat, but finally Flora came in.

"Flora!" he exclaimed, and they embraced. She looked nervous as they sat down. "How is the family? The school?"

She seemed detached as she replied quietly. "They sent us a new teacher."

"One that doesn't believe in God, I bet."

"Miguel Angel!" she exclaimed reprovingly.

"Sorry. I'll be a good boy." She looked upset, got up, and turned away. "Really—I'm sorry."

"That's not it." She turned to him, tears in her eyes.

"What is it?"

"I'm going to have a baby. Our baby."

He stared at her in shock for a moment. Then he got up and held her. "Don't worry. I'll do the right thing. I'll write a letter to your father, right away."

"Really? Then…you love me?"

"Yes," he said with conviction, "I do."

"Oh, Miguel!" She hugged him fiercely.

"Once I finish my three years here, then we will be married. If—I mean—will you?"

"Yes, Miguel!" They kissed.

A little while later, Miguel met with Hernesto and me in a dimly lit storage room. I said, "Miguel, we have decided that we're going to leave this place."

"What?" Miguel exclaimed in a soft voice.

"This is not the life for us," Hernesto said. "Only a little food, and it is bad…."

"The doghouse if we do something 'wrong'," I added.

"Yes," Miguel said, "I understand. I know. Why are you telling me?"

"Well," Hernesto said uncomfortably, "we, uh—"

"We need your help to escape," I finished for him.

"Oh, no!" he objected. "I have to be good now! My family, Flora...."

"It's only something small," I assured him. "When they call roll after bedtime, just call our names for us."

"It will give us a full night's head start," Hernesto added. "No one will know it was you in the dark."

"I don't know," he said uncertainly.

"Come on, Miguel," I said. "We are friends, right?"

"Yes, of course. I'll do it. When is the night?"

"Friday, after movie night," Hernesto said.

"Oh, thank God we only have to watch those movies one more time," I said.

"Good luck, my friends," Miguel said. "I'll pray that God watches over you."

"You'd better!" I said as we all put our hands in the middle of us in agreement.

That Friday night, Hernesto and I snuck out of the camp. We hid behind a building and ducked down as a guard passed by without noticing us. Then we made a break and went over the fence.

Back at our barracks, Sergeant Lopez patrolled outside it. He opened the door halfway in the darkness and stood in the doorway. As he called out the roll, a voice called out "Here!" after each name.

"Raffo! Moreno! Naranjo! Almazan! Navalles! Salas! Duran!" Miguel was sweating in his bed in the darkness as he waited for Lopez to continue the roll call. "Davis! Del Marmol!"

The Broken Rainbow: Mysterious Dark Karma

Trying to change his voice, Miguel called out, "Here!"

"Cox! Baumann!"

Using his natural voice, Miguel called, "Here!"

"Junco! Fuentes! Castaneva!"

Again, altering his voice, Miguel said, "Here!"

"Bazan!"

The last name called and everyone answering, the young men tried to go back to sleep. Miguel sat up in his bed and looked out the window. Quietly he said to himself, "Goodbye, my friends. Vayan con Dios."

Three years passed, and it was June of 1965. Young SMO soldiers marched and worked in the camp. Miguel Angel was sitting on his bunk in the barracks as he wrote a letter to Flora. He had now fully grown into manhood, and now sported a bloody bruise on one side of his face. A friend of his named Diego, a handsome man with curly hair who was also in the SMO, came up to him and noted the picture of the two-year-old boy next to Miguel's bunk and a book by Karl Marx.

"Hey, writing another letter, my friend?" Diego asked.

"Yes," Miguel replied, "to my fiancée. Only one more month and I'm finished with the SMO."

"Oh, you think I don't know that? It's all you've talked about for weeks!" He noticed the bruise. "Ah, I see you've displeased Sergeant Lopez again."

Miguel looked up from his letter. "It's nothing, Diego. What about yourself? You still have over a year left."

"Ah, I'll survive. Thanks for thinking about me."

"Break is about over; we'd better get back to work." Miguel put his letter away and got up off his bunk.

Diego gave him a mock salute. "Yes, Comandante!"

Miguel rolled his eyes. "I don't know how you can be happy in a place like this."

As they started to walk out the door, Diego said, "It's because I have my own guardian angel, Miguel Angel."

"Oh, boy," Miguel said in amusement. "This place has made you crazy."

Diego and Miguel were put to work setting up posts and then putting up a fence. Various other military personnel walked busily around the compound on their own tasks.

Diego said, "Why does it feel like we're building our own prison?"

Miguel answered, "No matter what they do, they cannot imprison the human heart." He tapped his chest.

They heard the siren signaling lunch, and so put down their tools to head to the SMO mess hall. They joined the line of other members for their daily food. No one smiled, and everyone looked thin and weary. The tiny portions of beans and rice barely filled the metal trays. They got their food and walked over to an empty table.

Miguel said, "Whew! I'm tired."

"How's your face?" Diego asked.

"It hurts."

"Well, a face that ugly should hurt."

"Shut up, Diego."

Diego looked amused but hid his laughter as Sergeant Lopez looked over at them and frowned. Once Lopez looked away, Diego leaned in and whispered, "Hey, Miguel. I'm going to sneak out tonight."

"Again?"

"I want to see my girl. She's so beautiful I can't resist."

"So you want my help again?"

"*Dios mio*[32], the guards are so stupid. Yes, I want your help. They never notice." He leaned back and winked.

That night, Diego climbed over a wire fence surrounding the camp in the darkness. He lands quietly on the other side, but suddenly found himself illuminated by a spotlight. His eyes widened in surprise as machine gun fire shattered the night's silence.

The next day, Miguel was bound to a chair in a small interrogation room in the camp. Sergeant Lopez entered, accompanied by Lieutenant Lenin, a stern communist officer with a thin moustache. Lopez closed the door after Lenin entered.

Lenin said, "I'll get straight to the point. How were you helping Diego?"

Nervously, Miguel tried to play innocent. "Helping him do what, Lieutenant?"

"Your friend Diego is dead, a traitor to Cuba. Do you wish to join him?"

"Dead? A traitor? How?"

"Attempting to avoid the mandatory service required of him. Stealing arms from our supplies. Apparently, he thought he could escape. We know you were helping him."

"No. Not Diego. He wouldn't steal."

---

[32] My God

"We know you are a traitor either way, even if you do not confess! Sergeant!"

Lopez produced the copy of Karl Marx that was by Miguel's bed. He opened it to reveal the pages were cut out and a Jewish prayer book was inside. He tossed it onto the table before Miguel, who asked, "Am I a traitor for believing in God?"

"You cannot be both a Jew and a socialist," Lenin said harshly. "Anything not of the people is against us."

"What about freedom?" Miguel asked. "I thought Castro fought for freedom!"

Lenin slapped Miguel across the face. "Don't you mention the *Comandante en Jefe's*[33] name! You sound like one of those worms from the United States, praying and talking about God!

Lenin forced himself to calm down. "Obviously, we have failed here. You have not learned how to be a proper citizen of Cuba. You will be sent to prison for treason."

Miguel slumped in despair as Lenin walked out. Lopez paused for a moment and took out the photo of Miguel's son. "Nice looking boy." He put the picture in his pocket. "One more little *pionero*[34] for the revolution."

A while later, Miguel was taken to a political prison. Outside a desolate concrete and steel room flanked by bars, he heard clearly as Che Guevara stood before a captive in chains, punching the bloody and battered prisoner fully in the face as two guards stood behind him. Guevara's blow was so hard that the captive was forced to the ground.

---

[33] Commander-in-Chief
[34] Pioneer

Che spat on the man. "You pig! You think to help those worms who want to flee?"

Che kicked the man, who replied quietly, "We only want to be free."

Che hauled him up by his shirt and pulled the man to his face. "Free? Free, you ungrateful dog? My men bled and died so you could be free from Batista! This is how you repay us? With treason?" The captive man sobbed. "Should I free you, then? Maybe I will free you from this life!

Che drew a military knife and drove it into the man's leg, who fell to the ground, bleeding and crying. "Get him out of here," Che said over his shoulder to the guards. "If he dies, he dies." Che paused for a moment in reflection as he mused out loud, "Why are they so ungrateful for what we have done?"

The guards then brought Miguel in, looking dirty and disheveled. They threw him onto the floor and Che looked up, instantly recognizing him. "I know you. The teacher. I told Perez you were hopeless. Traitor.

Che walked over to Miguel and punched him in the stomach, causing him to collapse to the floor, gasping for breath. Che then kicked him as he lay on the ground and continued, "Welcome to prison, traitor. I have given your case much consideration. This prison is much too nice for you. Instead, we'll send you to a very special prison, much more suited to a worm like yourself: La Cabaña."

Che walked back over to Miguel and stepped on his hand to crush Miguel's fingers.

Miguel, along with two other prisoners, was chained in the back of a truck under guard as the vehicle rumbled along a dusty road.

A high bridge crossing a river was up ahead. The truck rolled along it steadily as Miguel sat, hopeless, his crushed fingers hanging limply. The truck suddenly stopped. He could hear voices outside, then gunfire. The guard in the back jumped out, only to promptly be shot.

Chapter 30: Mysterious Karma Catches Miguel Angel

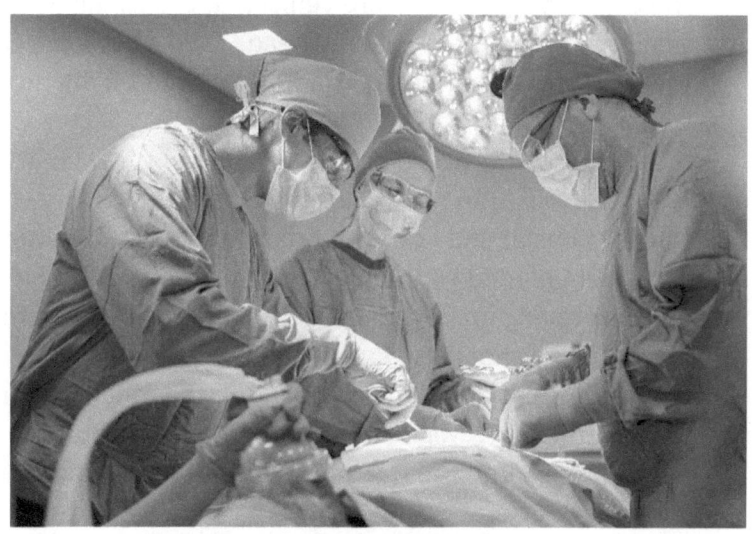

30 Wounded Miguel Angel

I walked around to the back of the truck with my machine gun. I smiled as I looked inside and said, "Good morning, Señor Baumann."

"Julio Antonio!" Miguel gasped in astonishment.

"Hurry! Your family is here for you!"

"What?" Miguel asked no further questions but jumped out of the truck, still in his handcuffs.

We came around the truck and started toward a military jeep and car that were waiting. Miguel's uncles, Solomon, Jacob, and Englebert were awaiting us, also carrying guns. They waved and called out.

Jacob called, "Miguel Angel!"

Englebert saw a military vehicle approaching the far side of the bridge and shouted, "Hurry!"

From the vehicle we heard a Cuban soldier yell, "You! Stop!"

All three uncles turned around and started firing. I said, "We can't go that way now!" We turned back toward the truck and saw two more vehicles approaching to block that escape route. I shook my head. "We'll have to fight them." I looked at Miguel's hand. "You can't fight. Run! Get away!"

"Where?" he asked.

"Just go!" The trucks closed in on both sides. Miguel's uncles and I opened fire at the trucks, but Miguel and I were pinned by the railing of the bridge. We climbed over the railing for cover. I started to say, "You need to...," but then two shots hit Miguel, one in the arm and one in the leg. A soldier had snuck around to the other side of us for a better shot. Miguel reached for me with cuffed hands but fell into the river, hundreds of feet below.

After that, Miguel never knew whether it was a vision or a nightmare while unconsciousness claimed him, but he was in the prison cell once more, only the shadows and lighting seemed surreal.

His mother, Sarah, sat on the floor crying, wearing her Star of David necklace. Then Che Guevara strode in, drawing his knife. Sarah shrieked in terror.

Then her harp was suddenly in the cell. Che slashed the strings and broke several with a screeching, unreal twang. Sarah screamed and held her ears. Che slashed again, destroying more strings and producing more screeches. Blood came out from under Sarah's ears, and

Miguel heard the sound of a heart pumping that grew louder.

Che grinned evilly and slashed away most of the remaining strings, producing a horrible, screeching hiss. Sarah screamed, holding her ears which now bled even more as the heart pounding grew to a crescendo.

Miguel's eyes opened with a start, freeing him of his nightmare. He found himself in a small bed in a strange house. His mother sat next to him as she watched over him.

"M-mother?" he asked weakly.

"I'm here," she answered.

"I thought I was dead."

"It was not your time yet." He tried to get up, but Sarah gently pushed him back down. "Don't. Not yet. We just took the bullets out."

"Bullets? My uncles! Julio Antonio! Are they alright?"

Sarah sighed and looked directly at him. "Your Uncle Jacob was killed."

"Oh, no!" He raised his good arm to cover his face.

"But the rest survived, Miguel Angel!" she said to give him spirit. "They are here, hiding with us! Your friend Julio Antonio is working on a way to get us away to Mexico."

Adela walked in at that moment, still a beautiful, innocent woman save for those mischievous eyes. "I thought I heard voices. He is awake? Good."

Sarah said, "Our gracious host is Adela. Her family has taken us in."

Miguel Angel said gratefully, "Thank you, Adela."

She replied, "I didn't know you knew Julio Antonio. He is also a friend of mine. Speaking of friends, Hernesto says to say hello."

"Ha!" Miguel Angel exclaimed. "He made it, too. I miss him."

As she left the room, Adela said, "Well, I'll tell your family that you're alive and awake."

Moments later, the small room was packed as the family trooped in: Rose, Solomon, Englebert were there, along with Flora and Miguel Angel's two-year-old son, David. The family swarmed around Miguel Angel, talking and laughing.

Solomon said, "We fished you out of the river a mile away! You must have gills!"

Miguel laughed. "Maybe I did—I don't remember."

Flora placed David on the side of the bed. He smiled at his father. Flora exclaimed, "He is so happy to see you!"

"I can tell," Miguel said as he smiled back.

Rose stood up and gestured to everyone. "Everyone, let Miguel Angel get his rest! Give him a quiet moment with his wife! Come on!" She ushered everyone out of the room.

Flora sat on the edge of the bed with David. "How do you feel?"

"I feel strange. One side of my body seems numb. I can't seem to move it."

"Well, my dear, you have been shot and lived. I'm sure it will get better." She kissed his forehead.

Miguel smiled weakly. "Yes, you're right, of course."

"Once we get out of Cuba we can find you a real surgeon," Flora said. "A couple of the local doctors and a great nurse here took out the bullets."

"Yes, that's good. We have to go now. I'm sorry—it's my fault."

"No, no—it's not you. You're a good man, Miguel Angel." He closed his eyes and fell asleep.

While my friend was reuniting with his family, I was discussing a business proposition with a local farmer outside his garage, which was open and filled with junk.

I asked, "Will it work for a large boat?"

"Yes, yes," the man answered confidently, "it should work fine. I should get rid of it anyway. The government does not want anyone to have these motors. They don't want us to leave. Did you know I could get arrested?"

I answered, "I'll pay you for it. Here." I handed him ten U.S. $100 bills.

His eyes widened. "Woo! Why so much?"

"For your trouble, and your help in loading it up. Let's put it in the jeep."

We covered the boat outboard motor and loaded it into the back of the jeep. I got into a Cuban military uniform and drove off. I came to a military checkpoint, a guard holding up his hand for me to stop, which I did. The guard walked over, looked at me, and saluted.

He looked at the cloth-covered bundle in the back. "What is that?"

I shrugged. "Transmission for the suction pumps at the dairy farm."

"Oh, really?" I handed him an ID card which stated that I was a special representative from the Prime Minister's Office. He looked embarrassed, hastily saluted, and waved me on. "You can go."

"Hasta la vista," I said as I waved at him and drove through the checkpoint.

Three months later, Adela was walking with David towards the playground just down the street from her house. She pointed towards it and said, "Look, David, there it is."

She helped him onto a swing and began pushing him. David giggled happily as he swung up and down. Suddenly, a hand grabbed the swing as it returned. Adela looked up to see Sergeant Lopez, who towered over both of them.

"Well, hello there," he said. Adela took a step back in fear, right into two other Cuban agents, who grabbed her. "Where is the rest of the family, whore? Tell me!"

Adela looked afraid and glanced towards the house. Her shoulders slumped in defeat. "I will tell you. Please don't hurt my boy. This way."

The agents let her go and she took David by the hand as she walked deliberately away from the house and down another street.

In the living room of Adela's house, Solomon and Sarah were talking quietly. The tribal decorations on the walls showed plainly that Adela was a follower of Santeria. Solomon said, "I'm tired of running. It seems like we're always running and hiding."

Sarah replied, "Soon we will have rest. I can feel it."

Solomon opened his mouth to reply, but at that moment I burst in by the front door. I said, "Tell everyone! Time to go!"

A few minutes later, Solomon, Sarah, and Flora were gathering up the family's possessions. Miguel, still partially paralyzed, watched from a chair.

Sarah asked, "Where is David?"

Flora said, "He went for a walk with Adela. Julio Antonio has gone to get them. He said he'll meet us there."

Soon, the family was at a dilapidated old pier loading up onto a boat equipped with the engine I had purchased. They have few possessions; Flora and Solomon helped Miguel onto the boat, and then Sarah climbed on board.

Miguel looked at Sarah. "Your harp?" Sarah shook her head sadly. "We'll get you another one, Mother." She smiled her thanks.

At that moment, I drove up in my jeep—alone. Flora ran over to me. "Adela? David?"

I shook my head. "I couldn't find them. I looked, but now there are soldiers coming. They must have found us!"

"I can't leave without David," she protested.

"Woman, the soldiers are minutes behind! You must go, now!"

"I can't! Not without my son!"

"Don't be a fool!" I snapped, trying to shock her into thinking logically. "You'll all die! David needs his mother alive! I will find him—now go!" I grabbed her by the arm and ran to the boat. I helped start the engine to help them get moving. "Go!" I said once again.

Solomon took the helm of the boat as it slowly moved out into the ocean. I jumped into my jeep and started it up. I glanced once over my shoulder and said under my breath, "Vaya con Dios, my friends."

I drove away quickly even as in the distance I saw the military trucks speeding towards the pier.

Dr. Julio Antonio del Marmol

Chapter 31: Che's Last Dance with the Devil

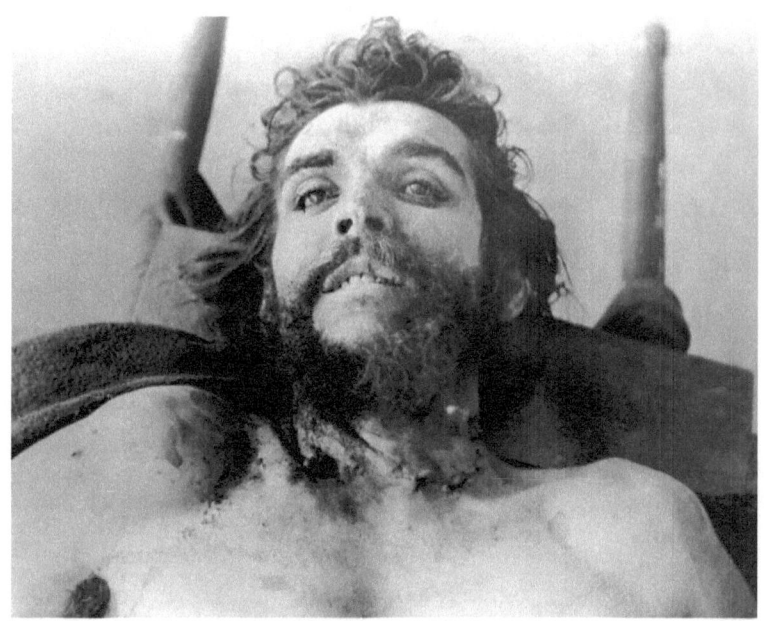

31 Che Captured in Bolivia

By December of 1965, the Baumanns had made it to Miami, Florida. There they managed to get Miguel to a hospital where he received treatment from a physician named Doctor Stone. Flora was abiding patiently in the hospital's waiting room when Doctor Stone walked up to speak to her.

She asked fearfully, "Is he...?"

Stone nodded. "The surgery was a success. We believe his nerve function will return fully soon."

Several weeks later, Miguel, now fully recovered and enlisted in the American military, walked in the front door of the Baumann house. Flora looked up from her knitting.

"Flora!" he said.

Flora got up and embraced him. "Oh, Miguel!"

"They accepted me into the Special Forces, my flower."

Flora asked dubiously, "Are you sure this is a good idea? You only just got better."

"We already talked about this, Flora. Remember our family, what we came from."

"Remember your father!" she countered.

Miguel sat down. "I wish I could remember him. But I am proud of him; he died fighting for freedom. I want to be like him."

"Even if you die like him?"

"Don't talk like that, Flora. Please. After I finish my training, I will join the fighting in South America."

"Where Che fights. In Bolivia."

"Yes."

That night, Sarah was in her simple bedroom which contained only her bed and nightstand as a faint blue light from the window illuminated the room. She prayed, "Protect my Miguel Angel."

It was now early October of 1967, and still hot in the jungles of Bolivia. A Bolivian captain and Felix Rodriguez led a group of ten Bolivian Army troops followed by an American Special Forces unit which included Miguel Angel.

Rodriguez said, "We have him trapped up there," as he pointed to a ridge.

The captain directed his men to flank one side of the ridge; the U.S. contingent was to take the other flank.

Behind his cover of rocks, Che was holding out, exhausted. He had been shot in the leg already and blood trickled from another wound on his left arm. Next to him was the dark man with six fingers. A handful of other troops took positions overlooking the ridge. Che's face was determined, and the sunlight briefly lit up the eyes of the dark man, and the catlike reflection shone once again. An aggressive piece of harp music was playing, but if Che or the dark man heard it, they gave no indication.

Back in Miami, Sarah had the curtains drawn and the lights turned down low. She played her harp passionately, almost angrily.

The harp music continued. In Bolivia, the American soldiers suddenly took gunfire. One of them went down and the others took cover and opened fire on Che's position. From the other side of the ridge, the Bolivian troops heard the gunfire and moved in.

Up on the ridge, Che and his dark companion were firing on the American troops. One of his men hit, Che glanced over his shoulder a moment and then kept firing. The dark man lined up a shot, smiled cruelly, and shot down another American.

Miguel saw the man go down. "Damn them!" he exclaimed. Just draw their fire a bit longer."

In Miami, almost as if she were seeing what was happening in Bolivia, Sarah played more fiercely.

The Broken Rainbow: Mysterious Dark Karma

Che was shouting orders when the Bolivians burst in on them from the other side, firing their weapons. Che turned to where the dark man was and said, "Cover me!" But the man was gone. Che looked around in confusion; the rest of his men were gunned down, fanatically screaming save for one other young soldier who threw his gun down in surrender. Che wearily dropped his gun, looking almost relieved.

Miguel noticed the firing had stopped. The harp music became more tranquil, eerie. He gestured for his men to move forward, and they started to move. Suddenly, the dark man was there, blood spurting as he stabbed a soldier. For a moment, the Americans were all stunned in surprise at the suddenness of the encounter. The man smiled, blood spatter on his mouth and teeth, and he raised his knife. All the men fired, riddling the man's body with bullets, and he fell over, dead.

In Miami, Sarah finished playing her song and then rested limply on her harp.

Miguel, Rodriguez, and the Bolivian captain discussed Che's fate outside the mud school building they were holding him in. The captain said, "We must kill him, now."

"Why?" Miguel disagreed. "Do you want to make a martyr out of a murderer? That's foolish! It's exactly what Castro wants!"

"Those are my orders, Mr. Baumann," the captain replied.

Rodriguez said, "Amigo, we have to listen to the Bolivians. They are the authority here."

Miguel said in disgust, "Fine. It's not my responsibility. Do what you must."

The captain pointed to one of his soldiers and entered the building, Miguel and Rodriguez following. Inside, they found Che tied to a chair, exhausted and bleeding. He looked peaceful and yet still defiant.

"Greetings, gentlemen," Che said. "I heard you discussing my fate."

"I do not wish for them to kill you here, Che," Miguel said.

"Do you wish mercy for me?" Che asked scornfully. "Is this because of your so-called God? I tell you; I don't believe in him."

"You will only see God for a moment because you're going to a different place."

"Ha! Where is he, then? Where is your God? You are the same weak man I met years ago. To think, they let you be a teacher! Do you even have the guts to kill me yourself, coward?"

The captain looked at Miguel, who shook his head slightly. "Who is the coward, Che—the man who comes to another country with his lies to spread oppression, or the man who tries to show them the truth? But it is not for me to kill you or even judge you. Let God be your judge, not me."

As Miguel walked out of the building, Che yelled, "There is no God!!" Miguel walked a few paces away and stared peacefully into the sky as Che continued to rant. "There is only death!" There was a brief pause. "Well, what are you waiting for? Shoot then, coward, shoot!"

A brief burst of gunfire was heard from inside, followed by another. Miguel looked back at the school for a moment, and then up at the sky where he saw a broken

The Broken Rainbow: Mysterious Dark Karma

rainbow form in the mist. After a moment, the rainbow formed fully, completed at last.

Back in Havana after the news of the execution was received, I was sitting with the other leaders on the podium behind Castro as he delivered his eulogy for Che. "Tonight we are gathered here, you and I, to try to express these sentiments in some way with regard to one who was one of the most familiar, one of the most admired, one of the most beloved, and, without any doubt, the most extraordinary of our *compañeros* of the revolution, to express these sentiments to him and to the heroes who have fought and have fallen beside him—his internationalist army which has been writing a glorious page in history...."

Later, we were gathered in the green room as we usually did after one of Castro's speeches. He was hot and thirsty after finishing his speech, and an aide brought him a cool drink which he gulped down rapidly. Waiting for him after he refreshed himself was Piñeiro, the head of the G-2.

Castro said, "Ah, Piñeiro, how much bullshit do I need to say to these imbeciles about that Argentinian bastard who was trying to take my place?"

"The man is dead, *Comandante en Jefe*," Piñeiro replied, "so I imagine not much more."

"Yes, dead! We get exactly what we wanted, an international martyr for our cause and at the same time that traitor is out of the way."

"What can I say? Comandante, you are a genius."

In Miami, Hernesto was driving his white Jaguar in a relaxed manner with the window down. He turned down the street towards the Baumann house, where

Flora was sitting out on the front porch, sewing. The day was very quiet, and she could hear voices from inside the house. She looked up as a new sound approached the house to see Hernesto pull up in the street. As she watched, Hernesto opened the back door, and her son David, now about six, ran out and up the porch to her.

"Mama!" he yelled.

Flora got down on her knees and held his head as she stroked his hair, scarcely allowing herself to believe it was him. "David? Is it really you? My David!!" She took him in her arms and began to weep.

Rose and Sarah came out the door, wondering what all the commotion was about. Rose started to say, "Flora, what is—" but stopped when she saw David. Sarah also stopped.

David saw his grandmother. "Grandma!"

Flora let him go and he jumped into Sarah's arms. Flora hugged Rose as they both started to cry. Sarah held David and looked into his eyes. "Just what I prayed for," was all she said.

A tear rolled down her cheek as she smiled at David; Hernesto, still in the street, smiled as he watched everyone.

From inside the house Miguel's voice was heard, demanding, "What is everyone doing outside?" He came out and was amazed and speechless for just a moment. Then he saw Hernesto and said, "It's a miracle! Hernesto, how? This is truly a gift from God!"

Sarah turned toward him and said, "David, look—it's your Papa."

David reached for Miguel Angel. "Papa!"

Miguel took him, smiling. The women all wept, the tears freely rolling down their faces.

The Broken Rainbow: Mysterious Dark Karma

Minutes later, the entire family was gathered: Solomon, Englebert, Rose, Sarah, Flora, and Miguel Angel. There was food and wine; a silver Kiddush cup was on the table and a harp in the corner of the room. Hernesto and David were the guests of honor.

Miguel said, "Hernesto, how did you do it?"

Hernesto replied, "I told you, I have some powerful friends. That reminds me, Julio Antonio says hello."

Miguel embraced Hernesto while Flora carried David around happily to all the members of the family. Miguel said, "Tell him I said thank you. Thank you as well, Hernesto."

"Rejoice, now you are free."

Miguel spoke very quietly to himself. "He has cut me free from the cords of the wicked."

As the gathering continued around him, Miguel looked at the black and white photograph on the wall which showed the family in Germany: Grandfather Solomon, Grandmother Livka, Rose, Jacob, David, Solomon Jr, Jacob Jr, Sarah, and Englebert. Beneath the picture was a Hebrew blessing.

Chapter 32: The Circle of Time

32 Grand Avenue, Santa Ana, California

October 1971

Through a great and terrible mistake by our own intelligence my real identity was exposed, blowing my cover beyond any repair. The intelligence community gave me the sad news that I needed to abandon my country and family within 72 hours, or I would be killed with all my family. The only possibility to prevent those I loved from being killed would be to leave immediately, dissociating myself from everyone I loved, as disappear into the darkness of a moonless night. This would give them the possibility to deny that they knew nothing about my activities. With only a snorkel and fins, I swam for twelve hours to the U.S. Naval Reservation at Guantanamo, where my associates had already prepared my entry. After I was processed, I was put on a plane with all precautions to avoid my being identified and flown to Florida.

Corona del Mar, Orange County, California
May 21st, 1988—17 years later

I opened my eyes, very happy from the beautiful dream of my childhood, and awoke to a very beautiful morning for my birthday. I woke that day and opened the curtains on my master bedroom. like always, to enjoy the patio with palm trees and bougainvillea and the water running down the long waterslide into the swimming pool installed to the right of the wet bar next to the huge jacuzzi. This view created a harmony, wonderful to wake up to, looking down the hills from the cliffs to the ocean. My friends had prepared for me a great surprise. To the right of the pool, I saw my friend O'Brien off to one side with a bottle of Negra Modelo beer, which caught me by surprise more than the beautiful decorations they had all over the patio with huge, multicolored bells with banners that read, "Happy Birthday, Julio Antonio".

As I opened the sliding doors of the master bedroom and everyone noticed that I was awake at that early hour of the morning, they started to sing "Happy Birthday" to me in unison, joyfully and with enthusiasm in a genuinely festive mood. I was confused and surprised and put the fingers of my left hand and caressed my forehead. With a little smile of gratitude, as they continued with their singing, I stepped out of my bedroom and walked along the deck to my swimming pool. To the left, I saw a huge, white table beneath a white canvas umbrella full of packages, wrapped in birthday paper. Evidently all my friends and family, including my Mimi and Papi, were in on it, but what surprised me the most was the presence there of my good friend and contact in intelligence, who continued to drink his beer by the wet bar with a huge smile as he raised the fingers of his left hand in a casual military salute.

I wondered who told him about the surprise party. None of my friends had his phone number or any way to contact him. I was still in my pajamas, not even having washed my face yet. I embraced Mima and Papi, who wished me a happy birthday. I greeted everyone and went towards the wet bar and O'Brien.

He said, "Happy Birthday, my friend. I hope you have many more years and more happy birthdays. I see the company of your mom and dad has brought to you a new smile and happiness in your life."

I nodded. "This is something I have to be grateful to you for the rest of my life. You're the one who offered me the contact in Spain to pull my Mima and Papi out of Cuba. I will never forget that."

He raised his left arm and shook his head. "You owe me nothing. Whatever we did was a very small sacrifice compared to what you've done for us and the country. This was just a token of our gratitude to you. Every corner of this country owes you much for the tremendous sacrifices and suffering you've endured in your life since you were twelve in your fight to stop malignant forces from coming to our country to destroy our families. Like the Nazis, the communist system, wherever they put their extremist ideological dirty boots, destroy like cannibals everything they touch until they have nothing to destroy anymore. And then they begin to eat each other."

I smiled slightly and gave him a small pat on the shoulder. "Well, why don't we say then that we're even, mano e mano? Both of us feel gratitude towards each other and the satisfaction to help each other."

With gratitude in his face, he replied, "I like that a lot more. Like you always say, one hand helps to wash the other and both of them are needed to properly wash your face."

I smiled once more. "OK. Your conclusion, I believe, is fair and square. Let's leave it there."

O'Brien smiled broadly and shook his head. "OK. How do you always manage, without 100% mastery of our language, you always manage to win the argument?" I smiled and nodded. He added, "Why don't you go and get dressed and tell your friends and family that I have a little surprise for you for your birthday, and we'll be back in a little bit?"

Is this true? Or is this an excuse to kidnap me from my birthday and take me to work as a slave?"

"To be honest with you, it's a little of both."

"I know you by now. This surprise comes with something else, like your hamburgers—they always come with French fries. By the way, how the devil did you know my friends were preparing this party for me? Have you been tapping their phones?"

"Shh. Remember, for your own security, I have to keep an eye on everybody." He pointed to his ears.

"Remember, we're like Papa God, we see and hear everything. Arturo didn't sleep at all last night, coordinating with Yaneba and Elizabeth how to keep you in the dark to surprise you."

I shook my head, not happy at hearing that. How many times have I told my friends on my team never to speak of anything of importance over the phone? Thank God this wasn't important."

O'Brien put his finger to his lips again. "Shh. Don't reprimand them, because they hardly slept last night so they could surprise you with all this." He gestured around at all the decorations. Even the mediation pool was decorated from side to side with the bells and balls.

I smiled and replied. "Don't worry about it. I won't reprimand them today, but I will tomorrow. Knowing like you do all the details for this party, imagine what would have happened if it had been the other side listening in."

O'Brien nodded. "Yes, you're right. And that's a very strong point. Let me tell you, though, with all the people you have around this place under the supervision of Chopin, you have really tight security. I don't think for a single minute that the most expert hitman would be able to penetrate this extreme security net he's put around nearly the entire block. To be honest with you, that was the first thing I noticed when I tried to get to your place. Luckily for me, Chopin recognized me and gave me the password so that I could get to the patio where everyone was patiently waiting for you to wake up. They didn't want to ruin your morning sleep since they know how late you work some nights."

"I know, I know. In my opinion, they're all admirable. But unfortunately, we're all human beings, not perfect, so when we engage in personal projects like this birthday, we get distracted and lower our guard. That is the precisely when they get us: while our guard is lowered because our emotions are highly focused on a project like this. This is something we cannot afford in our work in espionage. We cannot give ourselves the luxury of being distracted for a single minute, because that could cost not just our lives but those of our associates."

"Yes, I understand, and you do what you have to do. I'm not going to disagree with that. But you better go and get dressed. You don't want to make my two surprises wait."

"Uh-oh! I thought it was going to be one, but now it's two and with urgency."

"OK, go and get dressed. I'll give you more details in the car." As I walked to the master bedroom, O'Brien asked, "Can I take another of those Negra Modelos from your mini bar?"

"Of course, but don't take to many if you're going to drive."

"OK, but don't take too long dressing. I know you don't like to be driven by anybody, especially an old half-drunk man."

I told my friends and family that I had to leave for a little bit. They protested, and I said, "It won't be for long. O'Brien just wants to show me a surprise."

Amid the protests we left the house and walked toward O'Brien's four-door Ford sedan and drove to the Pacific Coast Highway. Chopin followed with three of his men to make sure we were safe.

As we drove, O'Brien smiled, "Well, if we look at your three surprises...."

"Oh, my God—they keep multiplying! It's not two anymore!"

"Well for security we divided one and put them in different locations."

I said, "Just keep your eyes on the road and stop playing with my curiosity. You won't achieve your purpose. You've known me very well after all the years we've worked together. No matter how much you've taught me, you won't get me to beg you for information. I know in the end you'll have to tell me anyway. You know my patience is like a rubber band: very elastic."

He shook his head and smiled. "There you go—another Marmolism! You could write not just one book but several, probably a dictionary!"

"OK, OK. At least tell me what the first surprise is going to be. It's my birthday, I deserve at least a little hint."

He shook his head. "Come on, come on. At least you can tell me that you're dying of curiosity."

I smiled vaguely. "Well, I have to be honest—a little." We approached the Balboa Bay Club along the PCH. I saw him put the signal light to turn left into the club. "Uh-oh! I know where you're going. Is this business or pleasure?"

He smiled mischievously. "A little bit of both, like I told you before."

He parked the car and we walked to the yacht moorings in the back of the club. We walked along the pier, and as we approached on of them, he called from the gangway bottom, "Captain Miguel Angel! Permission to come aboard."

A young man dressed in a U.S. Navy uniform climbed down from the bridge of the ship, grinning from ear to ear. He yelled, "Permission granted! Come on aboard, and welcome, my friends."

O'Brien hadn't exaggerated. That voice and large smiled brought me back many years with great joy. I

The Broken Rainbow: Mysterious Dark Karma

immediately recognized my old friend Miguel Angel. I wasn't surprised that O'Brien called him by that name, but my memory for the retention of facial expression and gesture, but the most characteristic one is one's smile. That was difficult to change, including with people who had submitted to plastic surgery.

Miguel Angel hugged me joyfully and seated us on the deck near the bow of the ship. O'Brien said, "You guys catch up. I'm going to go to the galley. I don't know about you guys, but I haven't even had breakfast and I'm hungry. The day is perfect for a few more beers."

After we exchanged several short stories and memories, Miguel Angel said that O'Brien contacted him at my suggestion. He gave me all the details so we could take to completion your project the Zipper with the final details in Berlin, Germany.

After we spoke for almost an hour, O'Brien finally came out with several beers on a tray and another tray with ham rolled with Swiss cheese, green olives with pimentos stuck with toothpicks. Since I had also not breakfasted, I was the first one to dip into the tray, as O'Brien's rush had virtually kidnapped me out of the house. As I chewed my roll of ham and cheese, I said, "It gives me great pleasure to see how you've been educating your palate, something we both have to give thanks to my mother, since without her neither of us would have learned the exquisite delicacies life offers to us."

O'Brien said with a smile as he nodded, "You're darn right. Please wait a little bit. My menu is more extensive. It's not just limited to ham and cheese."

I smiled again and cleared my throat. "I wondered what was taking so long. I began to think you were making a turkey for Thanksgiving or consulting with your boss, Addison. Now I see why you got delayed."

O'Brien, beer in hand and wearing an apron with the yacht's logo like a high cuisine chef, went back to the galley and returned a few minutes later with two trays of hors d'oeuvres of calamary in its ink, shrimp in garlic butter, and lobster tails with two containers on the tray of red sauce and tartar sauce, along with some crackers with beluga, black caviar and red salmon caviar, decorated with slices of different cheeses.

Miguel Angel had remained silent, entertained by our conversation and enjoying having plenty of excellent food. He said, "My great friend, I think I lost a great opportunity during the long years of absence from you. I expect, however, to catch up with this kind of treatment and this welcome you guys gave me today. You'll have to use the most fearsome dogs to chase me away."

I smiled and patted him on the shoulder. "You are on my list of the best friends I ever had. You are welcome yesterday, now, and forever to come to our side at any moment you wish."

He nodded in gratitude and satisfaction. "I know, thank you. Anyway, I need to say I'm very grateful to have you as a friend. You've always been generous and willing to die for the ones you love and care for. I remember how you saved my life and most importantly, returned my son to me—don't think I've forgotten. I owe you my life."

"You owe me only your loyalty and love, which I know I have without doubt. You've given them to me all your life."

O'Brien sat next to us, enjoying our company and his beer and the beautiful moment of our reunion. "Both of you guys should always remember this moment, because in these days and the difficult times we've gone through around the world, it's difficult to find priceless friendship like you have. It was born in the most terrible moments of your lives, the persecution, agonies you both lived in that horrible system in Cuba which, ironically, brought to your characters something extremely valuable, bonding you guys like steel with the most powerful union between human beings, which is when we go through Hell fighting against a common enemy. It brings to our warrior spirits blood and loyalty for the rest of our lives."

I smiled and patted him on the shoulder. "Thank you very much for your beautiful words. Not only beautiful, but of profound significance. Even though all you say is true, this bond also can exist from the beautiful and sincere friendship born between men who educate themselves about the crimes that this totalitarian regime made innocent people suffer from out of their ambition for money and power. Those men without scruples persecute everyone who doesn't agree with their ideology. Men like you, O'Brien, who have learned this are willing to die to stop these men from bringing the same misery to your country and family. You haven't suffered for yourself yet what we did, but you've learned from people like us." I took a sip of my beer. "That friendship which exists between us, O'Brien, is priceless, too."

"Thank you for your comparison, but with all my respect and gratitude, there's no comparison to what you guys went through and experienced in your own flesh and what I can learn from your sad and terrible experience." He raised his right hand to stop me from saying anything. "I really, really appreciate your friendship and comparison, but I've never been like you and Miguel Angel, gone through the horrible experience of losing a member of my family at the hands of those despicable people, the criminals who kill even children without mercy. That is an experience that you have to live for yourself in order to be able to understand the level of pain that men go through with something like that."

Miguel Angel looked sorrowful. "This time, with all my respect, my good friend and brother, Julio Antonio, I'm in complete agreement with your friend O'Brien. Even though I know that everything in life is different and there's no one way to reach Berlin. I learned in my own experiences that in different times we eventually get where we want to go in different ways if we do it all with determination. Maybe that famous wall dividing our great Germany will finally be demolished by history and our great effort.

He raised his beer to offer a toast. "I believe my grandfather and great-grandfather will be very proud that I put a little bit of effort into this operation that finally will return freedom and sovereignty in the reunification of Germany, which came from the horrible dictatorship of the Nazis to enter a worse one under the communist Marxists. Maybe we'll also send a message of freedom to other countries subjugated by this new Nazi Marxist ideology in Europe. Only Heaven and the Supreme Architect of the Universe can predict that maybe we could also achieve the collapse of the evil empire of the Soviet Union."

O'Brien raised his beer and smiled. "Even though this sounds like a Utopian dream, like you said before, Heaven only knows that the sky is the limit. Whatever we do, we're only the architects and engineers that will push the dominos on the table and will sit down to observe how one single piece collapses the whole game, using a very powerful gentleman, Mr. Franklin, that beautiful and powerful $100 bill might accomplish together with the intelligence community what the bullets of our Marines and soldiers have been incapable of doing for the past several decades in only a few weeks. Considering that our best contact is Colonel Vladimir Putin, who we bribed with only a few million dollars. He will open the gates for you guys. If he fails to do so, he will not receive the rest of the bribe.

He smirked as he paused to take a sip from his bottle of beer. He looked at me. "Remember, always, Putin is nothing more than another mercenary, another Nazi, without any scruples, principles, or decency. You know better than I, since you told me about meeting him when he was very young. You know his personality better than anyone. You remember also that the Devil is not smart by just by being a devil; he's a lot smarter because he's old. The older Putin gets, the more conniving he learns to be as do his diabolic ambitions.

"You should always also remember that you have a great advantage over him, since he doesn't know who you are now. Don't take this to the bank—let's hope our intelligence is correct because it's very important for you in case you have to establish a last-minute negotiation with this diabolical individual. Remember he's not a colonel in the KGB because he was born yesterday." He put one of his hands on my shoulder. "You know how much we're going to give him. If he asks for more, bargain with him to make it easier. Give him whatever he wants to get what you want. He doesn't have the slightest idea of the plans we have are not limited just to collapsing the Eastern Bloc in Germany. He doesn't even know he's putting a rope of $100 bills around his neck which will destroy the entire Soviet Bloc.

He added with greater emphasis, "I know that your extremely greater experience puts you far ahead of Putin, but don't forget you possess the most powerful weapon any member of intelligence possesses: your mental psychic abilities which you focused and molded when we sent you to Montauk. Use this weapon if necessary—it's a silent weapon no one can see or even expect. No metal detector can ever discover it; that little devil Putin will want to put his ass in a bag of ice because his tail will catch on fire when the Lightning lands in Berlin very soon."

I replied, "I hope I can live up to your high expectations."

O'Brien said with a smile, "You will exceed my expectations, I have no doubt about that, my friend!"

Chapter 33: Closure and Beginning

33 Exterior of the Hotel

A few hours later, we had covered all the details of the plan we would follow in Europe, particularly in Berlin, Germany. The principal objective there was that it would be the center of distribution for all the funds we were going to spread around during the final phase of the operation. After the debriefing with everyone in perfect agreement, we said goodbye to Miguel Angel with strong hugs, having already arranged our next meeting.

We headed for the city of Costa Mesa, leaving our sister city of Newport Beach behind. O'Brien had a big smile on his face as he drove his Ford sedan to the address of our final destination: 3050 Bristol Street, where we had one of our secure locations in the penthouse of this particular hotel, reserved exclusively for the activities of the Lightning team.

I found it strange that O'Brien would bring me to this particular location on my birthday, as he explained to me this phase of the last stage of the operation should not be linked with anyone who had been participating in the first phase of the currency's production. In case anything went wrong, one group would not be linked to the other, because the new group had no idea how or where the product had come from. Especially in case of betrayal, no one would ever be able to figure out who was behind it all and avoid the risk of losing the entire work. Given that, I wondered why he would bring me to a location linked to my primary team.

When we arrived at the hotel, O'Brien gave the sedan keys to the valet. We entered the lobby, passing by the bar on our way to the elevators. After we entered one of the glass elevators, O'Brien pressed the button for the penthouse suite. As we ascended, we could see the entire bar area, garden, and lobby. A couple that looked like they were honeymooning were also inside the car. They looked at us curiously when they saw the button O'Brien had pressed.

The young man said, "We are really, really impressed with our matrimonial suite we're staying in here. The penthouse must be breathtaking!"

The Broken Rainbow: Mysterious Dark Karma

O'Brien smiled slightly. "It is truly awesome."

When they got to their floor, before the door opened, the young red-headed freckled woman said, "Have a pleasant day."

This time I replied. "Thank you. You guys have the same."

They got out and we continued our ascent. When we got to the penthouse, my surprise was enormous, just as O'Brien had predicted. I recognized the smiling face of Sonya, who said, "Happy Birthday, Julio Antonio." Arms wide open, she received me with genuine joy and gave me a strong hug that I felt in my ribs. With a mischievous grin, she whispered in my ear, "I hope that you haven't changed your tastes and still enjoy a good bar of butter after all these years."

I wasn't able to keep from chuckling. We separated and replied in code, "I haven't' changed my taste, I continue to like it, and miss it very much when it's not on the table, as I've missed you and your beautiful, fantastic memory."

O'Brien looked on uncomprehending. I saw his puzzled face and tried to alleviate his confusion by saying, "Nothing important at all, just wonders of our memories."

Sonya smiled and nodded. She said to me with complete conviction, "That is right. It's unbelievable the things we can store in the drawers of our memories, including things that after many years we think many occasions forgotten." She offered us something to drink.

I replied that I was OK, but O'Brien, Irishman that he was, never said no to alcohol. I smiled and said, "I have to keep this Irishman on a leash. He's my lucky driver today. I'm not sure if I made the right choice."

O'Brien said, "Come on, please! It's just a beer. It won't get anyone drunk to complete the circle of this beautiful morning, celebrating the birthday of my great friend."

"You drink your beer, but don't use my birthday as an excuse. And only one beer—more than one, and I'll go back to my house in a taxi."

Sonya laughed and said, "Only one beer? Hm. I didn't know O'Brien was such a lightweight drinker."

I raised my right hand high to stop her. "Please don't go there. Don't encourage him! I've counted so far eight beers between my house and another meeting we had with Miguel Angel. I cannot for the love of God understand how somebody can drink so many beers in a very few hours in the morning!" I raised both hands in disbelief. "Believe me, if I drank even half of those beers, I would spend the rest of my birthday sleeping off the fantastic drunkenness."

She smiled and came back from the bar with three glasses of beer. "Come on, Julio Antonio—at least have a sip to toast with us. "

I picked up a glass. "This is a great problem, because you're becoming O'Brien's accomplice! You've not been with us all morning. If we continue to drink alcohol, I don't think we'll make it to noon!" O'Brien smiled as he hurriedly took his glass of beer off the tray like a little boy rushing to get a candy bar from someone with shining satisfaction in his eyes. I shook my head with a smile. "You cannot deny your origin, because there's an old saying in Cuba: God created liquor to keep the Irish from conquering the world."

O'Brien raised his glass high with a smile of satisfaction, savoring his beer before he even tasted it. He

The Broken Rainbow: Mysterious Dark Karma

said, "Also, God created Bacardi Rum in Cuba to keep the Castro communists from destroying the world."

I could not help but laugh at that, along with Sonya who found the remark very comic. I said, "As you can see, this is not the normal O'Brien—this is the Negra Modelo talking with his tongue." We all laughed, toasted to each other and they to my happiness ahead as a birthday toast.

Afterwards, Sonya asked O'Brien, "Have you already taken Julio Antonio to the Crowne Plaza hotel?"

O'Brien started and put a finger to his lips. "That is my last surprise for his birthday." They exchanged a glance and smiled mischievously as they both looked at me.

Sonya said, "OK, let's go." She picked up her handbag and slung it over her right shoulder. "I believe that surprise is the best one." We stepped outside and entered the elevator.

I said, "Guys, guys—why don't you stop? I woke up today with surprise after surprise. You'll drive me crazy."

O'Brien said, "Aren't you happy?"

I looked at Sonya and said, "Yes, very happy." She gave me a kiss and put her arm around my shoulder to cuddle a little with me.

As we entered the lobby, O'Brien got the car, and together we drove to the Crowne Plaza a few blocks away. When we arrived there, O'Brien checked the sedan in with the valet there and got his service ticket.

We entered the Plaza lobby and went to the bar. Before we even sat down at one of the tables, we were greeted by the smiling face of a handsome young man of middle height with wavy red hair who gave a big hug and kiss to Sonya. He looked at his watch and said, "Mama, I've been waiting for you for over an hour!"

Sonya pointed to O'Brien. "Blame your great Irish friend. He not only has been drinking too many beers this morning but also is our driver—imagine it!! But he is the organizer of this family event."

The young man stood next to the table as the waiter cleaned it with a wet towel. He held out his hand to me. "I'm Julius Christian."

I reacted in surprise as I looked at this young man in excellent physical shape, and Sonya stepped forward, anticipating my reply, "This is your father, Julio Antonio del Marmol. I don't know if you remember, but this is not the first time I've introduced you two."

Julius Christian grinned broadly and said with conviction, "Of course I remember, very well! I have a prodigious memory, and I remember he promised he would reunite with us in Costa Rica and never did."

I smiled, his hand still in mind and squeezed it very hard. "I never promised anything for the future because it's not in our hands but God's. How can we make a false promise in something that we don't know we can comply with? It doesn't depend on any of us. But talking about memories, which it appears you've inherited from me, mine says there's no doubt that I never promised anything. I always say my memory is longer and heavier than an elephant. I remember very clearly when you were perhaps four or five years old, a good-looking kid with a sad face. But you still bravely tried to smile, and asked me, 'Are you coming to Costa Rica with us, Papi, and com with us to that place where we can eat all the flavors of ice cream and never have to stand in line again?' I replied, if I remember correctly, that I would *try* to follow you very soon."

Julius Christian nodded. "You are absolutely right. I recall it that way as well, and that was a sincere answer I had from you at that time. Of course, not the answer I was expecting or the reassurance I was looking for, but I thought at that moment I would never see you again. I honor your honesty. Over the years my mother has told me all the stories about you and the great legacy you left behind of bravery, honor, and chivalry that inspired me to imitate you and follow in your footsteps as a spy. Something I can say to you today with pride is that I, at my young age, have become one of the best analysts inside the intelligence community."

I looked at O'Brien in surprise. He nodded. The waiter arrived with our beverages, and he said with a smile, "I hope you're pleased with Team #2 that I've put together very carefully. I made sure that everyone met your requirements. I considered that your birthday was the best possible day to introduce them to you, since you have plenty of time ahead to debrief all of them in luxurious details. If you consider any of them not completely up to your standards, you have time to train them, so we don't leave any room for error."

I nodded. "I believe you've done fabulous, excellent work, like you always do. I just wish you were more abstemious."

"You must be kidding! You take that away from me, you'll take the joy out of my life."

Julius Christian asked me, "How many years have you two known each other and worked together?"

"Over 17 years for both," O'Brien replied. "From the moment I met your father when he arrived in Florida from Guantanamo Base, we've worked together." He used the occasion to add something I always really appreciated. "Ever since your father arrived in our country, the Cuban government hasn't stopped trying to assassinate him. We had to relocate him multiple times in different states and cities, not just in the U.S. but around the world. He has 19 different identities and 25 passports as of this moment. I have no idea how many he'll have next week. I have to add that he never sleeps in the same place for more than a couple of days.

"Believe me," O'Brien reassured him, "I'm not trying to excuse your father for anything, but the best thing he's ever done in all these years, for both you and your mother's security, is to keep his distance from you. Now the level of danger has gone down after 17 years. Though it hasn't completely disappeared, what we're doing right now, we'll reduce it as if another 17 years has already passed. That is why you're going to have the privilege of saying in the future that you were part of something that changed history. That's also why I used his birthday as a reward for the multiple sacrifices and emotional distresses he's suffered so far away from his family, friends, and loved ones for nearly all his life."

I looked at O'Brien gratefully and understood his good intentions and motivations for what he said. I still had a little remorse in my heart. I had tried to contact them on several occasions; perhaps what O'Brien had said was partly true. I felt hadn't made enough effort precisely because I didn't want any harm to befall them. By the same token, I felt regret for not having tried harder.

Sonya looked at me with a great deal of emotion as she remembered the beautiful time we spent with each other in creating the young man who stood before us now.

I looked at Julius Christian in the eye, and in a moment of emotion our souls linked and both of us grew misty-eyed, without being able to control it. O'Brien's words and the memories of Sonya sharing the first tender kiss of love and gratitude when I defended her against her bullying brother combined to overwhelm my control, and two tears rolled down my cheeks. I tried to hide them by quickly wiping them away with the back of my hand. I opened my arms to Julius Christian. "I know we've shaken hands, but can I give you a hug now, the hug I've been dreaming to give you all these years of my absence?"

As if moved by a spring, he shot up emotionally out of his chair with tears in his eyes and came around the table. Tears rolled down his cheeks, caught by my emotional state, and we gave each other the biggest hug I had ever given and received. Sonya, watching us, stood up as well and came around the table. She walked over to us and embraced both of us.

I said, "I'm sorry for not trying harder in my efforts to reunite with you guys."

They both shook their heads and Sonya replied, "You have nothing to apologize for. The important thing is that we are together now, OK?"

"Yes, that's right, Mom," Julius Christian said firmly.

As all this happened, I caught O'Brien out of the corner of my eye drying his eyes, but the old fox didn't waste the opportunity to say something in the waiter's ear, politely asking her to refill our beverages, which were just apple and cranberry juices.

Or so I thought, but the fox was actually asking for a glass of Grand Marnier with warm non-cream milk, almost as if he was ready for a nap, as this was my remedy for a good night's sleep. In my emotional state, he felt that I wouldn't notice, and it would pass unobserved. He made the mistake of telling the waitress in a very low voice, almost in her ear; instead of throwing me off it opened my curiosity to know what the secret was they were sharing.

I surprised him then, when I walked back to the chair at the table, picked up his cup—which was supposed to be coffee—and he looked at me like a kid caught with his hand in the cookie jar. With a small smile, I shook my head and clucked my tongue. "I'm driving us all home from here, OK?"

He replied only with a nod. He knew he had been caught in the act; neither Sonya nor Julius Christian knew what had happened. We continued our conversation as if nothing had happened. We shared the details and debriefed them on the roles I wanted them to play in the final operation in Europe.

A little later, we left the hotel after saying goodbye to Julius Christian. As we walked out towards the valet, I pulled the ticket out of his coat pocket, retrieving the car with a generous tip for the attendant, and returned Sonya to the penthouse at the secure location. I told her I would come back at the end of the day to complete my birthday in her company.

After I returned to my home and the waiting crowd in Corona del Mar, who all recriminated me for the long time I was absent while O'Brien handled all the complaints chivalrously. After that bombardment from my friends and family, he had no energy to argue with me, and I

The Broken Rainbow: Mysterious Dark Karma

forced him to take a nap in one of the bedrooms of my house. The rest of us enjoyed the amenities of the pool and backyard, and I took the opportunity to debrief my #1 Team how they would continue the operation in my absence while I went to Europe. I was only supposed to take my pilot Chopin with me on this trip as a precautionary measure if I had to fly back in an emergency and leave Europe suddenly.

It was a beautiful day in the company of my friends and family, something very unusual. It was customary in the past for strange things to happen on my birthday. I looked at my wristwatch and saw that the day had flown by, like life does occasionally, without being noticed. I took into consideration that, after all, this birthday could be another exception like everything has in life.

I saw the sun beginning to set on the horizon and said to myself that it's better to be optimistic but at the same time not to take it for granted. It was still very early to sing about a victory. It was around 6 pm, and Mima, helped by Elizabeth and Yaneba, were serving the long, improvised table next to the barbeque and meditation pool. They removed a roasted suckling pig from the barbeque, placing it on a silver serving tray surrounded by yucca and *mojo criollo*[35]. There were fountains of fried bananas, salad, black beans and rice, and all kinds of tropical fruits. Of course, the fruit tartlets could not be missing, since Mima had made multiple small ones for dessert. At a different, smaller table, they had placed

---

[35] A Cuban marinade made from a citrus made from Seville oranges, garlic, olive oil, limes, and spices such as salt, cumin, oregano, and black pepper.

a tremendous *tres leches*[36] cake that she had prepared with so much love, decorated and with my name written in golden letters, *With Love to my Great and Beautiful Son, Julio Antonio.*

We sat down to eat the delicious food. After we finished our meal, I went around the table so I could blow out the candles. I said, "I think I've reached the age where there are too many candles on the cake. Next year, let's start over with only a single candle!"

O'Brien appeared finally after sleeping for many hours, stepping out of the sliding door that led to his bedroom. He came to my side and said, "Thank God I came back before you blew out the candles. I missed out on my roast pig. I'm sorry. I think I used your birthday as an excuse to drink a little too much, trusting my good Irish strong stomach and didn't calculate my brain would betray me."

"You have nothing to apologize for. Nobody is perfect. At least you woke up in time to sing 'Happy Birthday.'"

He smiled and gave me a big hug. "Happy Birthday, my friend."

The others began to sing to me, and I blew out the candles before cutting the cake. Mima made sure that O'Brien took two plates with him before he left: one with the food, and one with the dessert, along with a generous portion of cake.

---

[36] Literally, three milk. The cake is soaked in three kinds of milk: evaporated milk, condense milk, and heavy cream.

Chapter 34: Large Scale Betrayal

34 The Bar with the Elevators Just Beyond

After everyone left, I jumped in the shower quickly, because I didn't want to see Sonya too late. I took the XJSC V-12 hardtop convertible Jaguar and left Corona del Mar towards Costa Mesa to fulfill my commitment with her and end that day in her company. I arrived at the hotel, and, unlike my usual custom, left my keys at the valet parking. I took plates of the generous portions of that exquisite food and cake Mima had prepared for her from the passenger seat and headed towards the elevators.

As I walked through lobby, something caught my attention. The same couple O'Brien and I had encountered earlier that day were now standing with two other men who looked like gangsters, FBI, or Secret Service, gathered near the stairs which led to the bar. The Hawaiian man in charge of the bar recognized me, raised his hand affectionately, and yelled, "El Capitan!"

In his innocent, unfeigned affection, he pointed at me as he greeted me as if he had been talking about me with them and was identifying me. I replied cordially, "Nice to see you again, Dean!"

The most curious thing of all in this incident is the reaction of the others who were next to him. They abruptly, almost in unison, turned their faces away from me to avoid identification. I was about fifty feet from them as I passed by, my eyes not leaving them as I watched their movements. My reading was that they were completely confused, not expecting my presence there at that moment, much less that spontaneous greeting from Dean, a friend of many years who always provided great service to me and my team.

I knew something strange was going on with that group of people. I filed the information away in mind to get more details about their conversation with Dean from him later on. I didn't allow it to bother or disturb me and continued my way to the elevators. My senses were on maximum alert, and I immediately checked my various weapons, preparing to repel any personal attack in case an unpleasant surprise awaited me inside the elevator. I put not just my psychic but also my physical energies in readiness, hoping for the best but expecting the worst.

As the elevator door opened, I stood back a little bit, saw no one was inside, and entered it remaining close to the doors, ready to jump back out if someone suddenly entered the car. I got out in the penthouse without any confrontations.

Sonya was waiting for me with open arms. She sang "Happy Birthday" the moment I entered the door, just like I did to all my friends on their birthdays. I noticed she had a beautiful mezzo-soprano voice; when she was done, I handed her the plates of food, taking her by surprise.

"This is for me? Oh, my God! You know I'm hungry, and you know how much I love Cuban food, and how much I love your beautiful Mima. Did you have a beautiful party?"

I nodded and smiled slightly. She thanked me, opened the containers of food in the dining room, and picked up a piece of roast pork with her fingers. She smiled. "Yummy! It's so good!"

"Why don't you sit down and eat? You're going to start salivating at any minute."

"I know, I know."

"That's why I asked Mima to prepare two plates for you. Of course, I would have felt a lot better if you had been in my company at the party with my friends and family."

She shook her head. "No, no. Don't worry about it. O'Brien debriefed me in detail about the protocol. Besides, I have you at my side for the best of the whole day—the beginning, and now the end."

"Then let's enjoy the rest of the day. We have to thank God for what we have and not complain what we don't have."

I smiled as she put a small piece of pork in her mouth and closed her eyes in ecstasy. "Yummy, yummy! This had to have been prepared by your Mima. I have no doubt of that!"

I nodded and smiled. "Even though I could have made it myself, and according to Mima, even better than she. I think she's praising overmuch, and I didn't have the time anyway. She asked me to give you a big kiss from her, by the way."

She smiled mischievously and tapped her right cheek with her index finger. "OK. What are you waiting for? A kiss with that kind of love from one who had you for nine months in her womb is the most beautiful kiss I could receive today, and I've been waiting for years before I could find you again."

I moved towards her intending to give her a kiss her on the cheek, but she turned her face so that my kiss landed on her lips. Of course, the kiss that was supposed to be a peck turned into a passionate one. We separated and I said, "You cheated."

"Of course, I'm a cheater. That's why I've become a spy like you! "

"The kiss from Mima I don't think was supposed to be like that."

We continued kissing, and it began to raise our temperature, reaching the same heat we had at such an early age for each other. We separated a little in between kisses and she covered the food with another plate. With a big smile on her face she said, "This food can wait until later. I've been waiting for you for too many years." She

The Broken Rainbow: Mysterious Dark Karma

put her arms around my shoulders, drew into mine, and began to kiss me with even greater passion.

After a while we slowly walked to the master bedroom. She asked in my ear, "I didn't want you to do anything today. This is your birthday. I want you to let me do all the work. I want to leave you with the beautiful memory you left me so many years ago."

"OK," I replied with a smile and nod. "I like that."

She started to take my clothes off. As she did, I cautioned her, "Be careful with my undies—they're special."

"What do you have here?" she asked, seeing the unusual design. "I've never seen such strange underwear in my life. Are they designer?"

"No," I replied, "they're a weapon."

She chose not to ask anything further and proceeded to remove hers. Once we were both naked in the bed, she took a little container from the nightstand which had a small brush, much like those used by professional canvas painters used. She clearly had planned everything out. The liquid inside the container was yellow—it looked to me like butter. As she began to brush it on my chest, it felt warm.

I looked at her with a smile, as she brushed me as if painting a masterpiece, tickling me enormously, as the butter dripped against my chest.

She said, "Do you remember? Or have you forgotten with the passage of time?"

"No, I remember very well," I replied as I closed my eyes.

"No, no—open your eyes. I want you to see what I'm doing."

"It's too intense," I replied. She passed the brush across her bottom lip and then licked it as if she were a child with a stick of sugar candy. I said, "How can I forget my own creation which you and I enjoyed so much, and left such a beautiful memory for both of us for so many years?"

She smiled. "A-ha! Better be prepared. Today is your birthday, and I have decided to revive that experience and beautiful memory, with the difference being you will enjoy it the most and be the greatest beneficiary, just as I was so many years ago." Her smile became mischievous as she inserted the brush once more into the container.

As she brushed my chest and went down to my stomach, allowing the butter to drip all over my body, I felt a twinge go from my head down to my toes. I could no longer keep my eyes open and closed them, transporting myself to aphrodisiac dreams with guttural sounds of pleasure as she continued to go lower in her playing with the brush. I can only say in conclusion that this was one of the best birthdays of my life. Until that particular moment, the tremendous joining of physical pleasure and spiritual from our souls that left us completely satisfied in a beautiful, unforgettable encounter as she went farther and farther down my body.

That unforgettable night ended as I checked my wristwatch and saw it was 8 pm. After Sonya ate like a very satisfied lioness the food I brought her, we looked at each other across the dining room. I asked her if she wanted to enjoy going to the bar with me. "I have a curiosity I need to satisfy over something that happened on my way to meet with you."

She with a beautiful and spontaneous disposition replied, "Of course. That's not a bad idea at all. Give me a few minutes to pull myself together and put on some makeup. I don't want to scare anyone in the bar. I'll go down with you with pleasure."

The Broken Rainbow: Mysterious Dark Karma

A little while later we left the penthouse and got into one of the elevators. Sonya was dressed in a beautiful red night gown, very elegant, for which I complimented her about how beautiful she looked in that dress. As we came down, we looked down at the lobby through the glass wall of the elevator.

So far, my psychic senses gave me no abnormal readings, and I was grateful to be able to take Sonya out to have a good time. Even so, my psychological antennae were up, because the last thing I wanted to do was put her in any kind of danger. I knew she needed some entertainment as a recompense for all the years I had been absent in her life. I was looking forward to giving her some more memories and joy.

As if God read my mind, as we walked out of the elevator the musical group at the piano bar played the soft rock song, "The Lady in Red," which was one of my favorite songs at that time. Sonya looked at herself in a reflection and smiled. She said, "Oh, my God, it's like our telepathy is working overtime. I read that you would bring me down here to give me a good time, and you probably sent a signal to the musicians in the bar."

As we came out of the elevator, however, I began to feel uncomfortable. My reading had changed, and as we slowly walked to the bar, that tremendous negative energy multiplied at a very high speed as we drew closer to the bar. I felt my face grow hot, like my face was too close to the fire in a fireplace, like my face was burning and my vision wavered as if I were looking through the distortion caused by heat waves on the highway. I said nothing to Sonya lest I hamper her enjoyment, but the more I felt these signals from my psyche, the more this uncomfortable feeling grew.

Finally, the tingling on the back of my neck raised my neck hairs as if in protest, which always was a sign that extreme danger was close at hand. I tried to hide it as best I could, but Sonya, guided by her feminine instincts, detected my emotional state. We sat at one of the tables near the bar in the most strategic corner I could locate and continued listening to that beautiful song. I had remained quiet the entire time but broke my silence by absently noting, "This is my favorite song."

She replied, "Welcome back to the world. What happened to you? The song is nearly finished, and you only now just noticed it. It's like your spirit has been out of reach, like your body was here but your spirit has been floating away."

I smiled. "Truthfully, that is exactly how I've been feeling. Even though I've tried to control it and bridle my feelings after so many years, and I'm very grateful to God for this extraordinary gift He's sent me, I've learned that unfortunately we have to grab the bull by the horns and never by the tail. We should never show fear or turn your back on the bull because he will take advantage of your weakness and nail his horns to your butt."

Sonya smiled. "You and your Marmolisms! Believe it or not, a long time ago you scared me with your daredevil attitude, but little by little, I've studied your actions very deeply in the years of your absence. I've come to the conclusion that I love it. I understand now that when you learn to master your fears no one can control or intimidate you."

I smiled again, this time I leaned forward to give her a small kiss on her cheek. I said, "I not only believe that you've grown physically over the past years but also mentally and spiritually as well. I love it very much. I'm going to write it down as one more attribute on the long list of good qualities you possess."

She smiled and said, "Thank you very much for your beautiful words. It has a great effect on me."

The waitress came over to take our order. To my surprise, when I looked up from the menu and saw the waitress' face, it was the woman with the long red hair that O'Brien and I had met that morning in the elevator who was supposedly on her honeymoon. I asked, "Where is my friend, Dean?"

She pretended to not understand my accent. "Who?" she asked.

"Dean. The Hawaiian man in charge of the bar."

"Oh!" she said to cover it. "He is off today. My name is Laurie. What do you want to drink today?"

I looked at her distrustfully. I didn't want to confront her, but I didn't want to order anything from her, either. There was something about her I didn't feel previously, and that made me extremely uncomfortable--it was like when I was around the socialists and communists in the beginning; I felt the passion and caught the desire to help the poor, but when I finally met them, I realized how ugly, poisonous, and destructive they really were.

I understood more clearly why I had those feelings when we were walking towards the bar. They were my psychological signals and before she left, I could not hold back. I approached her with a single question to verify what I already knew as for the real reason she was there. "How long have you been working here, Laurie?"

Without hesitation, with a fake smile on her face, she replied in an exaggerated manner, "Oh, a long time!" She spread her arms wide. "A very long time."

That answer corroborated to me immediately what a professional compulsive liar she was. What she either didn't know or had forgotten from her screenplay was that I've visited this place for fifteen years, where we discreetly had a safehouse for secure meetings, not just with my team but also with O'Brien and some of his associates. Of course, only the highest levels of management and security knew in any limited way who we really were. If she had been working there for such a long time, there was no way I would never have seen her face before that morning.

I didn't know why she was lying, but a huge doubt entered my mind. And when there's doubt, I stop. As soon as she left to bring the juices we ordered, I said to Sonya, "Don't even touch the glass when she brings the drinks. Let her put them on the table by herself."

I had noticed one important detail that I've never seen with any waitress here—she was wearing white gloves on her hands. Even though I have seen that done in very elegant restaurants as a requirement for their service staff, I never saw Dean or any other worker in the bar wear such gloves. Another doubt in my mind.

I remembered recently some attacks to some of our agents in Europe and other places with radioactive substances and I decided to take some extreme precautions. When she returned with the glasses, neither of us touched them. The cranberry juice we ordered remained untouched on the table. I decided to leave that place at once and communicated my concerns to Sonya. I pulled out my beeper and dialed the emergency code to Chopin and his crew.

I didn't give her a great deal of detail, so as not to worry her. "I need to take a rain check for you. We need to get back to the penthouse as soon as possible."

As we walked back towards the elevators, I saw Laurie following us with her eyes. I kept an eye on her and saw her pick up the $20 I left there for her, but she didn't touch the glasses. I missed not one single movement of hers, and saw her doing the same with me, watching every step we took and the direction in which we headed.

35 The Jaguar XJSC Use the Lightning

Chapter 35: Mercenaries with Intelligence

36 *The Stalls in the Men's Room*

As we came around the gazebo heading towards the elevator, and I saw through the windows Laurie hurriedly pick up an in-house telephone and speak to someone as if she was providing the details of our movements to another person.

We didn't even reach the elevators when a huge explosion inside the women's bathroom shook the whole place. People were screaming in confusion, running around mindlessly, and smoke poured out of the bathroom. I said to Sonya, "Stay here." I ran over to the elevators, pushed the penthouse button for one and jumped out. I went to the second car and did the same.

I had changed my plans because I knew those explosions were the perfect decoy for a plot to assassinate someone. I took Sonya by her right arm. "Come with me, please." I took her inside the men's room.

Apparently, due to the explosion, the few men who had been in there left in a rush to see what was happening. I went to the end of the stalls in the men's room and selected the one before the last, entered it with Sonya, and locked the door. I got on top of the toilet and put my back against the wall, instructing Sonya to do the same and face me.

Screaming continued outside, and we heard weapons discharging. Minutes later, we heard the door to the bathroom open and the steps of several people come inside. A man's voice said, "No one's here."

Another voice replied, "Check everything anyway."

I slowly drew my pistol and carefully cocked it.

A third voice, which sounded like Laurie's, said, "Don't waste your time. I saw them go into the elevators. I believe each of them took a different car. The security team will be here soon, and we only have a few minutes to eliminate them both and leave."

One of the men had a hand on top of our stall, but we could see through the crack that he was wearing an electric blue shirt as he turned and left. We heard the bathroom door close once more. My pistol was still ready for firing, but I breathed a deep sigh of relief. Sonya did as well and whispered in my ear, "They almost found us here."

I made no reply but motioned for silence as I nodded in agreement. We heard more gunshots outside. Sonya wanted to leave that place, which she signaled to me by pointing at the door. I shook my head no and held up my index finger to caution for silence once more. I held up my palm and made more signals to her, but her face showed confusion. I whispered in her ear, "We need to stay here until some of our people arrive."

Then she understood and silently nodded. A few seconds went by, and we heard the door open once more. The very deep voice of a man said, "If there's anybody hiding in here, you guys can come out. I work with the private security of the hotel." Sonya moved forward, but I grabbed her and held her back. He said again, "This floor is on fire."

I continued shaking my head no, my pistol pointing right at the door at the stall. I held the index finger of my lips again. This could be a trap; my long years of training and intimate familiarity with that hotel, enabled me to know every single member of the security force there. My elephant memory was not just natural; it had been sharpened by my intense training in Montauk, and I had never heard that voice before in any man I had met there. Besides, normally these people worked in pairs, not alone, especially during an emergency.

My instincts told me that probably this man was the leader of these terrorist assassins. In frustration, as his men reported that they could not find us, he made a desperate attempt to locate us himself before he left with the sour pill of defeat. He was doubling back to check all the places his people had told him they could not find us.

We heard the fire alarms going off, and people outside were still screaming in panic. Every time the door of the bathroom opened and closed, the ambient noise increased and decreased, but we maintained our composure and moved not one muscle in our bodies. We both knew that the man had not left yet due to the strange silence—the door had not opened yet. He was standing there, listening for any movement or sound, as he tried to trick us into thinking he had gone.

Several minutes passed, and we heard that voice again along with several crashes as he kicked the stalls. We could feel the vibration right through the metal struts connecting all the stalls. "I'm sick and tired of playing your game. I know you're here, and I'll get you out, if necessary, by burning this bathroom down or shooting into every single stall."

As we felt his kicks against the doors getting closer to us, I knew that he would not stop until he reached ours. I signaled to Sonya with my hands and mimicking with my face for us to change positions so that she was to the side and against the wall in common with the final stall, still on top of the toilet. I now had a clear field of fire in front of me. Balancing myself by holding both elbows against the wall, I put one heel against the edge of the toilet and prepared to kick against the stall's door. I very gently unlatched the door.

As soon as I saw his silhouette through the crack between the stall frame and door's edge, I kicked so violently that the door flew off its hinges on the frame and right into him, sending him sprawling onto his back on the marble floor. He fired once harmlessly into the air before his pistol flew out of his hand, breaking the plastic of the false ceiling and shattering the florescent light inside. Pieces of glass fell onto the floor, and his pistol skittered across the floor and stopped beneath the sinks.

37 Men's Room Sinks

I took him by surprise by jumping out of the stall, pulling the door off him, and kicking him solidly in the jaw. Sonya jumped out behind me, ran to the sinks, and got his pistol. She returned and put it against his head, yelling, "Don't move, if you want to live another night, murderer!"

The man was in his late 30's, skinny and middling height, but looked very fit. He had a peculiar look, a little slovenly with an unshaven face, but with extremely expensive clothing from high end designers, and sporting a splendid Rolex wristwatch.

Sonya pulled his wallet out of his pocket and opened it. She looked up at me in surprise as she checked the photo of the man and him and said, "You won't believe this. This murderer doesn't work for hotel security. He works for the FBI."

I shook my head as if I had been jolted by electricity. "What are you saying?"

"Exactly what you heard." She held out the ID badge with his photo next to it.

It was true. He was an FBI agent. I looked down at him and checked the ID to verify the truth of this. The ID read in large green letters, *Special Agent, Counterterrorism Division, National Security Branch*. His name was Jaime Marquez Garcias. I stepped forward, pistol in hand. I placed it against his head as Sonya had and said, "Can you explain what this means, Jaime?"

He looked at my cynically and with a challenging look in his eyes replied, "It's very simple. You and your girlfriend will both be dead, along with all your associates involved with your secret operation for the CIA, the Zipper. None of you will live to tell the story, including your mentor, O'Brien."

"Oh, really?" I replied mockingly. I showed him my left hand, which shook exaggeratedly. "Look! You've frightened me incredibly. Can you tell me who will be the super hitman that will take on such an extremely delicate mission and kill so many people? You?" I shook my head. "I think your plans or whoever came up with them will fail miserably, the same way many others have failed. The same way, also, that your plan to assassinate us has failed miserably just now."

Jaime said in a challenging tone, "If I were in your shoes, I wouldn't be so sure of that. We have many associates outside there." He thrust his chin towards the door. "They're still looking for you guys." He smiled cynically. "I might not have made *you* afraid or caused your hands to shake but look at your girlfriend. She can't even hold her pistol steady. She's shaking so bad it looks like she's got Parkinson's. I don't think all the toilet paper in this restroom will be sufficient to calm her symptoms of diarrhea."

I glanced at Sonya, who held the pistol in her left hand and his ID in her right, and she snatched both hands towards her chest in embarrassment. Her eyes were moist as she looked at him spitefully, holding her tears back to avoid giving him any satisfaction. It was clear she was a little confused by all that was happening, especially since this individual was supposedly on our side, but now merely a mercenary, contracted to kill and humiliate us. He might be feeling powerful because he had a certain position within this federal agency.

As Sonya changed the ID and pistol from one hand to the other, she held the ID upside down, and another ID fell from one side of the wallet onto the floor. She bent down and examined it, holding it in her fingers high. "Oh, my God! This murderer isn't just a professional assassin; he's holding a membership to the global communist organization created in Cuba by Che Guevara—the Tri-Continental Union. He had it proudly in his wallet! Can you imagine it? He's more dangerous than the typical mercenary the communists bribe and buy in this country. He's a double agent, implanted here by the KGB years ago."

The Broken Rainbow: Mysterious Dark Karma

I looked up to examine the ID she was showing me. Jaime used the small distraction to grab my wrist which held the pistol while hitting me with his elbow. I momentarily lost my balance slightly, even as Sonya yelled a warning, but it was too late.

In frustration she tried to train his gun on him, but we wrestled on the ground, ruining her aim. She yelled, "Stop, or I'll shoot you in the head!"

Of course, Jaime ignored her, knowing full well she didn't have a clear shot. As we wrestled, my pistol discharged twice. One bullet struck the long mirror over the sinks, shattering it in pieces. The other bullet hit Sonya in her right shoulder, causing her to drop the pistol, which skittered across the floor. She bent down into a half-crouch to avoid being shot again even as she tried to recover the dropped pistol.

It was clear Jaime had been trained for combat. We rolled around in one-handed combat, striking each other when we could get a blow in with our free hands. We both showed bruising as we each took a severe beating. He tried to trip me by tangling one of his legs between mine, frustrated at the iron grip I maintained on my weapon.

I recovered from the trip attempt, opening my left to get back on the toilet stool to gain my equilibrium. Unfortunately for him, he used that opportunity to knee me in the testicles and discovered the special protection I had against such a maneuver. He screamed in intense agony and began to bleed all over the place as he released his grip on my weapon hand. He fell onto his knees on the marble floor, still in shocked confusion, trying to understand what had happened.

Jaime looked at me in frustration and yelled, "You guys not only have a huge problem with the FBI for attacking a federal agent, but you'll both be dead before the sun rises this morning."

Sonya had retrieved his pistol and went to the paper towel dispensers, pulled out several towels, and put them over her wounded shoulder, checking herself in the mirror. She took some more paper towels, much thicker bond this time, and wrapped several layers around the muzzle.

She put the pistol to Jaime's forehead and said, "There's a very slight possibility of that happening, but it's remote due to your position right now. What I'm going to tell you right now is reality, and that is that you are going to die in a few seconds, before us. All I can guarantee is that you will never hurt anyone ever again or take innocent lives for a handful of dollars. This is right now, not waiting for the sun to rise. All I ask you is to give my greetings to Che Guevara, because you're going directly to Hell to keep that stinker good company. Are you sure that you don't need toilet paper here you're going?" She pulled the trigger. She then shook and began to cry.

I said, "You didn't have to do that."

"Yes. I *needed* to do that, for my son, so that he wouldn't have to deal with people like that in the future." She turned away. "Not for you or any of us. For my son."

"OK, calm down. Everything is over, and we need to look at your shoulder."

"Don't worry about it. It's just a flesh wound. I've already stopped the bleeding. Let's get out of here immediately. You must tell O'Brien everything that happened here." She handed the documents she took from Jaime and cleaned his pistol with the toilet paper and left the pistol next to his body.

The Broken Rainbow: Mysterious Dark Karma

We left the bathroom to the surprised eyes of the fire department, who helped guide us out of the hotel, past the police lines and the paramedics, who offered her help, which she declined. As we walked through the lobby, we met Chopin with two of his men.

Chopin exclaimed, "Thank God! We've been looking for you all over! Where have you been?" His reaction was a blend of joy and concern. "Where did you hide? We were beginning to think you had been kidnapped."

I smiled. "Hiding in plain sight. Always in the most obvious place where your enemies won't look for you. In this case, our friends as well."

"Well, the most important thing is that you guys are both OK. I want to let you know we have that red snake, Laurie, in the marinating room in Corona del Mar. She's already vomited some of the stuff that you're going to want to know. She's ready for you to complete the interrogation."

"Very well. Take Sonya to the Crowne Plaza to be with her son, Julius Christian. Don't move an inch until I get to the bottom of this. This location has been burned for a while. Please get in touch with Dr. Hector Zayas-Bazan to examine her shoulder. Even though she says it's a flesh wound, she needs to have it looked at. The last thing we want is for that small wound to get infected and complicate things by not being able to make our trip to Europe."

"OK," Chopin said with a big smile. He gave me a big, unexpected hug. "Doc, I'm glad you're both OK and you're alive. Don't worry—I'll take care of everything for you, and Sonya and your son will be safe."

I said goodbye to Sonya, we hugged and kissed, and she left with Chopin and his men. After I retrieved my Jaguar from the valet, I drove to South Coast Plaza and went to a public telephone to call O'Brien with the emergency code.

The Broken Rainbow: Mysterious Dark Karma

Chapter 36: O'Brien Calls the Cleaners

38 Balboa Ferry

Anytime either of us received the emergency code from the other, the protocol was to immediately drop everything to go help the other. I gave him the location code for the Balboa ferry. A little while later, I arrived at the location and saw him waiting for me, seated at a small table on the patio of the French café near the ferry. I had known the owner of the establishment, Bill, for quite some time, so we would leave our cars near there and walk to the ferry. Especially during the summer, the parking problem in the area was nearly impossible, so we had made a mutually beneficial arrangement with Bill. This strategic location had become so important for our work that it was sometimes a life-or-death situation to be able to detect anyone following us.

Using the ferry was an idea I had suggested to the intelligence group and had served us for a long time now. That street which ended at the ferry was so congested that it was impossible for anyone to follow us without giving away their obvious intention and so expose them, especially when we never got onto the ferry in our vehicles. We would park in Bill's private parking slots, walk on the sidewalk that was only 200 feet from the ferry, boarded it, and cross from the island to the peninsula. We would repeat that crossing seated on the bench as pedestrians to talk about our most secret and delicate information. Anyone that was trying to listen in on our conversation would be completely exposed to us.

That is why we called this particular location "the end of pursuit" or the "island of mystery." It was where so many plans that brought changes all around the world and altered the course of history had been discussed and formed with the goal of improving the lives of millions if not billions of people, protecting their freedom, and on many occasions, preventing horrible events of catastrophic consequences for all humanity at large. From a global perspective the events we dealt with were of historical, social, and political significance of the gravest kind.

O'Brien ordered his typical, favorite beverage, his cup of skim milk with Grand Marnier, and I my typical glass of heated Grand Marnier in a brandy sifter. We sipped our drinks for a little while as we each brought the other up to speed. We picked up our beverages, and I left payment for them along with my usual generous tip. As was our custom, we took our glasses from that place, also with Bill's knowledge; the entire service staff knew us well and that we would come back to pick up our vehicles, leaving the empty glasses when we did.

We left the café and walked to the ferry along the very narrow sidewalks. O'Brien said, "We have a little problem." His face was extremely worried as he spoke. I was able to read that he was extremely frustrated, and I immediately understood that the problem was not a small one by any means. Perhaps he didn't want to alarm me as we walked to the ferry and sat down on the long bench for the pedestrians.

He continued, "I'm sorry to tell you this, but we just discovered quite recently, and too late to warn you, that one of the highest executives within counterintelligence has been sharing with our enemies in the most minute details what has transpired during the Zipper operation. Our enemies, in turn, have informed their allies inside the FBI, State Department, and other federal agencies, whoever they've been able to bribe with enormous amounts of money. Unfortunately, the man who tried to kill you and Sonya tonight in our secret location at the hotel was not the only attempt. It was also tried at the same time in the Balboa Bay Club with Miguel Angel as well as Corona del Mar with your other team.

You have nothing to worry about. Even though this was done simultaneously, the first one was against Miguel Angel, and we were able to neutralize it and immediately sound the alarm. The other team has such fantastic security that they put everyone down without any casualties. Unfortunately, you were the last one, and we were unable to warn you in time. The man we're holding prisoner from the first attack at the club sang like a canary; he's wounded, but not seriously so. We managed to question him intensely and get him to confess to the whole plan, how they intended to destroy the operation, and the fruit of our work. They wanted to get the money to use for their perverse plans to spread their Marxist ideology around the world."

"Is Miguel Angel OK?" I asked.

He put his hand on my shoulder. "You have nothing to worry about. He's OK and is navigating right now on the high seas in that beautiful yacht, on his way to Europe with his valuable cargo and his entire crew. I added a few extra security operators, considering what happened in the past couple of hours and the extreme situation."

I replied, "This is not a small problem like you said at the beginning. This is a gigantic one. This will impact every single one of our plans. We'll have to alter everything we planned to do in Europe, because we've lost the element of surprise if our enemies here communicate with our enemies there. This could hamper our part in the plan." I reached into my pocket and pulled the documents that we got from Jaimie Garcia and handed them to O'Brien. "This agent won't reach his retirement. He took a little shortcut, converting himself not only into a mercenary assassin but also into a despised ally of the Marxists."

O'Brien took the documents and examined them wordlessly. He nodded. "Yes, he took a shortcut to Hell. I hope he received a warm welcome from his father, Lucifer. But the most important thing right now is that you guys leave for Europe immediately before another attempt happens. We have to get ahead of our enemies and not give them the time to regroup. Like you say, we cannot let them to take away that factor of surprise."

"When do we leave?"

"If possible, tonight."

"Very short notice, but I'll do my best. I'll communicate with Chopin immediately. What do you want to do with Laurie?"

He looked at me in surprise. "Who's Laurie?"

"The redheaded bartender at the hotel. We met her this morning in the elevator on our way to see Sonya in the penthouse." He still looked puzzled. "You remember? You had a small talk with her supposed husband. They commented when you pressed the penthouse button on the elevator."

"Oh! Maybe she was another mercenary, contracted to eliminate you and your team. What's up with her?"

"Nothing of major importance. My guys took her prisoner when she tried to escape and have her in the marinating room in Corona del Mar. You say they made an attempt on that location, so I don't know now if she's dead or alive. We might find her with bandages on her eyes and a gag in her mouth or we might find her with a bullet in the head. From the marinating room, the next place to go is the oven."

"Oh, that is fantastic!" he exclaimed. "A female mercenary! In precarious, chaotic situations like this she could be a fountain of information for us. We might get a lot more names than we already have to clean up in our agencies. We shouldn't waste this opportunity, but not you. You have much more important things to do in Europe that might decide the future of freedom not just in our country but in the free world. I'll get in touch with your team; you get Sonya, Julius Christian, and Chopin ready to get out of here as soon as possible, not just for the security of our country but also for the personal security of each of you until we can put our house in order. The more distance you put between us here, the better for everyone.

"We'll put all these traitors, as you say in Cuba, in *mojo criollo*. One by one, everyone at the highest levels involved in this miserable plot will pay with their lives, because the President has given me carte blanche and said that I am to make sure this never goes to a trial, and I'm going to follow the orders of the President to the T, no matter what position they have in the government right now. I won't take any prisoners in this spring cleaning. We will do exactly and follow what your friend Sonya did today, based on the debriefing I had with my contacts, who were the first ones to arrive in the bathroom of the hotel and found the body of that FBI traitor."

I looked at him in surprise and doubt. "How do you know it wasn't me who executed him?"

O'Brien smirked and shook his head. He pointed at my chest. "You? No. Don't forget you've been around me for so many years, and I've never seen you take the life of any other human being, especially when you have ways to neutralize any individual no matter what level of skill that person has. As soon as they described the scene to me, especially the punctures on one of his knees, I put two and two together and concluded this miserable assassin had a very violent and physical encounter with you, and you activated our self-defense technology we provided you.

"Of course, as I figured it, Sonya came to your defense and finished the job. She doesn't know how you act because she's been absent for too many years to be aware of your techniques and ethics, or how unaccustomed as you are of taking the lives of your enemies. You neutralize and incapacitate them, though I don't know if you do that to make the suffer a little longer in their miserable, diabolic lives until they in time, as I've seen myself, find some doors of redemption and repentance or maybe find the true doors to Hell and enter with Satan through those doors which open only one way."

I smiled and shook my head without replying. I wondered how O'Brien knew the doors of Hell opened only one way. O'Brien noticed and asked, "What are you smiling at?"

"I just was thinking about your comment about Hell's doors." We were near the café on our way back from the ferry.

We walked to our cars after leaving the glasses with the waitress. O'Brien and I said goodbye but not before he said, "Please, when everything is in motion, for my tranquility, give me a jingle."

"OK, Pop," I teased. We left the island of Balboa in different directions.

That same night, we left for Germany in our private plane, Chopin as pilot, Gervasio as his co-pilot. There was only Sonya, Julius Christian, and one of O'Brien's most trusted men, a tall, skinny, man with thinning blonde hair, blue eyes, and a very muscular, sculpted body. According to O'Brien, he was a skilled martial artist, and that was why he was along, but I didn't like it at all. I preferred to work with people I knew, not strange faces, but due to what had happened that day and the pressure to close this final stage of the operation while maintaining our surprise element, I accepted it. I simply expressed my unhappiness to him and left it at that. O'Brien had given him strict orders to obey anything I said and not to take orders from anyone else in the agency; only from me.

I had nothing against any man who worked directly with the CIA or any other department of the intelligence community, but to me it was very difficult to completely trust someone that received a paycheck in payment for their services. My theory has always been that, unless the individual was an extreme patriot with great integrity, he could easily be bought but a much bigger check than what they received from the agency. This theory of mine had been repeatedly proven right in the past.

On the trip to Europe, we had the opportunity to discuss the details of the plan we were going to follow. I informed the team step by step as we advanced what the following step would be along toward the final objective, but not in minute details. I left those to wherever we were in Germany, in West Berlin.

May 25, 1989, a few days later
West Berlin
Miguel Angel, Sonya, Julius Christian, Chopin, Gervasio, O'Brien's man, Mike, and I were meeting in a beautiful cabin which belonged to the Baumanns. Two blonde-haired, blue-eyed cousins of Miguel Angel were hosting us. Sarah was the elder, and the younger one, Helga, the most beautiful; otherwise, they looked like they were twins, with their long blonde hair in braids and beautiful big blue eyes filled with life. They were in their late 20's, only a few years apart in age. Sarah was the contact in Berlin with the colonel in the KGB, the hard man in the communist party, Putin. He made the last decision in every plan, according to Sarah, and controlled all the

movements from one side to the other with regards to espionage.

Sarah had been a double spy for many years and one of the most trusted confidants of Putin. Very recently, she had been recruited by American intelligence when she manifested her wish to abandon the Russians. She felt no more loyalty to the communist party in Berlin and even less to her boss, Vladimir Putin. We didn't get any details, but Putin did something to her which created a lot of hardship and embarrassment. No one ever reacts until someone stomps on their own foot. Apparently, she realized, once and for all, that this ideology didn't function well, saying one thing in public and doing something else completely different out of the public eye.

She had been a master spy in the service of our enemy and proved her loyalty to Putin during multiple operations. She also had been responsible for exposing many of our agents and those of our allies and in doing so had earned the ear and trust of Putin. She was a key, quite literally, that would open the doors in Berlin and bring democracy into the Communist Bloc. We were using the same methods of corruption used by them, especially Putin, who never even dreamed or expected what was coming. It never even crossed his mind to guess what we were really doing.

We were sitting around a huge, circular table, typical of European preference, eating cold meats: salami, sausages with different cheeses, olives, crackers, in the unique villa constructed roughly of logs. This cabin belonged to the Baumann family, who had managed to survive the persecution of the Nazis, only now to face that of the Marxist communists, who had continued as an experimental extension that totalitarian ideology which never worked anywhere in the world it was tried, bringing with the destruction of family and countries.

We raised our glasses and took a sip of the great wine stored for years in the vast cellar. Miguel Angel offered a toast. He stood up and said, "For the freedom of Germany and the rest of the Communist Bloc."

The rest of us stood and said, "Freedom to all of Europe and the world!" We took another sip, reaffirming our feelings which kept us continuing our fight in history against oppression from every single totalitarian government in the modern world for many generations.

I added, "The abuse of people's freedom is the beginning of the extermination of our own freedom and the views of freedom itself, without exception of race or any religion. This is a clear lesson for future generations."

Miguel Angel, who was sitting next to me, put his hand on my shoulder. "Will you please come with me?"

We excused ourselves and left the table, taking with us the half-filled glasses of that exquisite wine and went down to the basement of that beautiful villa. As we approached a thick double door, all the locks painted with shiny varnish like that used on ships, he took a set of keys from his pocket and opened them. We entered the room as he turned the lights on, revealing thousands of bottles of wine stored on shelves built into the walls.

We walked to the center of the room, where there was a metal pole with a large tungsten halogen lamp on top of it. He pulled the cord for the lamp to turn it on, revealing a tarp like those used to cover cars in storage. He pulled that aside, revealing around twenty duffel bags. He picked up one of the bags, untied the cord, and emptied the contents out for me so I could see that the job was done. The bundles of $10,000 spread out over the remaining bags.

He smiled in satisfaction as he handed me a key to the room. "Only you and I have access to this room. Temptation is the son of the Devil, so as a security measure we should keep it this way, at least until the moment when this vast amount of money gets distributed according to our plan."

I smiled and grabbed his shoulder affectionately. "It gives me great pleasure not only that you followed my instructions to the letter, but also that you maintained your integrity intact as I expected." I added affectionately, "Your father and the rest of your family should be proud of you. The ones still with us will show it and those who have gone on are having a big smile in Heaven. Even though they're not with us now, with their eyes and spirits have guarded our backs. This was not easy to do. Our great ancestors have been protecting us against false temptations which are constantly putting us to a test throughout our lives."

Miguel Angel smiled a little in satisfaction. He looked me in the eyes and asked, "Don't you agree with me, Dr. Antonio Rada Montiel, famous cardiologist and multimillionaire businessman? How has the export/import business been lately?"

"I believe it's booming in Germany. I'll let you know if it gets better or worse in a few years."

"Well, I can assure you of is that you and I have gone through life's ups and downs multiple times. In the process we unfortunately met Satan but managed to leave with only a few emotional scars and some small burns. This proved to everyone that Satan is nothing more than the composition formed from those individuals filled with envy and frustrations that not happy with themselves. They've been searching for power and material wealth with no consideration to the men who sweat every day in their work to survive in their good will to follow the Word of God. But these individuals only seek to destroy every single beautiful thing made by God and men that they find in their path. Like their sinister teacher, Satan, they use different names to hide their true nature, changing as often as need be, whether it's daily or by decade. Nazis, communists, Marxists, Progressives, or whatever; in the end, they bear only one single banner: cannibals of the beauty, structure, and unity of our society and against all the men of goodwill in life."

I grinned broadly. "I don't have the smallest doubt that God brought us our souls together even before we were born from the uteruses of our mothers. That is why it doesn't make any difference how many turns you and I have circled around the Sun, and we always find ourselves at the same point from where we departed. We are linked by the same principles and the same divine cause to stop and destroy those powerful diabolical forces that try to dominate, control, and destroy this beautiful world that our Creator has given us to live in peace and harmony with no hatred, division, or tyranny."

Miguel Angel stepped forward, his face and eyes emotional, barely containing a couple of tears which threatened to escape. He controlled himself, opened his arms, and embraced me in a massive fraternal bear hug. Sarah entered the room at that moment. Miguel Angel jumped back uncomfortably, since should not have been there.

She said, "I'm sorry to interrupt you guys, but I just got off the phone with Colonel Putin. He will meet us in the place previously agreed upon, where we'll conclude our business."

I replied, trying to alleviate Miguel Angel's tension, with a smile, "Good news. Then the plan continues to be in motion as we expected."

Miguel Angel, with courtesy but strong, firm conviction, took Sarah by the arm and guided her from the room. "OK, Sarah—everything is great. Let's go."

I could not help but notice Sarah eying the $10,000 bundles on top of the bags in the center of the room. I gave it no particular importance, as it was a natural thing to do. I followed them wordlessly. Miguel Angel stopped at the door and proceeded to double lock those heavy wooden doors, leaving behind the room with that valuable load.

After we left the room, with a small smile on his face, Miguel Angel said to his cousin, "Sarah, very good work. How much will it finally cost us for this safe conduct and the assurance that we won't be bothered by his KGB dogs?"

Sarah said, "Only five million. This is, if he doesn't change his mind at the last minute like he normally does. He's not a man of conviction. But that was my last offer to him and the limit I had been authorized to offer at that time. Of course, it's all in the hands of Dr. Montiel and his skills in negotiating now. I know from his file that his reputation is considered by intelligence to be unparalleled. I have to warn you that Putin is not an everyday lion. He's the genetic cross between a lion, hyena, and the anaconda snake. These three species are very dangerous because they are more complicated to predict their movements and their capacity to camouflage themselves to hide from their enemies."

Miguel Angel smiled. He could not contain himself and in a spontaneous reaction in my defense replied as he finished locking the final security on the doors, "Sarah, if there's anything I can assure you of is that those three species you just mentioned would run for their lives in panic during a dark, stormy night when the lightning and its powerful discharges from the sky hits the trees and burn them down." He put an arm around my shoulder as he put the key to the money room in his pants pocket. He added, "Don't worry about it at all, Sarah. My friend, Dr. Montiel not only possesses the capacity of being a great negotiator and will probably have Colonel Putin wrapped around his finger, but he also possesses the capacity to give that communist the worst surprise he could ever have or even imagine."

"OK," Sarah replied in an unconvinced tone. She smiled vaguely and shook her head.

I said, "Thank you very much, Sarah. I appreciate most sincerely all the information and precise details concerning the personality of our enemy. This could be extremely beneficial and of critical importance, sometimes even life or death. I just advise you not to take your cousin Miguel Angel too seriously. He and I grew up together. We are like brothers, and when he was very little always looked at me like his protector. Now, of course, he continues to look at me in the same way, and nothing through the years has changed his mind."

We returned to the round table and sat down. Nearly everyone had finished eating and the table was cleared off. Sarah pulled out a cardboard tube and extracted from it a map which she spread out over the table. She showed us the schematics for the drainage tunnels beneath the city of Berlin and how they interconnected with each other. She traced the route to the place where we were supposed to meet the next night with our enemies who were now, for the moment, our allies in this strange convenient arrangement.

We also looked at the place where we were to transport the massive quantity of money contained within those seabags, where we were supposed to give the final bribe money for Colonel Putin to close his eyes and allow us to do our business in East Germany. The rest of the money would go to the resistance in the anti-communist movements who were in charge of distributing it around the Communist Bloc in the attempt to collapse the already weak Soviet economy—an aspect of the plan he knew nothing about.

After several hours of debriefing, everyone was assigned their individual functions and protocols to follow to the letter, we broke up to rest from the trip and be prepared for the next night when all this would take place. Even though we had meticulously planned everything, we knew from experience that nothing ever came out in practice the same way that it had been planned in theory. Each of us had to be mentally and physically prepared for any circumstance that could suddenly happen during our mission. In the worst-case scenario, if we didn't follow the and proceed carefully to protect the lives of the others, the price we could pay could be the total failure of our mission and possibly the even higher price of all our lives.

Having all this in mind raised my level of stress and the sleep which usually came to me very easily every night in a matter of seconds, this night took a long time. I don't know how long I had been asleep, but I felt something like an insect trying to crawl into one of my ears. Perhaps I was dreaming or having a nightmare, because that image changed to the barrel of a pistol putting a lot of pressure on my ear. I didn't open my eyes yet. I carefully moved my hand under my pillow in search of my pistol. I located it and wrapped my fingers around it. I whipped around suddenly, sitting up on my behind, my weapon in my left hand, and reached around with my right to grab a wrist. I rolled over on top of the intruder, only to discover that it was Sonya.

Her eyes flew open wide as she saw me on top of her with my pistol to her head. She said in a low, desperate voice, "Julio Antonio, it's me, it's me. Sonya."

Though I was still half-asleep, I had to smile to see what she had held in her hand. It looked like a bar of butter. I shook my head and shook my finger at her. "What you just did could end very dangerously."

Sonya saw my smile and from my relaxed posture realized I had recognized her. She put her index finger to her lips and whispered, "Lower your voice if you don't want to wake up the others. That would ruin my plan with the yoga butter I carefully and specially prepared for you to help alleviate your nervous tension."

I smiled broadly. I put on an innocent look. "What nervous tension? Whatever you provoke with that bar of butter?"

Sonya rapidly answered by jumping out of the bed and opening her transparent silk bathrobe by pulling on a lace at her neck and allowing it to whisperingly to fall onto the black bearskin rug which covered nearly all the edges of that rustic log bed painted to a shine by the same marine varnish. She bent over and got down onto her knees and beckoned to me and enjoy her nakedness.

The Broken Rainbow: Mysterious Dark Karma

With the bar of butter still in her right hand, she brought it slowly to her lips in a sensual manner, as if she were painting her lips with lipstick. She then sensuously ran her tongue across her lips, as if savoring the butter in satisfaction. She locked eyes with me and then let her hand go down her body slowly. The only light in the room came through the windows from the moon outside. The shadows in that dim light made that image became more sexual than she had intended. I jumped out of bed and went to her in great excitement. I lay on top of her on that comfortable, soft, thick bear rug. We made love a long time until both of us were completely exhausted ad fell into a profound sleep.

I woke up suddenly, sensing the vibrations through the wooden floor rather than hearing footsteps. I checked my luminous dial on my Rolex and saw that it was 4:30 am. Someone was outside my room, coming closer and closer. I could see the handle of the door move as if someone were trying to open it, doing it slowly to minimize the noise.

I reached under the pillow I had brought down onto the bear rug, not even realizing that I had left my pistol by the bed in my half-asleep state. I looked down at Sonya's naked body and realized that though I was at a disadvantage without my weapon, I would wake her up just stepping over her. I kept my eyes half-closed, watching the door steadily.

When it opened, I saw a silhouette enter the room and move towards my bed, not realizing that I was on the floor. The figure tripped on Sonya's feet, waking her up after all. The intruder fell to the floor, and the sound of a glass container shattering broke the silence. Something else rolled along the floor.

I jumped up from the bear rug and dashed to the bed, looking for the pistol I had left on the nightstand next to it. Pistol in hand, I reached under the candelabra with multiple bulbs and switched the lights on. To my surprise, it was Sarah, who now was on her knees trying to get up off the floor.

A broken cup lay by her side with a dark liquid spreading across the floor. It looked like chocolate, based on what was spread across her transparent white night gown. She tried with both hands to wipe up the mess on her clothes under that powerful light, revealing her athletic figure, cultivated with extreme discipline, and showing off her beautiful, firm breasts along with the long, blonde hair braided over her head.

I froze, not just filled with surprise at this unexpected visitor but also fascinated by that magnificent, sculptured body which looked like Venus di Milo, the only difference being that she had arms. Sonya was also frozen and mute, completely naked and exposed herself. In the midst of all this commotion, I didn't even realize that I was also wearing only what God clothed me in when He sent me to Earth.

Sonya looked down at me and then back into my eyes, with her eyes widened in surprise. I looked down to check myself and saw my nakedness. Pistol in my left hand, I rapidly grabbed a decorative pillow with my right to cover myself with a small guilty smile of embarrassment at being confronted by so much feminine nudity.

I asked Sarah, "To what do we owe the honor of your visit? Or maybe we left some untied knot in our previous conversation?"

Sarah remained mute, contemplating Sonya's beautiful nude body. All three of us were confused. Sonya also looked at Sarah's body, perhaps wondering what this woman was doing in the room wearing a translucent robe. They both looked at me still not attempting to cover themselves. "There you go," I said as I tossed my pillow onto the bed and went to go put on some clothes. Their eyes followed me with shocked expressions.

I figured that by the time they took checking each other out I would already have my clothes on and be ready to go. Once they noticed that I gave them no further importance, they began to talk to each other as Sonya dressed. Sarah apologized for the abrupt interruption, adding, "I didn't know you two were together."

"Whether we are together or not is no one's business," Sonya added. "There is no need to publish it in the newspapers."

"I'm sorry, I just stopped by to speak with Dr. Rada Montiel. I first heard voices and later steps of people walking very quietly in the wine cellar. This seemed strange to me at these early morning hours and thought perhaps they were associates of Dr. Rada Montiel's bringing more bags from the yacht."

I raised my arms up high. "Wait a minute," I said. "Are you sure you heard voices and movement? And that they came from the wine cellar?"

"Yes," she replied. "I'm very sure. The wine cellar is right beneath my room."

Hearing her response, I turned around double-checked that my pistol was ready to fire. 'Sarah, go at once and wake up Miguel Angel; share with him what you just told me. Meet me in the wine cellar. Be careful when you approach it. No one except Miguel Angel and I have a key, and no one is going to bring anything from the yacht. Besides, I believe all the bags are already here, according to my latest debrief. If you heard noises down there, there's no other answer than that there is an intruder that is trying to steal them from us."

Sonya had put her bathrobe back on. She said to me, "I'll go back to my room and put some clothes on as well as get my pistol so I can cover you from the driveway. I want to see how they came in, how they plan to get out, and plan a little surprise for them. If they're here, they either have parked in front of the cabin or somewhere nearby."

I smiled. "Very good idea." I nodded. "But be very careful. These individuals more than anything are either agents of the KGB at Putin's personal service or they've been sent by them."

Sonya replied with a grim face, "You had better be more careful than us. This premature movement by Putin might not be limited just to the money; it may be to eliminate all of us once and for all."

Sarah's face was long and deadly serious. "Knowing Putin as well as I do after all the years I've worked within his circle, I can assure you guys that he isn't accustomed to leaving any witnesses behind in any operation he's involved in, sometimes eliminating even his own people in order to cover his tracks. He adds them without further thought to the glorious martyrs to the Motherland of the Soviet Union." She smiled cynically as she shook her head. "Why do you guys think that Putin has risen to the rank of Colonel inside the KGB at such a young age? He has to have extreme savvy and Machiavellian personality to advance so quickly inside such a humongous tank of sharks."

All three of us nodded in agreement. Sarah said to me, "I'll meet you in the wine cellar after I wake Miguel

The Broken Rainbow: Mysterious Dark Karma

Angel along with the others and debrief them. We need everyone to stop these people. Some of them can cover our exit in case we need to leave this place. Don't worry, I'll handle and organize everything. One thing I need to tell you—we need to get our hands on one of our enemies. At least one. They never work solo in these kinds of operations—they work in teams. This will show to Putin your psychological superiority, and that will give you more power in your negotiations with him, especially if we can manage to get at least one alive to provide us with enough details to incriminate Putin and anyone else with him. That way, it will be hard for him to deny that we grabbed one of them with the hands in the cookie jar."

I replied, "I think that's a great idea. You coordinate the rest." We left the room, each heading in a different direction.

The Broken Rainbow: Mysterious Dark Karma

Chapter 37: Putin's Double-Cross and the Traitor

39 Alexanderplatz, East Berlin, East Germany

As I walked towards the wine cellar, I saw a very tall, physically fit man coming up the cellar stairs with one of the bags of our money over his shoulder. I knelt down and hid behind a suit of armor. I waited until he was close to the top of the stairs so he wouldn't be able to defend himself with the added encumbrance of the duffel bag over his shoulder. I crept over to him and stabbed him in the neck with my poison ring, taking him by complete surprise. I held him by the arm holding the bag and, with a strong tug, I yanked him up the rest of the stairs. I took the bag off his shoulder to prevent it falling down the stairs or thumping onto the wooden floor, thus alerting any others that might still be down below.

The effect of the injection began to take hold almost immediately. His eyes were glassy, and his gaze confused. He put his right hand to his neck and looked at it, seeing a small dot of blood. He was an old KGB fox and realized he had been hit and that his life was now measured in minutes, if not seconds.

I pointed my pistol at his head and held my index finger to my lips. I whispered very softly, "If you make any noise, you will die. I've just injected you with a potent poison. If you don't get the antidote in the next 30 seconds, you'll be dead in a few minutes."

He raised his hands, and he wobbled uncertainly in his dizziness. He nodded to show he would comply with my orders. He rested his shoulder against the railing of the stairs, looking for a place to support his body. The effects of this poison first started with disorientation and instability as well as balance, followed by a loss of consciousness and convulsions. I had to rush before he reached that stage and forced him with my pistol to walk in front of me.

I opened the utility closet filled with cleaning supplies, ladders, and tools. Shoving him inside, he heavily fell onto the floor in a seated position. I gave him the antidote, grabbed the heavy bag of money, and put it next to him. With a small smile on my face, I touched his shoulder and whispered, "Don't go away, OK? Watch this valuable cargo for me."

I knew that by this time he wouldn't even hear what I was saying, for the convulsions had begun. The antidote would take hold soon. I started to leave the utility room when I heard steps in the hallway. I closed the door leaving a crack so I could see who it was. I saw the silhouette of another man much like my captive, taller and more corpulent, coming from the direction of the back door, his pistol in a shoulder holster. From the extended barrel, I could tell he had a silencer fixed.

It appeared that Sarah's assumption was correct. All these individuals were apparently working in a team, and it appeared that their intention was to empty the cellar of those bags of money. After this second gorilla disappeared down the stairs, I started to leave my hiding place, and saw Miguel Angel, pistol in hand, was coming my way from the front of the villa.

I held high the pistol I had taken from my captive in my right hand and raised the index finger of my left hand to my lips to caution for silence. I walked towards the stairs, signaling the danger to my friend. When we got to each other, I whispered in his ear, "I already have one as a prisoner in the utility room, but I saw another one heading down. You get on one side of the stairs, and I'll get on the other, and we can ambush him when he returns."

I took the right-hand side of the stairs, Miguel Angel on the left. The gorilla returned upstairs, but he had no bag over his shoulder. His pistol was out, and he began to fire at Miguel Angel, who he had spotted. We both ducked down quickly before he was completely up the stairs.

We lay down on the floor to avoid the low level of the bullets, which hit the big logs of wood, splinters flying from the impact. Nearly immediately afterwards, a shot rang out, and the man fell backwards down the stairs, a hole in the middle of his forehead. The tremendous noise of his fall down the stairs was loud in that silence. We looked and saw Sarah, pistol in hand.

She asked, "How many more still around?"

"I don't know. But this one at least is out of commission, and I have another one in the utility closet as a prisoner." I pointed in that direction.

"Good!" she said. "You guys should be very careful. I figured at least two more of them are still around."

Sonya appeared right behind Sarah, coming in from the driveway. Sarah jumped in surprise as Sonya said, "No, not two. Four, my friend Sarah. But they don't represent any danger to use. We can wrap them in ice and ship them as a package to Putin. I believe this will give him a little idea who he's really dealing with and playing his games with."

I smiled and replied, "That's really a great idea, Sonya."

Sonya smiled with a small smile of her own. "We had better be thinking big or go home."

Miguel Angel asked in a low voice, "Do you really think that's a good idea?"

"Yes. Without doubt Putin just tried to rob us, maybe hoping he won't have to fulfill his agreement. He didn't make it with me; he made it with the intelligence community, which is a no-no in our business. He has already received a generous advance as a good faith deposit. What he just did here by sending his gorillas to rob us shows us no signal of loyalty or even good intentions in complying and fulfilling his agreement."

We went down to the wine cellar to see what had happened there. We got to the bottom of the stairs and saw both wooden doors wide open. As we expected, not only the lock but also the hinges had been cut off. From the clean cut and lack of melted leavings, they must have used some kind of laser rather than a welding torch. This was no surprise, coming from Putin. The sad part in the whole thing was finding the body of O'Brien's man, Mike, in a black plastic body bag, body riddled by bullet holes. The bag was under the tarp we had used to cover the money.

The bag of money taken from the gorilla leaving the cellar was the last bag they had removed. Sonya said to me, "Thank God for Sarah, who heard those insignificant noises by these delinquents. We nearly missed it ourselves. As I surprised them in the driveway, I saw they had a van completely loaded with all the bags we had in here before. They've saved us the job of loading the money, since we can use their vehicle now, and it's ready to go. They were probably waiting for this last man to check everything out to make sure they didn't leave anything behind."

Sarah looked at the body of the man she had shot. She noticed the white shoes made with a special material, similar to suede—they were specially designed to make no noise and leave behind no footprints. They were similar used by the crew of luxury yachts. She pointed this out to us and said, "I have no doubts that these men had been ordered to not just take the money but also kill all of us."

Sonya smiled and nodded. "I agree with you a hundred percent. They wanted to turn us into *chicharrones*[37]. I found containers full of gasoline in very strategic places around the entire cabin. They were prepared to be set it on fire and kill us while we slept."

Miguel Angel said, "Well, this means they've planned on relocating the money as well as killing us. Normally, when the first team sent to do this kind of work, there is another team already in motion to complete the work the first team failed to do. I don't think any of us have any wish to get to know any more these criminals in service to Putin."

I smiled. "Precisely what I've been thinking. That's why we'll send an emergency message to Mr. Putin with the package containing the bodies of the five men on ice, confirming our meeting but also explaining to him that due to the last occurrences in our cabin where we're staying, we regretfully have to report he lost his men, but as a courtesy and goodwill gesture, we're sending back their bodies. If he decides to conclude our agreement as previously arranged with the intelligence community, we won't meet tonight. We will meet today at twelve o'clock noon in the same place, or the deal is off."

Sonya came over to me. "Are you sure, after all that's happened, that it's worth the risk of meeting with this crazy, egotistical maniac?"

I nodded. "The future of Europe and maybe of the world is on the table in this game Putin is playing with us. Don't you think, if we made it all the way to here, we shouldn't at least play it to the end? At least to try and finish it with Putin and his assassins?"

---

[37] A dish consisting of fried pork belly or fried pork rinds; may also be made from chicken, mutton, or beef.

Sonya said, "Yes, you're 100% correct. We should complete our mission."

I replied, "OK. The only thing is that we will completely change the initial plan and will start with Plan B. I will explain to you guys in luxurious details in brief after I take a long shower. I need to put in order all my thoughts." I turned to Helga. "I need one of those ice cream trucks. You told me before that you work in one of those places. I don't care how much it costs; I want to give Putin a big surprise. Do you think you can manage to get that?"

"Of course," she replied. "I have no doubts. With money, anything is possible." She smiled mischievously. "But why buy it? That would leave a trace. I believe the best thing would be to steal it."

I smiled. "Of course, if it doesn't complicate things. Especially in the short time we have."

Helga looked at her wristwatch and looked back up to me. "Is an hour good enough? Or do you need it sooner?"

I looked at her in surprise at that and shook my head. "No, one hour is good enough. Don't rush. Remember, things done in a rush never turn out well. I'll explain to you when you get back what we're going to do with that truck."

"OK," she replied with a bit smile on her face. She checked her watch again. "Consider it done."

"Thank you. We will talk after I finish my shower."

I went back to my room and began to take my shower. It took me longer than I had thought, because I needed to marinate all the alternate plan with extreme caution. My showers normally took ten to fifteen minutes, but this time it took half an hour. It was necessary though, because when I finished, I was very alert, physically and mentally capable of moving mountains. As I left my room and went back to my friends and give them the details of the new plan, I really was shocked and surprised when I heard in the front driveway of the cabin the music from an ice cream truck.

Helga was at the wheel and Julius Christian sat in the passenger seat. I received both with joy, hugging them both in turn. I looked at my watch and said, "This is in record time. How did you manage it?"

She pointed to Julius Christian. "To be completely honest, he helped me tremendously." She put her arm around his shoulders in friendly affection.

Julius Christian raised both arms high and said, "No, no, no—she did all the work. I only gave her a little help, and that's the truth."

"Don't you want to take credit for what you did?" she asked him.

I stopped them with both arms high. "You guys can tell me about the adventure you had in getting that ice cream truck later. But now we need to go inside so I can debrief you about this operation we're going to conduct in a few hours. Or on the contrary, the efforts we just made up will be wasted. That is the last thing any of us wants to see happen."

They both realized my sense of urgency and nodded their heads, following me into the cabin where we sat down around the large round table with the rest of our friends who were already there.

Sonya spoke first as she put the documents she had obtained from the prisoner, including his identification papers as a KGB agent. "This is not an ordinary agent." She spoke with emphasis. "This is one of Putin's officers and the guy in charge of the entire team he sent to rob us. As we thought, their mission was to not only rob us but also to kill us all, taking no prisoners."

Everyone was disturbed by what she said, but I noticed Sarah was even more dismayed. I thought it even looked like an expression of profound betrayal or disgust. She shook her head as if she had been taken by surprise. Sonya and Chopin had interrogated the prisoner by themselves in the cellar at the request of Miguel Angel. O'Brien had already shared with him the high level of technical and psychological training that they both possessed to extract information without even having to pinch the prisoner, no matter how prepared and trained that prisoner might be.

I took the prisoner's documents in my hands and said, *Dimitrich Ivanov. Lieutenant of the KGB, Special Forces Operations.* I raised my right arm as I displayed the documents. "This will be our passport and ticket to cross from West to East, with safe conduct without paying a single dime to Putin. We might be able to penetrate the Iron Curtain with our precious cargo right under the noses of all the KGB agents, using the same methods and vehicle they sent to rob us." I pulled out of my shirt pocket a paper with a code number on it. I handed it to Miguel Angel and said, "After you pass this around to everyone, destroy it. This will be the emergency code we use if the operation for any reason goes wrong to abort it. You guys will maintain the walkie-talkies on the same frequency off until you cross the border to East Berlin. We will divide into three teams.

"Team #1 will have Dimitrich Ivanov as the driver along with Miguel Angel and Chopin with the precious cargo. Team #2 will be the ice cream truck, Helga and Julius Christian. Team #3 will be Sonya accompanied by several crewmen from the yacht. They are all professional snipers. They will not only watch our back during the negotiations with Putin but afterwards as well.

"If all goes well, and Team 1 tells me it went through and we don't need to pay Putin, Team 3 can send him to his ultimate afterlife. We need to remain alert, because Putin thinks he has the winning hand in this game. He might try to pull off a very dirty cheat to win no matter what. That is why we have this emergency code for retreat, so it cannot be in the hands of our enemies under any circumstance, as it would completely destroy our mission by dividing and creating confusion among us."

Sarah asked, "How can you be so sure that Dimitrich Ivanov won't betray us when he gets to the border?"

I smiled. "That is something our friend Sonya can give better details on than I." I raised my right hand and motioned for her to take over.

Sonya nodded and stood up. She pulled a device out of her briefcase and set it on the table. It looked like a collar one used with fighting dogs to protect their throats, except this was not leather or had the spikes such collars usually had. It was metallic, with a hinge and a seal. She held up a remote control. "Another such device is locked around the neck of our prisoner; we have shown him a video demonstrating what it can do to someone's neck. After it's activated, a very small laser beam begins to circle around the neck, cutting away the first layer of skin; it then readjusts to a tighter circle, continuing around and cutting deeper skin layers with each successive pass, growing smaller and smaller. After producing in hours of agony, the neck gets fully severed. Only then, when the head is cut off, will it automatically disconnect.

"This is one of the demonstrations that we showed Dimitrich Ivanov, along with other psychological methods that induced him to agree to cooperate fully with whatever we ask. As you know, even the bravest individual of these terrorists would want to leave this world in that painful and excruciating way. This device is our insurance policy. He knows I have the remote control in my hands and could activate it at any second; of course, the code to stop it is in my head. No one can find it." She tapped her temple with her index finger. "He will drive with us wearing this collar with a scarf covering it. Any questions?"

Everyone shook their heads. She sat back down. I took back over and continued my debriefing, giving them all the details, we were going to execute in the next few hours. After everyone was on the same page to complete the operation, the Closet of the Zipper, we left the cabin in different vehicles after sending the body of Mike with the cleaning crew to return it to the United States.

I was sitting in the passenger seat of Sarah's car, looked over at Chopin, who sat in the van with the precious cargo, and saw him crossing himself. With a small smile, I gave him a thumbs up, which he returned as a salute as the van drove off.

A little later, we crossed the border. We arrived at a plaza which was a giant circle. We selected that particular place, not only to be a public place but also for the magnificent and strategic qualities it possessed. The same way it served us could likewise help our enemies. Knowing them as we did, the location could be for any of us a double-edged knife. Both sides had complete knowledge of this, and after studying other options we decided to keep the location, concluding that it was the most indicated one on the menu.

People were walking around the plaza, some taking pictures, couples getting their portraits taken, and others sitting beneath the umbrellas outside the various sidewalk cafes and restaurants. I looked at my wristwatch a little impatiently. Putin was twenty-five minutes late for our meeting. It bothered me and worried me a little. Even though I was always an eternal optimist, as a human being at the end, I could not avoid thinking that my plans could be exposed if anything had happened at the border with Lieutenant Ivanov.

I could not help that the hairs on the back of my neck raised up, not because of what I was thinking but by the proximity of Putin. I had identified him by his peculiar, waddling penguin-like walk. He was accompanied by six men, all with disguised as Jews with long beards, but I was prepared from the moment I identified him.

They came over to us and Putin approached, putting one of his arms to tap Sarah on the shoulder, taking her by surprise. She looked at me in shame, since she was supposed to be there to identify him. My walkie-talkie crackled as I heard Miguel Angel's voice giving the code I had been waiting for, which told me that Mr. Franklin was at peace with no issues at all. "We will retreat to our place of origin," he said. "Over and out."

That call meant we no longer had to deal with Putin. I felt a lot more relaxed, not just because of Miguel Angel's message but also at seeing Putin pulling the beard down with a smile to Sarah. Putin, at least for now, had no intention of assassinating us.

Had that been the case, his men would have put bullets in our heads already. I understood then that he had no idea where the money was. I regained my composure and confidence.

Putin said with a very cocky attitude and tone of voice, "If I wanted, you would already be dead, Dr. Antonio Rada Montiel, the man who collapsed the operation in Panama which destroyed General Ochoa and his team. Or, if you prefer, Dr. Julio Antonio del Marmol, aka the Cuban Lightning. You owe me a debt of gratitude…."

Before he could finish, I interrupted with a big smile as I knew for a fact I had the winning hand, "I don't remember in that invitation you sent me to meet you here, by the way for which you're actually half an hour late to, any requirement to dress for a carnival."

He looked at me, scrutinizing me with his little eyes in an attempt to penetrate my brain. "What about it? You don't like Jewish people? Are you an Antisemite?"

I smiled ironically. "To be honest with you, you're being hypocritical like a good communist. Under Stalin's regime, the communists were the only ones in the entire world who continued the legacy of Hitler, killing Jews in greater numbers than he ever did and sending into exile millions more. That is the reason it seems to me humorous that you guys chose to disguise yourselves as one of your worst enemies."

Putin looked deeply into my eyes once more, trying to verify my features were who he vaguely remembered from childhood, searching through the drawers of his memory. At that moment, the ice cream truck entered the plaza with Julius Christian and Helga, who had come to stop right next to us. All of Putin's men reached into their overcoats for their pistols, preparing for the worst and repel any aggression.

The Broken Rainbow: Mysterious Dark Karma

A few seconds later, as Putin realized that this was really an ice cream truck, he waved to his men to relax. It appeared that Putin loved ice cream, as he walked to the window counter of the truck. He asked Helga, "What kind of flavors have you brought today?"

Helga didn't answer his question. Instead, she brought buckets of ice cream and placed them on the counter, with small paper sample cups and spoons. After placing the five buckets on the counter, she said, "Various flavors."

Very pleased at all her work, he said, "Thank you." Putin opened the first bucket and his jaw dropped in shock as he saw the head of one of his minions he had sent to rob and then burn us all alive.

With a cold expression, Helga asked, "What's the matter? Is so much ice cream making you lose your head? You can try the others." Without waiting for him, she opened the other buckets.

Putin stepped back, completely petrified when he saw the contents of the buckets. The rest of his men, ten or fifteen feet away, were not able to see what was impacting their leader so greatly. Finally, he recovered himself and yelled, "Arrest this man and woman! These are criminal terrorists!"

The men with Putin began to pull their weapons out, not having the slightest idea that they were already surrounded by Sonya and the men from the yacht, who immediately moved in and disarmed them. They were handcuffed and gagged, and then placed inside of the ice cream truck. The last one to be put in the truck was Putin. His eyes bulged out in shock when he saw ten five-gallon cans of gasoline, the ones intended to burn me and my team alive. Cowering, like every bully, he said cynically, "Why don't you ask your friend Sarah who provided us the exact address of where you guys were staying and where you had that load of money?"

I looked at Sarah in shocked surprise, doubts in my eyes. She didn't deny it, nor did she agree with Putin. Two tears ran down her cheeks. She yelled at him, "Traitor! You intended to kill all of us, including me! You deserve what you're going to get." She crammed a gag deep into Putin's mouth before he could say anything further.

I looked up at the sky, looking for an answer for this magnificent betrayal. But I only saw a large broken rainbow on that dark overcast day which now began to sprinkle. Lightning illuminated the sky as I gave Sarah the keys to the truck. "You do with them whatever you think is best. I don't like to kill people, but some people, like Hitler, Che Guevara, Fidel Castro, and Putin, are better off not being born into this world. If you can find room in your heart to forgive yourself and forgive him, maybe you can become a better person."

The Broken Rainbow: Mysterious Dark Karma

Epilogue

    I discovered somewhat later that Sarah and Putin had long been involved not just in espionage activities but more deeply in a sexual relationship, to the shame and dismay of the Baumann family. Though neither of them was loyal to anyone, they evidently learned to forgive each other. With Sarah's help, he returned to Moscow.

    Birds of a feather may flock together, but little did Putin know that he became a key component in our plans. Blinded by his ambition for power and money, he never dreamed of the contribution he made to the destruction of his glorious Soviet Union. He only thought that they would lose East Germany. A few months later the Berlin Wall collapsed, starting an economic chain reaction which caused complete and total ruination of the evil Soviet Empire.

    If I ever had any doubts in my mind up to that point about my psychic, extraordinary gift from birth to clearly see the future, they disappeared after that day in 1963. When I met and shook the hand of Vladimir Putin on that day, I saw, as if on a large television screen, his evil spirit growing with age. I saw how he grabbed power, committing horrible crimes all the way from 1960 until 2000, leaving behind him a trail of death, converting himself to become the reincarnation of Adolf Hitler, another son of Satan, sending their dark karma to the Earth and bringing destruction of humanity at large. Those images played through my mind as if an emergency warning from God, saying "Watch yourself, your brothers, and all of humanity, because Satan has sent to Earth another of his evil sons."

40 The First Stage of the Soviet Union's Collapse

The Broken Rainbow: Mysterious Dark Karma

41 All Evil Forces Collapse Thanks to the Zipper

2021: 33 years later

As the Lightning's vision comes true again, history repeats itself. Putin invades the Ukraine, committing another genocide there and putting the peace and stability of the rest of the world at risk like his predecessor, Hitler, did nearly a century before.

Dr. Julio Antonio del Marmol

The Broken Rainbow:
Mysterious Dark Karma

The past, present, and the future, **1937, 1987**, and **2047**: the Lightning's precognition for the future.

In the year 2047, the first step will be taken towards the end of the world as we know it. The three forces of dark karma unite in their ambition for power and control over humanity. This escalation will use the three most powerful tools in their arsenal: genocide, famine, and pestilence. When these three nuclear giants release these destructive forces against the human race, this devastating technology will open for the first time the doors to the Black Hole in the universe, which in turn will precipitate the Apocalypse. But even they, knowing it will be demise of all the peoples of the entire world would rather cause the end of this beautiful Earth than not feed their unscrupulous ambition for domination. They would rather condemn us to extinction and eternal flames which the forces of Nature would prohibit any human being ever to come back from.

The Broken Rainbow: Mysterious Dark Karma

Let's hope to God, the Supreme Architect of the Universe, that the forces of Good will unite, once and for all, in an extreme effort to stop in time this vision, or what I see will be an inevitability.

Dr. Julio Antonio del Marmol

Dr. Julio Antonio del Marmol

Agnostics and Atheists

Agnostics and atheists, stay away from them because they are empty vessels floating in the ocean of life. Those who deny their Creator and the love of God probably hate themselves, their country, and their flag. They will never be capable of loving you or anyone else because love doesn't exist in their hearts. Their resentment toward God and society makes them completely blind. These people only find comfort by Satan's side.

Dr. Julio Antonio del Marmol

The Broken Rainbow: Mysterious Dark Karma Press Release 9/16/2022

A new book by Dr. Julio Antonio del Marmol, the Cuban Lightning.

Like its 13 predecessors, this book reveals a tremendous and different story. In a departure from previous stories, this one incorporates that of another family, beginning in a much different part of the world.

In this magnificent true spy story, the reader is taken on a very fast ride from the 30's to the 90's as two families unite in combatting the evil forces motivated only by their desire to help humanity. With that load on their shoulders, they also carry the dream of a free world where everyone is able to live in peace and harmony, free of diabolic tyrannies, whose only objective is the full destruction of humanity. The two families are the Baumanns and the del Marmols, who are each betrayed by the false promises of prosperity from the diabolical men infesting the political systems. These men were sent to Earth at the command of their master with the sole purpose to plant the seed of division, hatred, and destruction, and on occasion genocide, creating the perfect ground for their king and his mysterious dark karma to drag the entire world to live in eternal darkness.

In this story, the reader finds out how from generation to generation the seed of evil ferments to repeat destruction and corruption over the Earth. The reader also discovers how the seed of love, dignity, and generosity is planted by the positive energies of these two families. They manage to stop that evil force, bringing about the destruction and perishing of many of these leaders, sent back to where they really came from: Hell. This story has romance, intrigue, action, and betrayal in abundance, keeping the reader in suspense from beginning to end.

The Broken Rainbow clarifies history and corrects elements of historical, political, and social events which leave one in complete awe. The facts, the documentation, pictures, and evidence are so overwhelming as to leave the reader with absolutely no doubts as to why the dark forces have been hiding these important details of history. Line by line, the reader discovers why those historical events have been distorted and sometimes altered by governments in power to mislead others. Political figures fear the consequences that this truthful information could produce.

Those who love uncensored truth, freedom of expression, and democracy will be entertained even as they receive a fountain of knowledge that contributes to enhancing their intellectual capacity to see the world as it is. This literature brings stories from the past to open the reader's hunger for knowledge, making us all understand that those mistakes, wars, famine, and genocides from the past should never be repeated again. With this fountain of

The Broken Rainbow: Mysterious Dark Karma

knowledge and corrections of history offered, we can obtain a better future as we see a world of beautiful peace and harmony where everyone lives in respect for each other with dignity, as any human being deserves to live and die.

Dr. Julio Antonio del Marmol

Other Works by the Author

Rites of Passage of a Master Spy
1) *Cuba: The Truth, the Lies, and the Coverups*
2) *The Havana Conspiracies*
3) *The Dark Face of Marxism*
4) *The Deadly Deals*
5) *The Evil Rituals*
6) *JFK: The Unwrapped Enigma*

7) *The Cuban Lightning: The Zipper*
8) *Cuba: Russian Roulette of the World*
9) *Montauk: The Lightning Chance*
10) *The Lightning and Montauk: Reality vs. Fiction*
11) *ISIS: The Genetic Conception*
12) *The Lightning and bin Laden: Genetic Trail of the Lightning*
13) *Black Tears: The Havana Syndrome*

Graphic Novel
Options in Your Mind Equals Freedom

www.ingramcontent.com/pod-product-compliance
Lightning Source LLC
Chambersburg PA
CBHW031701230426
43668CB00006B/70